25 Ways to Make College Pay Off

Advice for Anxious Parents from a Professor Who's Seen It All

Professor Bill Coplin, Ph.D.

AMACOM

American Management Association

New York • Atlanta • Brussels • Chicago • Mexico City • San Francisco
Shanghai • Tokyo • Toronto • Washington, D.C.

Library of Congress Cataloging-in-Publication Data

Coplin, William D.
    25 ways to make college pay off : advice for anxious parents from a professor who's seen it all / Bill Coplin.
        p.   cm.
    Includes index.
    ISBN-13: 978-0-8144-7456-3 (pbk.)
    ISBN-10: 0-8144-7456-X (pbk.)
    1. Career education—United States.   2. College student orientation—United States.   3. Career development—United States.   I. Title.   II. Title: Twenty-five ways to make college pay off.

LC1037.5.C684   2007
378'.013—dc22   2007006947

Printing number

10   9   8   7   6   5   4   3   2   1

This book is dedicated to my students past and present and their parents.

Contents

Preface

"Let the buyer beware."

—English translation of the Latin legal term *caveat emptor*

A father of a college sophomore approached me for help starting a support group called No Basement-Dwelling Grads. Having seen other families find their empty nests occupied by children who do "well" in college but are unable to get jobs, he didn't want it to happen to him and his children.

He had good reason to worry. Here are some gruesome facts:

- About 46 percent of college freshmen will not graduate from four-year programs in six years.[1]

- About 60 percent of college graduates say they plan to live with their parents after graduation.[2]

- Only 20 percent of the 450 business and political leaders in a 2004 survey said yes when asked whether schools are preparing students to meet employers' needs.[3]

Who's responsible for the swarms of overqualified, underemployed, still-living-with-mom-and-dad twentysomethings? Well, there are the professors who love their subjects more than their students and college administrators who are more interested in winning research grants and filling seats than educating undergrads. Many critics (and victims) of this consistent failure have been given a voice over the past decade by state and federal politicians who have issued reports and proposed legislation to hold colleges and universities accountable for high costs and low achievement.

Although colleges and universities could do a much better job of helping undergraduates pursue satisfying careers after college, students don't seem to know how to get the most out of their college educations. Parents paying the freight need to provide guidance to their children on how to make the college years pay off.

I'm not saying undergraduate education does more harm than good for its students. But I know it could do a lot better. And as a parent, you can help your child use his entire college experience, not just the courses, to prepare for a satisfying career. You can maximize your child's opportunity to find and pursue a satisfying career path after college by following the advice provided in this book.

This book suggests a no-nonsense approach toward your child's college experience. That means no nonsense with your child and no nonsense with the college program. You may find it difficult to follow all of the book's recommendations, and you may disagree with specific suggestions; like any self-help book, you can pick and choose from the advice provided here. If nothing else, it will show you how seeing college as a chance to gain work-related experience is the key to preparing your child for a successful career. But I recommend following through on the specific strategies at the end of each chapter. They will make a huge difference in your child's success.

I developed and tested the tips in this book during my forty years of student advising, lots of research, and interviews with some of the nation's most prominent employers. But they are also advice I gave my own children. Now in their late thirties and early forties, they each had a different college experience, but all found worthwhile work and happy lives. I will give you some details on them and their spouses in chapter 3.

If nothing else, I hope this book helps you and your child become better consumers of undergraduate education with respect to career preparation. There are other purposes for a college education: Children need to mature, have a good time, become good citizens, and learn for the sake of learning. But this book's focus is on helping parents help their children prepare for rewarding careers after college—the number-one reason parents pay as much as $200,000 for a four-year undergraduate program.

I decided to write this book for parents rather than students for a very simple reason. In discussing my previous book, *10 Things Employers Want You to Learn in College*, with parents, I realized that writing directly to students was not enough. Students rarely read the book; their parents and relatives did. Moreover, I realized that parents approach their children in a variety of counterproductive ways. It's as if they're at the race track spending money and watching from the sidelines. Their primary activities are cheering for high grades or letting loose a torrent of four-letter words when their children appear to be faltering. Parents have to become investors, not gamblers, in their children's college educations.

The book is divided into six sections:

■ **PART ONE: Three Goals for Career Success Through College.** This section describes the three goals that your child should have to prepare for a viable career path after college. The three goals are to (1) develop skills employers want, (2) build the character employers want, and (3) explore a variety of career paths.

■ **PART TWO: Building a Good Relationship with Your Child.** This section describes how you can establish a working relationship with your child to support his career preparation during the college years. The advice recognizes that you can't make your child do anything, but you can coach him to be successful.

■ **PART THREE: The High School Years as Career Preparation.** This section provides suggestions on what parents should do during the years before college, including the application and college-selection process. If your child is already in college, you can skim this section, but you may gain some insight into his college performance by looking back on his high school years through the lens provided by these chapters.

■ **PART FOUR: Academics: The 50-50 Principle.** This section describes the academic component of a college education. It shows why academics constitute no more than 50 percent of your child's college education with respect to his career preparation. It also provides answers to other academic questions relating to grade point average (GPA), transferring, and graduating early.

■ **PART FIVE: The Other 50 Percent.** This section provides ideas on how your child should use her college years to develop skills, build character, and explore careers by engaging in activities outside of the classroom. I discuss the vital importance of student activities, jobs, internships, and the career-services office as well as the key roles these things can play if your child uses them intelligently.

■ **PART SIX: Post-College Paths.** Graduate school should not be a default option. This section shows how the twenties can be used by your child to hone skills, enhance character, and discover a career while earning enough to live on his own.

Because I have spent most of my career teaching at a university and have been effectively "out of the job market" for some time, I invited two colleagues of mine to contribute the final chapters on job searches and career development.

This book is not about finances, dealing with roommate problems, how to get good grades, or how to get admitted to the best graduate schools. Many other books and websites are available for such purposes, and I encourage you to check them out. This book is about how to help your children maximize their college experiences in order to pursue satisfying careers. The primary audience for this book is parents whose children are planning to attend or already attend a traditional four-year undergraduate program; however, much of it can be applied to those planning to attend two-year programs or vocational postsecondary programs.

Each chapter closes with a section titled "What Parents Can Do." These sections list a few very concrete and specific strategies that you can follow in coaching and encouraging your child. They provide a simple and common-sense approach to helping you help your child be on track when he graduates instead of spending his twenties (and possibly longer) getting the career-savvy education he should have gotten in college. A "Useful Resources" section at the very end of each chapter will also help you gain additional perspective.

Throughout the book, I have drawn examples from students I have worked with over the past forty years. I asked current students and parents, mostly from Syracuse University, to provide sidebars elaborating on the points in the text. Their anecdotes illustrate my point but should not be taken as comprehensive evidence. Helping your child use college as a launchpad for a career after graduation is not a science. Even though I based my advice on the best research available, research is often contradictory and not easily transferred into reasonable strategies for real-world problems. All I can tell you for sure is that I have seen it work for my family and my students. Take what you find sensible and think will work for you and your child.

Notes

1. *The Chronicle of Higher Education*, Almanac Issue 2006–2007, p. 14.

2. Peg Tyre, Karen Springen, and Judy Scelfo, "Bringing Up Adultolescents," *Newsweek*, March 25, 2002, p. 34.

3. *USA Today*, December 28, 2004, column B1.

Acknowledgments

I have received a great deal of help from a variety of sources in preparing the manuscript for this book. Students played a central role in this project, as they do in most of my projects. Emily Pecachek performed wonders on doing the initial copyediting and critiquing the early draft as well as writing a few comments of her own that appear in the book. Lauren D'Angelo and Asher Epstein provided reactions and suggestions as well as conducted research. Bradley T. Warren assisted in researching and documenting important parts of the manuscript. Several other students and alumni, including Kevin Smith, Ry Bloomdahl, Lauren Rupard, Heather Bowes, and Patrick Hoyle, provided comments and research help.

Parents of current college students have also provided suggestions and comments, including Jim Arey, Gail Benedict, Mark Lichty, and Steve Canale. Steve, who also happens to be (much to my good fortune) corporate recruitment director for General Electric, has spent much time reacting to drafts and providing suggestions as well as insightful quotes.

Colleagues at Syracuse University provided suggestions and advice, including John Fiset on concurrent enrollment programs; Bruce Hamm on offerings by the continuing education division of the university; Colleen O'Connor Bench from the Parent's Office; Michael Cahill, Karen McGee, and Gregg Victory from career services; and Suzanne Mettler, whose study on the GI Bill proved relevant. Barbara Risser, a vice president from Onondaga Community College, tried to help me understand the full range of services and benefits offered by community colleges. Robert Oliva, who

2 5 WAYS TO MAKE

Although there are far more than twenty-five specific tips and strategies presented in this book, this list represents the twenty-five key ideas I would like to convey. If you take nothing else from my book, incorporate these twenty-five principles as you help your child find a satisfying career through the college experience

This list is divided into two groups. The first group describes things you can do (or avoid doing) to be sure your child is on the right track. You can think of it as advice to you as an investor in your child's future. The second group addresses actions your child must take, but you have a lot of influence on those actions.

For You
1. Use the Goldilocks principle—not too hot and not too cold. Just the right mixture of hands on and hands off.
2. Have your child prepare a written or verbal plan about how college is contributing to his career focus.
3. Perform a "focus check" every four months to check his commitment to that future career.
4. Require your child to pay for at least 20 percent of his college education.
5. Don't be held hostage by the fear that your child will not earn a college degree.
6. Don't worry about your child's GPA if it is 3.0 or above.
7. Take strong action if your child's GPA is heading below 2.0.
8. Don't fight your child's urge to transfer; just try to minimize additional costs and lost credits.
9. Tell your child before she enters college that you will not pay for more than four years (unless it is a longer program, such as architecture or pharmacy).

COLLEGE PAY OFF

For Your Child

10. Pursue the three goals of developing skills, building character, and exploring careers.
11. Determine how your college years will help you achieve these goals.
12. Consider taking a year off before college to work or investigate nontraditional programs and colleges.
13. View the application process as a test of your commitment to skills, character, and career exploration rather than as a test of your future success.
14. Gain between six and fifteen college credits while in high school.
15. Assume that no more than 50 percent of your course work will help you prepare for a career; the other 50 percent comes from internships, part-time jobs, student activities, and social experiences outside of the classroom.
16. Hit the ground running and aim for a valuable work or internship experience the summer after your freshman year.
17. Take courses that emphasize skills, use hands-on activities, and require team projects and writing.
18. Don't obsess over grades as long as you are near or above a 3.0.
19. Spend at least one semester and as many as three semesters in off-campus, credit-bearing programs.
20. Avoid summer school unless it can be used to eliminate pesky requirements.
21. Don't make graduate school your default option instead of getting a real job; in most cases, graduate school should be preceded by two years of full-time work experience.
22. Go to your college's career-services office early and often.
23. Remember that temp agencies can provide summer jobs and a career launch for the confused and undecided.
24. Put as much time into searching for your first job as you should have put into applying to college.
25. See your first job after college as a step that can lead in many directions you never anticipated.

PART ONE

Three Goals for Career Success Through College

Motivated college students should pursue three goals in college if they want to be on a successful career track when they graduate:

1. *Develop skills*
2. *Build character*
3. *Explore careers*

Parents can show them the way.

CHAPTER 1

Skills

"If we don't change our direction, we are likely to end up where we are headed."

—Chinese proverb

Students have many misconceptions about how college can help them prepare for satisfying careers, but the biggest is that a college degree and a high GPA will guarantee a good first job and a successful career. Anyone in the work world knows that over the long run skills and character ensure success. The GPA provides employers with only an indication that the student may have some of the essential skills they want. They need much more information than that.

A 2006 survey of U.S. employers by the National Association of Colleges and Employers (NACE) reveals what employers value in their new hires.[1] The most highly rated soft skills were communications and teamwork. Character traits sought most were honesty/integrity and strong work ethic, and important technical skills included analytic and computer skills.

Since the mid-1980s, employers have consistently reported in many different studies that college graduates have solid technical skills for their specific fields but lack general professional skills. The conclusion from these studies and my conversations with corporate recruiters is clear: Skills and character determine career success; a college degree guarantees neither.

I'll discuss character in chapter 2; this one focuses on skills. After reading this chapter, I hope you will be convinced that you need to deliver the message "skills matter" every chance you get. Employers don't want just degree holders; they want professionals who have the general skills that every job demands.

It sounds simple and obvious, but most college students just don't get it. Brainwashed from kindergarten to believe that getting into a good college will guarantee their futures, they have been turned into grade-getting machines. They see college as just one more set of classes to get through. Because most of these classes require taking tests to unload or synthesize information, students assume that learning the content is what's important—not learning the skills.

The sooner your child gets the point that skills matter the better. It will change her focus from degree requirements to ways she can develop skills. It might convince her to take an accounting course even if she hates numbers or do some community service so she can improve her interpersonal skills. It will help her see that the summer is as important for her skills development as the academic year.

What Parents Can Do

As you probably already know, you only have limited influence on your child's attitude. There are some things you can do, however. Here are three strategies you can follow to the letter or, more likely, in spirit.

Strategy #1: Drive home the message that skills are key to success. Be sure to understand the importance of skill development in your child's college education and to provide advice based on that perspective. Tell her to *take every opportunity to develop skills not just through course selection but in everything she does outside class.* If your child asks you about course selection, for example, talk about skills she thinks she might develop rather than give an opinion on which courses she should take. If she asks whether she should take a job for the second year in a row as a lifeguard, your response should be, "Is that the best opportunity for making money and developing a broad range of skills?" This question can be a starting point to reexamine her options. For example, if she does return to lifeguarding, she should ask for more management responsibility, which will raise her employability a great deal. If you consistently respond to these career questions by asking about what will be learned from each opportunity, she will get the message.

Strategy #2: Place a list of skills where your child can see it. Give your child a list of skills that are important. My list is based on years of advising students, extensive discussion with career counselors and employers, and the consistent research findings of employers. Feel free to make a copy and post it on your child's bedroom or bathroom mirror. It provides a target for your child to aim at as she progresses through her high school and college years.

You may want to add, delete, or rephrase some of the skills on the chart. If your child has a specific career focus such as accounting or social work, you could add a career-specific list. Just make sure you have some list of skills. The list defines your child's mission during her college experience. Regardless of the field, she should try to develop all these skills to the highest level possible before, during, and after college. In looking through my list, you will note that "establishing a work ethic" is more a set of attitudes than skills.

I first presented the list of thirty-eight skills in ten categories in my last book, *10 Things Employers Want You to Learn in College*, and it has taken on a life of its own. In speaking engagements over the past three years, I have presented it to thousands of people. I have asked parents, teachers, employers, and career experts to react to the list and suggest additions. Many of the additions were slight variations on the listed skills. For example, people have mentioned *ethics*, which is close to my term *be honest*, and they have mentioned *continuous learning*, which is covered in several of the skills I listed. On the whole, however, the list was confirmed by audience after audience.

The Ten Things Employers Want

Establishing a Work Ethic
Kick Yourself in the Butt • Be Honest • Manage Your Time • Manage Your Money

Developing Physical Skills
Stay Well • Look Good • Type 35 WPM Error Free • Take Legible Notes

Communicating Verbally
Converse One-on-One • Present to Groups • Use Visual Displays

Communicating in Writing
Write Well • Edit and Proof • Use Word-Processing Tools • Send Information Electronically

Working Directly with People
Build Good Relationships • Work in Teams • Teach Others

Influencing People
Manage Efficiently • Sell Successfully • Politick Wisely • Lead Effectively

Gathering Information
Use Library Holdings • Use Commercial Databases • Search the Web • Conduct Interviews • Use Surveys • Keep and Use Records

Using Quantitative Tools
Use Numbers • Use Graphs and Tables • Use Spreadsheet Programs

Asking and Answering the Right Questions
Detect BS • Pay Attention to Detail • Apply Knowledge • Evaluate Actions and Policies

Solving Problems
Identify Problems • Develop Solutions • Launch Solutions

The list recognizes that in today's global economy the ability to work on a team, to constantly learn, and to solve problems when new conditions arise are the keys to a successful career. Technical training in a specific field like accounting, computer programming, or engineering is important for that first job, but long-term success grows from general professional skills.

Strategy #3: Encourage your child to periodically complete a skills assessment. A great way to help your child understand the importance of skills is to encourage her to do a self-inventory. An inventory worksheet based on my list of ten skill categories appears on page 57 in chapter 6. It might be fun for you and your child to complete the inventory and compare your relative strengths and weaknesses. In addition to driving home the point that skills matter, your child might conclude that she is already on her way to building the skills she needs to succeed.

This revelation is particularly important for B and C students who may think that because they are not at the top of their classes academically, they have no future. A few years ago a high school senior wrote to me after reading my book *10 Things Employers Want You to Learn in College*. He said he was glad to see the list of skills because with his B average, he thought he would have no career. Now this senior is graduating from college and is on his way to becoming a high school history teacher. Students who have very bright futures but just don't get As are beat up by a K-12 education system that makes grades the only tangible measure of success.

Conversely, if your child is a high academic achiever, working through this inventory will drive home the point that academic success is only part of the key to her future. It will help her understand that even though she may not have to take a skills test at school, skills are the ultimate goal of her education. Every year, alumni send me e-mails marveling at how very high-achieving students from the "best" colleges in the country don't know how to write a memo, use the change-tracking features in Microsoft Word, or even use a copy machine. They also have the same complaints about students from graduate schools. One of my former students at the Harvard

Graduate School of Education was astounded at how poorly many of her peers were using basic computer programs like Word and Excel.

These three strategies will reduce the confusion students have over the purpose of a college education. Be patient. You are presenting a viewpoint that counters the prevailing mythology that college is about grades and degrees. It also challenges the competitiveness of our education system, where students are pitted against one another to determine who ranks highest. The emphasis on skills provides an absolute standard against which students can measure themselves. Winning the search for a satisfying career isn't about beating others; it's about playing the game well.

Useful Resources

Consult a very useful website, https://www.collegeparents.org, that touches all areas of college, many, like financial aid, not covered in this book. It also provides access to resources for all of the topics covered by this book.

How to Win Friends and Influence People, by Dale Carnegie (New York: Pocket Books, 1982). This book provides a time-tested way to develop human-relations and communications skills, which are so critical to career success. A CD set is also available, which makes it even easier for you to use. Try to sneak it into some CD player your child listens to. If you listen to it too, you will be able to approach your child through Carnegie's philosophy. It works on everybody.

My book *10 Things Employers Want You to Learn in College* (Berkeley, CA: Ten Speed Press, 2003). This book is written directly to college students and precollege students to help them focus on the skills they need to develop in college.

Note

1. Andrea Koncz and Mimi Collins, "Employers Cite Communication Skills as Key, but Say Many Job Seekers Don't Have Them," National Association of Colleges and Employers, April 26, 2006. Available at http://www.naceweb.org/press/display.asp?year=2006&prid=235.

Character

"A man's character is his fate."

—Heraclitus

This main point of this chapter is really a no-brainer. What employer wants a lazy, dishonest, and self-indulgent employee? The challenge is to figure out how to help your children develop the character that will make them great hires, not to mention good people in all aspects of life.

Defining the term *good character* is like defining the term *pornography*. As Justice Potter Stewart said in a 1964 Supreme Court decision, "I know it when I see it."[1] Consequently, you don't need to study philosophy to define the essence of good character in order to help your child have what employers want. As a parent, you know it when you see it.

The sidebar shows Benjamin Franklin's definition of good character. Ben was quite serious about improving himself. In his autobiography, he tells the reader how to make a table using thirteen rows of virtues and columns for each day of the week.[2] He explains how he works on one virtue each week. Character, like skills, requires a conscious commitment to self-improvement, and for Franklin, a table was the way to go.

A conscious commitment to good character is crucial to your child's career success. In a study by education researcher Kathleen Cotton, employers described what she calls "affective skills and traits," an academic way of saying what employers value as good character.[3] Here is her list:

Dependability/responsibility
Positive attitude toward work

Conscientiousness, punctuality, efficiency
Interpersonal skills, cooperation, working as a team member
Self-confidence, positive self-image
Adaptability, flexibility
Enthusiasm, motivation
Self-discipline, self-management
Appropriate dress, grooming
Honesty, integrity
Ability to work without supervision

Ben Franklin's Thirteen Virtues

1. Temperance
2. Silence
3. Order
4. Resolution
5. Frugality
6. Industry
7. Sincerity
8. Justice
9. Moderation
10. Cleanliness
11. Tranquility
12. Chastity
13. Humility

You may not want to require your child to place either of these lists on the bathroom mirror. It could easily threaten your credibility by sounding so "preachy," but clearly you will want to communicate the spirit of good character with respect to the workplace in a variety of ways. Just as emphasis on the skills presented in chapter 1 is key to career preparation, good character is an important target of learning for any college student, as it is for all of us.

Although employers want employees who are honest, forces in our society encourage dishonesty. These forces manifest themselves in illegal behaviors such as drug use and underage drinking, but they also affect schoolwork. A 2006 survey released by the Josephson Institute found that of 36,122 high school students, 60 percent had cheated on a test and 92 percent were satisfied with their personal ethics and character.[4] Unacceptably high rates of dishonesty have become the standard. College faculties are finding increasing incidents of such behavior, and employers are on the lookout for it.

Teaching these types of attributes is part of parenting from the day your child is born. It would be fruitless to be comprehensive in my discussion here. However, money is one topic worth discussing.

Money Matters

Although the saying "money is the root of all evil" is clearly a gross simplification, getting, spending, and managing money presents a test of character. How your child handles decisions about money creates a great opportunity for building the character necessary for a successful career.

Employers want someone who can manage his own money. For example, an article in the *Boston Globe* presented stories of people who were denied jobs because of poor credit history. Yes, employers check credit histories. According to Matt Fellowes of the Brookings Institution, 35 percent of U.S. employers checked credit reports in 2004.[5]

Parents can help their children develop character by emphasizing that a college education is an investment and that they expect a payoff from that investment. Clarity of costs is a great character builder. When your child takes on some of those costs, as I will discuss, it is an even better one. Investors don't try to hide what they are providing to those whose businesses they invest in. Why not make the amount of your investment clear?

I am frequently surprised about how unclear students are about the cost of their education. Many parents, and not just the wealthy ones, want to "protect" their children from the ugly reality of the high cost of a college education. How can this protection build character? How can it motivate students to work hard if they feel like they are on a free ride?

Clarity about financial costs also helps with another problem that plagues the parent-child relationship with respect to college: guilt. In my conversations with students and their parents, I find that many students feel guilty about costing their parents so much money, and many parents feel guilty about not providing more financial support. If the amount of financial support is not clearly established and mutually accepted, this guilt can create unnecessary anxiety and stress. There will always be some level of guilt, but transparency is a way to minimize its negative effects.

Chapter 6 calls for your child to develop and write a plan for his college years. The plan includes goals like graduate on time, have summer internships, complete activities to gain experience, and work with the career-services office. The more specific and detailed the list of activities, the better.

The plan should be revised yearly to adjust for the progress made, or lack thereof, in the previous year. In making and updating the plan, your child will be honoring a commitment, which is one of the most important aspects of good character and something employers demand.

The plan will also force your child to share the bad news with the good news. Most people like to overreport the good news and avoid mentioning the bad news. Employers don't like that for obvious reasons. Neither does the Securities and Exchange Commission or the American people.

The investor's mind-set naturally leads to one of the key principles of good investing: The principals should have their own money in the investment. Many parents think that providing full financial support allows their children to be free to get the most out of college. Footing the entire bill for a ride on a merry-go-round for your five-year-old makes sense; putting up $150,000 so that junior can be free of financial worries in college makes no sense. Benjamin Franklin would not see this as a way to build any one of his thirteen virtues, especially frugality; industry; and, given the high cost of beer, temperance.

Future employers are wary of parental generosity. Employers want to see evidence of work ethic and money management. They love to see a consistent employment history (unpaid internships count). If your child can write on her resume that she contributed 50 percent of the cost of her college education, employers will be even more impressed. Even 20 percent would work for some employers. It's not the amount as much as that the applicant wants to show she paid at least part of her way. Every employer I have talked to throughout my career has complained about the arrogance, tardiness, unwillingness to work hard, and general feeling of entitlement of new hires. Demonstrating a significant financial stake in their own education helps students convince employers of their good character.

In my experience as a professor, the students who have a financial stake in their own education tend to be more focused and organized about the fact that a college education is a gateway to a rewarding career path. In contrast, I find that students who are given a free ride tend to stay confused and unfocused throughout their four years of school. I have not seen studies on this topic, but it is something worthy of investigation.

Teenagers, like the rest of us, pay more attention to money spent when it is their own. They realize how much work actually goes into buying an iPod or a new outfit. This realization is vital to future successes. If students realize the cost of an undergraduate education, then they might be inclined to take it more seriously. That's why it's important for your child to have a financial stake in the game. Whether it's paying for his books or all or part of the tuition, requiring your child to spend some of the money he has earned is important for his success down the road. Loans can count if you and your child know he, not you, will be paying them off.

I suggest that you implement a plan similar to the one Lauren's parents followed during her junior and senior year (described in the sidebar). They gave her a large lump sum of about $10,000 to last nine months. This is a scary thought. If you can do the same when your child is a senior, you can have some confidence that your child is on the right track to a satisfying career. If your child does well under the plan, then it's a lock.

The question of "financial stake" provides another opportunity for character building if two parents disagree on how big the financial stake should be for their child. It is typical for one parent or the other to resist placing too much of a burden on a child, and there can be legitimate differences of opinion. The natural inclination of the child is to play one parent against the other and in some cases get the parents to compete for the child's affection. If this kind of family politics can be resolved through a fair and open agreement, it's a wonderful way to teach good character!

Trust Me with the Money

For my first two years, living on campus, none of my university expenses went through me. My parents paid my tuition and room and board. The last two years, when I was living off campus, they continued to pay all university expenses, but at the beginning of each semester, gave me a check that covered rent and estimated food and utility costs. It was then up to me to write the checks every month and keep on top of my own living expenses. I was also in the process of buying my car from them, so rather than deduct that amount from the money they were giving me, they still left it up to me to write them a separate monthly check, just to reinforce the point.

Throughout all four years, I was always responsible for my own spending money, so I had a series of work-study and off-campus local jobs. Mom and Dad always told me that if I chose to blow the whole amount they gave me on beer, that was my prerogative, but then I'd have to find my own way to pay my rent. Luckily, it never came to that (which of course they knew it wouldn't, which is why it was a safe risk to take).

—Lauren Rupard, a 2003 Syracuse University graduate who is now enjoying a fine career in Washington, D.C., and is not living at home

What Parents Can Do

This section does not even pretend to provide advice on how parents can develop good character in their children. There are an unlimited number of sources of information and ideas on this topic, including other parents, religious leaders, peers, and school-district programs for character education, as well as books and magazine articles. I focused on money because I believe it is the biggest leverage point you have as a coach in helping your child develop the character employers hope to find in their employees. Here are three more strategies for doing this.

Strategy #1: Role modeling is the best way to teach. St. Francis of Assisi said, "Preach the gospel always and if necessary, use words." Demonstrating good character in conversations about your own career and workplace experiences can help your child develop many of the attitudes and traits employers want. Talk to him about how you and others have done so well professionally by working hard, doing the best work possible, and practicing continuous improvement.

The trouble with role modeling as a teaching method is that it is sometimes a pain in the neck. You know the idea "do as I say, not as I do" is wrong, but that doesn't mean you will not use it. When I complain about my students' grammar and typing mistakes, my wife, who reads my manuscripts, suggests that I do what I tell my students to do. When your children were little, perhaps you could justify eating a bag of potato chips right before dinner with the authoritarian statement, "I am an adult and you are a child." For college-age or even high school–age children, you will just have to bite the bullet and avoid complaining about your boss in front of your children. Who said parenting got easier when your children are out of diapers?

Let me illustrate my points by bringing up a touchy subject. Many students I talk with about financial aid tell me that their parents figured out illegal, if not at least unethical, ways to become eligible for more financial aid. For example, they might put their businesses in someone else's name. It could mean thousands of dollars in savings, but what does it mean for that student's character?

Strategy #2: Act as an investor and require a financial stake in the game. Parents can be calculating and rational about how much money they spend on their children's education, but they become confused and emotional about what their children do with this investment. An investor's mind-set will help your child build character.

The financial components need to be spelled out clearly. You should

Parental Financial Aid Scams

I once had a student hand deliver a letter from his parents. The letter explained the hardship the family was experiencing due to the parents' separation and divorce. However, apparently the student forgot to remove the "sticky" note his parents wrote, telling him that everything was really okay and that they were just telling this to the financial aid office to appeal for more money.

The more common practice is to shift assets. People do it all the time to "outwit" Medicaid, beat taxes, shelter property from lawsuits and ex-spouses, and also to "beat" financial aid. Families can legally transfer a student's assets to a sibling, the parent, or spend them on a "noncountable item" (like buying the family car with the student's college account).

—Chris Walsh, chief financial aid officer, Syracuse University

estimate the total cost of tuition plus living expenses and books along with financial aid. Indicate the amount that you will contribute and the amount of your child's contribution. The trade-offs among different kinds of loans and future debt should also be explored.

As already noted, a key investment strategy is to require the principals to have a financial stake in the game. Even as little as 20 percent would be enough to require money management and the practice of deferring gratification. A Hartford Financial Services survey of 2,245 parents of high school and college students revealed that 80 percent of all parents say they require some financial contribution, and 41 percent say they required more than half.[6]

Like every suggestion throughout this book, moderation is the key when determining the size of the financial stake you request of your children. Students who work more than twenty hours a week and take a full course load do not graduate on time as often as those who work less. Some students are so busy earning money to pay the bills that they do poorly academically and cannot take advantage of outside activities. But on the whole, money worries should be part of a college education.

Strategy # 3: Encourage your child to practice Dale Carnegie principles. In several sections of this book, I recommend the use of Dale Carnegie's principles, many of which are provided in his book *How to Win Friends and*

Influence People. It can guide your work to establish a good relationship with your child and model how to get along with others. Dale Carnegie can help you help your child build character. Get yourself a copy and point out to your child how you used a principle or two a week. Practicing the principles in the book can make a big difference if my experience with undergraduates is any example. In my classes I often ask students to choose a Carnegie principle and use it for a time. Later, I have them get up in the front of the class and give a one-minute talk on how it worked. Many send me an e-mail or mention in casual conversation how a principle like "smile" helped them.

One of my sophomores read the Carnegie book over the summer while she was a camp counselor. She was not getting anywhere with the fourteen teenage girls in her cabin—they were not making their beds or keeping things neat. She would yell and lecture and threaten, but after reading Dale's principle "talk in terms of the other person's interests," she sat them down and explained how getting good marks on inspections would result in more pizza and other perks. She was amazed that her cabin won the top awards, and she was even more excited when she got more gratuities from parents than ever before—and more than any of the other counselors.

On occasion, some students will say that Dale Carnegie is about manipulating people, and you might think the same. Carnegie was a deeply religious man dedicated to helping people succeed, and that spirit comes through in his book. I tell them that of course the book is about sales, but selling is noble if you care about the customer. Talking about this book with your child can help you model character.

Dale Carnegie principles are basically about good character. To make them work, people have to be genuine in their concern for others, and through their enthusiasm they inspire themselves and others. You probably have already helped your child do that or may have a favorite book or plan to help your child develop a healthy ability to treat people well. The point is that some conscious and consistent attempt on your part to generate such character traits during your child's college years makes sense.

Useful Resources

How to Win Friends and Influence People, by Dale Carnegie (New York: Pocket Books, 1982). This book is as much about character as it is about skills, and so I mention it again here. Students find it to be more than just a book on how to influence people. It is really about demonstrating character by listening to and respecting others.

How You Can Help: An Easy Guide to Doing Good Deeds in Your Everyday Life, by William D. Coplin (New York: Routledge, 2000). This book suggests how to weave doing good into everyday life without it getting in the way of other goals.

The 7 Habits of Highly Effective People, by Stephen R. Covey (New York: Simon & Schuster, 1989). This is one of the most widely read books in the business world and elsewhere on getting along with people through good character.

The No-Cash Allowance: A Practical Guide for Teaching Your Children How to Manage Money, by Lynne Finch (New London, WI: Walnut Row, 2004). Money may be the root of all evil, but money matters provide an opportunity for practicing good character.

Character Matters: How to Help Our Children Develop Good Judgment, Integrity, and Other Essential Virtues, by Thomas Lickona (New York: Touchstone, 2004). Written by the most well-recognized authority on the character-education movement in our schools, this book speaks to both parents and teachers.

Benjamin Franklin's the Art of Virtue: His Formula for Successful Living, by Benjamin Franklin and George Rogers (Eden Prairie, MN: Acorn Publishing, 1996). This book provides a quaint and entertaining discussion of Ben's old-fashioned views of character—views that our society could benefit from today.

Notes

1. *Jacobellis v. Ohio,* 378 U.S. 184 (1964).

2. Benjamin Franklin, *The Autobiography and Other Writings,* edited by L. Jesse Lemisch (New York: Signet Classics, 2001), pp. 94–100.

3. Kathleen Cotton, "Developing Employability Skills," School Improvement Research Series, Northwest Regional Educational Laboratory (November 1993). Available at http://www.nwrel.org/scpd/sirs/8/c015.html.

4. The Josephson Institute of Ethics, "2006 Josephson Institute Report Card on the Ethics of American Youth," October 15, 2006.

5. Diane Lewis, "Qualification: Must Have a Good Credit History," *Boston Globe,* September 5, 2006. Available at www.boston.com/business/globe/articles/2006/09/05/qualification_must_have_a_good_credit_history/.

6. Inside *USA Today,* September 25, 2006, p. 3.

CHAPTER 3

Career Exploration

"I always wanted to be somebody, but I should have been more specific."

—Lily Tomlin, comedian and actress

Career exploration starts at a very early age. Children want to be firefighters, police officers, teachers, chefs, and mechanics soon after they start walking. These early signs should not be ignored by you or them.

When I was about five years old, I started teaching kids on my block how to tell time. I also played bus driver, collecting fares when I was confined to bed for illness. In high school and college, I ran a tutoring business that grossed in its last year about $100 a week and showed my interest in business. Despite these indicators, I was uncertain about what career I should choose and considered many paths including law and the Foreign Service. While pursuing a master's degree to get into the Foreign Service, I was asked to teach some classes and only then realized that I wanted to teach. Years later, my father reminded me that I had always had a talent and inclination to teach, starting at a very young age.

By the time your children become teenagers and start thinking about careers, they usually forget about their early inclinations. They look toward the media, particularly television, and see athletes, entertainers, TV broadcasters, lawyers, and doctors. They tend to think money is synonymous with success, so they seek careers that promise big money. But people who make the most money are passionate about and skilled at what they do, regardless of field. Sometimes it just requires being innovative and persevering.

Obstacles to Career Exploration

The biggest obstacle to career exploration today is that teenagers have no understanding of the millions (and by millions, I mean *millions*) of career options out there. There are 12,000 specific occupations according to the U.S. Department of Labor, with many variations and employment opportunities for each. Your child might end up in the career she dreamt about as a child, a career that you or close family members are in or, in rare cases, something she saw on TV. But chances are she will land someplace she never knew existed, doing something that incorporates the interests and skills she demonstrated as a child. This is particularly true in today's economy with the rapidly changing job market and the unforeseen impact of new technology.

College curricula often mislead students in the career-exploration process. Students who are the most confused and unfocused usually end up in a general or liberal arts program, where bewilderment is considered a sign of education. Moreover, liberal arts faculty members tend to steer students away from business careers, even though these careers compose about 80 percent of all jobs in America. They try to steer some into Ph.D. programs, which accounts for the large oversupply of Ph.D.'s in most fields in the United States. Others are encouraged to pursue nonprofit work. Students in professional schools with faculty who are researchers rather than real-world practitioners are likely to be misled also. Except teaching a student how to become a professional academic researcher, many college faculty members lack the experience to provide guidance on career options.

Guidance counselors and career-service staff respond to this problem in high school and college primarily by giving talks, bringing people from different fields into classes, and having students take personality inventories and explore career options that fit their interests. These activities have some impact but are not enough to put most students on a promising career path. Learning about careers in the counselor's office doesn't put the student any closer to actually working in the field; only a program of career preparation can do that.

In high school, the question, "What career paths might you follow?" inevitably gets redefined into "Are you going to college?" and then "What college?" This is a convenient transformation because it is a more concrete question. It puts off the inevitable uncertainty and risk associated with choosing a career. It avoids the dreaded question, "What are you going to be when you grow up?" The proper question should be, "What college do you plan to attend and how will your choice help you explore and prepare for careers you may want to pursue?" College selection should be connected to exploring career options.

In chapter 7, I will discuss the "college for all" attitude encouraged by our high schools and pose the question, "Is your child college material?" The "college for all" attitude contributes greatly to a gap between career goals and actual achievement among high school students, and it reflects a failure to look broadly at the infinite range of careers open to students. Sociology professor John Reynolds suggests that the prospect of earning high salaries drives students more than what interests them. The system misleads them because they may shoot to become professors when in fact plumbers earn as much or more money. No wonder, according to Tim Conway (who authored chapter 22, on getting that first job), that 80 percent of college freshmen are uncertain about an academic major and 65 percent of college students change their majors two or three times.

Most of what I say in this book is based on existing research and my experiences with thousands of students, but my personal experience with our four children and their four spouses might be helpful to you. You might say I have in-depth and long-term knowledge. Ours is a middle-class family, and all my children are now in their forties. Their experiences not only demonstrate that skills and character are the keys to career success, but also that career exploration is more about what you like to do and less about where you study or what your major is.

Son number one was a straight-A student through the ninth grade, at which time he discovered *girls*. By the time he was a senior he had moved from an A average to a cumulative B− average; his SAT scores were in the top 20 percent. He interviewed with an admissions officer at a second-tier school, hoping to get into the engineering program. The admissions officer basically said, "Not a chance unless you go to community college and maintain a B average." So, he shifted to the management program and was admitted. He switched fields because above all he wanted to go to college—or at least, he thought he did as a senior in high school. After doing B work (to his surprise, because he didn't study very much) the first quarter, he "achieved" a 0.00 average the next. He tried a few more semesters at Syracuse University, where he attended for free because he was the son of a faculty member, but he eventually failed out there as well. He then went to a community college in Florida, but because he didn't go to class or even take the tests, you can imagine what happened. You might think I was furious about all this, but fortunately for him, I know that college is not for everyone. My wife and I discussed the situation with him and as a family we agreed that graduation was not a realistic expectation for him at that time. Instead, we agreed that he should become financially independent (a euphemism for "You're on your own, kid"), and he started to work full-time.

He tried to start a trucking business, but that didn't work, so he got a job at one of the office-supply stores. He was a hard worker and was quickly promoted to store manager; he was on the road to regional manager and who knows where after that. But he wasn't ready to be serious, so he quit and got a new job in the mail room at a big insurance company in Atlanta. His work ethic and professionalism got noticed, and the general manager of the company suggested that he take the underwriter's exam, which he passed easily. After several moves, he is a manager of underwriters, has a wife, three kids, a sailboat, a house, and two cars. He's happy and has no inclination to go to college. He may have regretted not getting a college degree, but he is too busy coaching his son's lacrosse team.

His wife was also a college wannabe who didn't feel like paying her dues. She met my son when they were both pretending to go to community college in Florida. She worked for the same insurance company where he was a mail boy, and she became an adjuster. She moved up the ranks and followed her husband to different areas. She quit her job when they had three kids but worked part-time for L.L.Bean on holidays. She liked the job, especially the discounts. Then she got a job doing graphics and general computer-based work for a small company. She is working almost full-time; is very active in her children's lives; and, among other things, is a force in school-board politics.

Son number two got a college degree at a small Catholic school in Rochester, New York. He enjoyed the learning experience and picked up a lot of skills. He worked in customer service for two furniture companies after receiving his bachelor of science degree in management and now is working for a very successful company that produces road-construction machinery. He deals with marketing, customer service, and delivery. He is a hard worker who has great social skills and a tremendous sense of responsibility. He is married and has a house, two kids, and two cars.

His wife completed a two-year degree in an executive-secretary training program at SUNY-Alfred and promptly got a job in that position. From that job she moved up the ladder to a sales position. She was doing very well, traveling to New York City and elsewhere from her base in Rochester. After a few years she decided to quit the job because it was too much pressure and kept her working too many hours. She became a waitress, where she met my son. She's still a part-time waitress two nights a week at an upscale restaurant. She likes people and food, so she's happy.

Daughter number one was the typical high achiever: thinking about medical school, maintaining a high GPA, and involving herself in all kinds of activities in the honors program at the University of Maryland. She applied but never made it to medical school. Instead, she got a master's degree in hospital administration from the University of Minnesota, which required an internship. From her internship, she got a full-time job at the same hospital and moved up the ranks; before long, she was making more money than I was. She moved to another hospital and is on track to become a CEO or COO. Her career prospects remain robust because she's highly skilled in just about everything. She has two kids, an expensive house, and a job she loves. Her friends say she makes "the best &$#!!%$ brownies in the world" and she is thinking of trying a side business.

Her husband received his bachelor's degree in chemical engineering from the University of Maryland (not surprisingly, he met my daughter at school). He says he wants to be something else but sticks to the job because he actually likes it. He feels pressured to move up, but he doesn't want managerial responsibilities. I think he wants to start a rock band or be a cartoonist. Multitalented, he is happy also.

Daughter number two got a bachelor's degree in psychology from the University of Maryland and started working in a nursing home. She couldn't take the pressure and reprehensible methods that administrators were using to fill empty beds with people not on Medicaid. She tried one of the make-a-teacher-in-a-month programs in Baltimore but smiled too much, so the little monsters ate her alive. She then worked in customer service for a very big jewelry company and was so good that they gave her outrageous bonuses and raises even though she wanted out from the day she got there. After twelve years, one day she just quit. Now she is happy as a lark working two days a week for a friend as an office worker. She didn't develop many computer skills in college (much to my chagrin) because she hated them. But when her friend needed someone to keep the books, my daughter applied herself, became a computer whiz, and found that she actually loves it. She has a house, two cars, and two dogs that make her very happy. She and her husband are angling to start a bed-and-breakfast, which will probably happen.

Her husband, my son-in-law, takes the prize for career shifting. An economics major at the University of Maryland, his real major was having fun. He swears he learned nothing in college, but he met my daughter there, so it wasn't a total loss for him. He had several real estate jobs before he started working for a private school for the developmentally disabled. He was so good that the school paid for his master's degree. Upon almost receiving it, he realized that he was burned-out and took a state job finding employment for people with serious disabilities. After about six years of doing very well, he quit and became a house painter. Now he is really happy and making as much as he was in his other jobs. He could actually make a lot more, but he just wants to pay his bills.

So what's the conclusion from these eight cases? First, all eight are competent in both technical and general professional skills. Some are more skilled than others, but all are skilled enough to pursue diverse career options. Second, they work very hard and take on a lot of responsibility whenever they make a commitment. Third, they move around to different jobs, sometimes switching fields. Finally, for most of them, their undergraduate majors have nothing to do with where they are now. The graduate portion of their education is related to their current profession in two out of three cases.

As a parent, I'm satisfied with where they are in their lives. They're not just out of my house (and my wallet). They're living the American Dream. Enjoying life in a responsible and self-sustaining manner is a reasonable, modest, and satisfying goal.

What about you? Is that your goal as a parent, or do you have expectations that your child will go into a certain field or accumulate a lot of money? If you do, you are forgetting that your children are not your trophies or your property. It is hard to avoid these feelings sometimes, but everyone will be better off if you do.

Career Services Are Essential

Although career exploration is a very confusing thing for most college students, the career-services office is the one place at every college where your child can get a start and the direction he needs. Students and parents tend to think of career services as part of a strategy to get prepped for the job market. The truth is that it should be part of a career-development strategy from the day students step on campus as applicants.

Students treat career-service staff like most of us treat doctors. When we get sick enough, we go to the doctor for some medicine. Preventive medicine still is a hard sell for most people. The same is true for students pursuing careers. They want a quick fix from the career-services office, like *Get me a job now!* Chapter 22 will provide specific suggestions on how seniors can get jobs and how you can help your child. To take advantage of those suggestions, your child needs to make friends with the career-services staff early and often.

Career-services programs have emerged as an ever-increasing administrative expense over the past fifty years because parents expect such services, and it is clear that faculty members can't provide them. That is good news for parents. It means that somebody's job depends on helping your child achieve her career mission. In my experience, career-services staff members are talented, caring, and dedicated.

Your child can visit the career-services office during the second semester of her senior year and get a poor start on her career when she graduates, or she can start working with the career-services office when she arrives on campus as a freshman, get a spectacular job, and a really good education.

Students tend to think that the only thing the career-services staff is good for is writing resumes, teaching tricks to pull on interviewers, and getting leads on open jobs. This limited view brings most students to the career-services office when it is too late. It also leads to an underuse of this critical resource—a crucial link to the major reason for your huge financial investment.

Career services can offer help in all of the following areas before a student's senior year and job hunt begin:

■ **Exploring Skills and Interests.** Students can take a variety of tests to assess what they are good at and what they like to do. Professionals interpret the tests and counsel students.

■ **Exploring the Characteristics and Requirements of Many Career Fields.** Students can use several different online services like eChoices, Discover, and SIGI Plus.

■ **Writing Resumes and Cover Letters for Internships.** Career-services offices provide templates for resumes, access to online programs, training in writing resumes and cover letters, and personal consultation.

■ **Preparing for Internship Interviews.** Students can take training sessions on interviews and practice interviewing using videotaping.

■ **Understanding E-Recruiting for Internships.** Students have access to e-mail systems that alert the career-services office to job openings, career fairs, and visits by employers.

■ **Meeting Employers Offering Internships on Campus.** Students can benefit from the contacts career-services personnel have with employers, especially when campus visits are arranged. They will screen students for interviews, so early and frequent contact with staff will pay off.

■ **Networking with Alumni for Mentoring and Intern Searching.** Increasingly, career-services staff members are getting help from alumni who can serve as mentors and advisers as well as provide information on available internships.

■ **Obtaining Internships and Summer Jobs.** Given the growing importance of internships and summer jobs, career-services offices are devoting more resources to helping students find these positions. They can provide books and online services as well as leads through their contact with alumni.

■ **Exploring Graduate Schools.** Students can get information on graduate programs, their connections with certain careers, and information on tests for graduate schools.

■ **Choosing a Major and Selecting Courses That Will Help Pursue Careers.** Students can talk to career staff about useful courses on campus from a career perspective. This will help to provide a more complete picture than they might get from relying solely on faculty.

■ **Identifying Faculty and Staff on Campus to Serve as Advisers.** Career-services people know the faculty and staff members on campus who are willing to help students find appropriate career paths, and they will introduce students to these individuals.

■ **Identifying Student Activities That Might Be Helpful.** Students should think of student activities as a way to build skills and character. The career-services staff will have insight into which organization's activities would be most helpful given a student's interests and talents.

■ **Keeping Students Focused on the Career Mission.** Just the act of visiting the career-services office once or twice a semester helps students focus on their career missions in college. They will always find something useful in their pursuit of this objective.

From this list, it is obvious that the career-services staff can play a critical role in helping your child develop the skills and character employers want. The staff can also help your child explore career options. Your child should think of the staff members as personal career coaches. It is also obvious that many of the services they provide to help your child get internships during the first three years of college can also be used for the senior-year job hunt.

What Parents Can Do

In chapter 4, we'll talk about why college students have difficulty focusing on career preparation. Students tend to live in the present and often forget to pursue the objectives that will put them on the path to career success. Even if they are committed to gaining skills and developing character, they may still avoid career exploration.

To open your child's eyes to the possibilities, career exploration must be an integral part of her college education. Your child may be hesitant to embrace this mission; like most of us, she seeks to avoid uncertainty and risk. Plus, she has many more pressing social matters to attend to. Here are some strategies to help you generate an interest in and provide help for career exploration:

Strategy #1: Remember, the apple doesn't fall far from the tree. Your child sees you and your relatives as models to emulate (or rebel against). Long-time personal contacts shape your child's view of the kinds of careers she may pursue. This principle has its limits; just because Uncle Ed is a circus clown doesn't mean your child should be, too. However, if your child is sincerely interested in your profession or the profession of a relative, have him ask questions, shadow you at work, or possibly set up an internship.

In advising students, I find that the parents' careers often color their advice to their children. Lawyers want their children to go to law school. Teachers tell their children not to go into education. The majority of parents place no pressure either way.

The last course is the best. Give your child an understanding of your own career and be realistic about the benefits and costs. Above all, make it clear that her career choice is up to her.

Strategy #2: Have a conversation about career options. Before your child takes off for college, encourage her to think about what would be interesting to her. You could start the conversation off with the question, "Would you like most of your job to be dealing with people, analyzing information, or working with your hands?" The answer is likely to be a combination. The purpose of the conversation is to get the topic on your child's agenda, not to reach a conclusion.

Don't worry about ability at this point. Ask her how her activities, especially outside of class, will allow her to explore these three general interests. Encourage her to look for jobs, student activities, and internships that will let her see if she likes what she thinks she likes. Thousands of would-be lawyers have been stopped cold in their tracks by a summer internship in a lawyer's office, which is usually a good thing for their parents' pocketbooks and for society as a whole. Internships are important in helping your child see what he doesn't want to do; through process of elimination he will learn what he does want to do.

Strategy #3: Encourage career-exploration activities, especially early and frequent visits to the campus career-services office. You can encourage career exploration by suggesting that your child participate in a variety of experiences both inside and outside of class. By far the most important are jobs and internships where your child explores her career interests as she seeks to please her boss or supervisor. Without these experiences, the lectures, books, and "interest inventories" will not provide much help.

One of the most important things you can do is encourage your child to visit the career-services office at her college. Start early; go together when you and your child make campus visits in high school. Review the list of services provided in this chapter.

Some useful experiences can happen in the classroom, but more will take place in activities outside of the classroom. Parts four and five of this book suggest many ways in which your child can use academic and nonacademic activities to explore careers.

Useful Resources

High schools and colleges, public libraries, and other organizations providing job support make one of several computer-based career-advising programs like eChoices, Discover, or SIGIPlus available. Every day, the site provides engaging occupation features as well as articles about building skills and exploring education programs. You can also sign up for a free weekly e-mail newsletter full of career-exploration and skill-building articles.

Igniteyoungadults.com is a website by Tim Conway (author of chapter 22). It is designed to promote his services but also to help students explore careers. He and his website are excellent sources of information on career exploration and career coaching.

Major in Success: Make College Easier, Fire Up Your Dreams, and Get a Very Cool Job, by Patrick Combs (Berkeley, CA: Ten Speed Press, 2000). This book oversells the possibilities of dream careers and has too much of "you can be anything you want to be" in it, but if your child needs some enthusiasm, it might be useful.

Making a Life, Making a Living: Reclaiming Your Purpose and Passion in Business and in Life, by Mark Albion (New York: Warner Books, 2000). Written by a former Harvard Business School professor who decided that life was too short to stay in a job that had no purpose beyond making money, this book will help you think about how to have a fulfilling career.

What Color Is Your Parachute? A Practical Manual for Job-Hunters and Career-Changers, by Richard N. Bolles (Berkeley, CA: Ten Speed Press, 2006). This is the best-selling book providing general career advice. Written primarily for people changing jobs and careers, the book provides a more elaborate discussion of the questions raised by figure 3-1. Bolles's website, http://www.JobHun tersBible.com, may also be helpful.

PART TWO

Building a Good Relationship with Your Child

Parents have to act more like coaches and investors and less like cheerleaders and charities. Chapters 4, 5, and 6 show you how.

Focus, Focus, Focus

"Insanity is often the logic of an accurate mind overtasked."

—Oliver Wendell Holmes

I have a terrier (a Westie, in fact) that is particularly susceptible to what I call the "focus problem." When he pays attention to me, he doesn't do bad things like run away, bark at other dogs, or chase squirrels with me in tow. But when he focuses on something else, like a strange smell, a fleeing rabbit, or the personality defect of another dog, he can be very bad.

My dog's "focus problem" consists of two different patterns. The first is Instant Gratification Syndrome (IGS), where he flits from one pursuit to another. During obedience training, he has trouble paying attention for more than three seconds. His desire for instant gratification destroys his focus. If I could keep his attention long enough, I'm sure I could get him to do anything, even play the piano.

The second is Can't See the Forest for the Trees Syndrome (CSFTS), where he focuses on a woodchuck and will not even stop for a treat or a mighty tug on his collar. He could spend half an hour in extreme agitation, driving everyone but the woodchuck crazy.

The same is true of college students. One of my students described college IGS perfectly:

College students have so many things running through their heads from "How drunk am I going to get tonight?" to "I have a paper due in five hours, which I have not started," to "Where am I going to eat?" Faced with

29

an infinite number of choices on what to do with their time, they tend to be overwhelmed by the crush of the present for all of the decisions they make. Most are so excited to make friends and stay out late that they can't focus on anything except living it up.

What "it" is, I'm not sure, but my students assure me it can be quite distracting.

College students tend to focus on the wrong thing to the exclusion of others. CSFTS takes many forms. If students are academically uninclined or conversely scared to death of not doing well, they worry about grades so much that they often avoid courses that will help them in their careers. They may even focus on just doing well on the tests rather than learning the material. Outside of course work and career activities, their focus can be on the entire range of social activities or specific obsessions like video games, gambling, alcohol and drug abuse, or soap operas.

Helping your child to focus long enough to do things right and to engage in the variety of activities necessary to prepare for a career is no easy task. Ultimately, maturity is the determining factor, and we all know that it requires time and patience on the part of any parent.

College Requires a New Level of Maturity

In their book, *Helping Your First-Year College Student Succeed: A Guide for Parents*, Richard Mullendore and Cathie Hatch list the major differences between high school and college (see figure 4-1). The biggest difference is that the support systems and structured environment are virtually removed in college. Your child will have to take responsibility for his own self-development and the consequences of his actions. It's like letting my Westie loose in the woods and hoping he comes home better able to cope with nature.

The entire college experience requires students to handle much more freedom than they had in high school. It tests their maturity and good judgment. Living at home or at a boarding school during high school does not present the same kinds of temptations as the 24/7 freedoms available in college. Moreover, the influence of peers becomes even more predominant than in high school. Unfortunately, risky and negative behavior tends to crowd out good behavior. College life itself has always been a force to encourage immature behavior. Remember the film *Animal House*? Need I say more?

Parents have to step up and be the positive influence that counteracts this peer pressure. Dr. Mel Levine, a practicing psychiatrist and an academic researcher at the University of North Carolina, approached this idea in his

Figure 4-1. Major differences between high school and college.

HIGH SCHOOL	COLLEGE
Teacher/Student Contact—Contact closer and more frequent (five days a week)	*Teacher/Student Contact*—Faculty is available during office hours (only a few hours a week) and by appointment to address students' concerns.
Competition/Grades—Academic competition is not as strong; good grades can often be obtained with minimum effort.	*Competition/Grades*—Academic competition is much stronger; minimum effort may produce poor grades.
Status—Students establish a personal status in academic and social activities based on family and community factors.	*Status*—Students can build their status as they wish; high school status can be repeated or changed.
Counseling/Dependence—Students can rely on parents, teachers, and counselors to help make decisions and give advice. Students must abide by parents' boundaries and restrictions.	*Counseling/Dependence*—Students rely on themselves; they see the results of making their own decisions. It is their responsibility to seek advice as needed. Students set their own restrictions.
Motivation—Students get stimulation to achieve or participate from parents, teachers, and counselors.	*Motivation*—Students apply their own motivation to their work and activities as they wish.
Freedom—Students' freedom is limited. Parents will often help students out of a crisis should one arise.	*Freedom*—Students have much more freedom. Students must accept responsibility for their own actions.
Distractions—There are distractions from school, but these are partially controlled by school and home.	*Distractions*—The opportunity for more distractions exists. Time management to students will become important.
Value Judgments—Students often make value judgments based on parental values; thus, many of their value judgments are made for them.	*Value Judgments*—Students have the opportunity to see the world through their own eyes and develop their own opinions and values.

SOURCE: Mullendore, Richard H., and Hatch, Cathie. *Helping Your First-Year College Student Succeed: A Guide for Parents.* Columbia, SC: University of South Carolina, National Resource Center for The First-Year Experience & Students in Transition. © 2000. Reprinted with permission.

book titled *Ready or Not, Here Life Comes.* The tagline for the book is "America's top learning expert shows how today's society makes it hard for kids to grow into productive adults—and what we can do about it."[1]

We don't have an MRI that detects levels of immaturity. We know a lot about it, having been that way ourselves. But that doesn't make it any easier to counteract.

If your child's grades are down or he drops courses, misses deadlines, does his work at the last minute, or doesn't plan ahead for next semester or a summer internship, immaturity is probably the reason. This conclusion may be difficult to accept, but it shouldn't be ignored.

Parents tend to ignore the massive role immaturity plays in poor focus. They don't want to face the reality that their child may not be ready for college. Fearing their child will be doomed to a life of misery and poverty if he doesn't graduate from college, they remain in a state of denial. The fear and denial prevents them from providing the counsel and pressure that will hasten the maturation process.

Another factor that you must consider is the role of alcohol and drugs in your child's life. Many students flunk out of college because they were already addicts or alcoholics. Peer pressure and easy access are constant forces that many students cannot resist. If you see drugs and alcohol playing a role in your child's life in high school, you can bet that it will only get worse in college.

College Requires Balancing Competing Interests

College students are faced with an infinite number of opportunities to be distracted from their career missions in college. An overconcern with grades can prevent them from getting the nonacademic experiences essential to developing skills, building character, and exploring careers. The desire to have fun or just hang out can prevent them from graduating and taking the time to pursue their career missions. Working to earn money to pay for college can get in the way. Activities to change the world can also become a preoccupation that garners too much attention.

One of my students who left the university without graduating after six years was missing in action for weeks at a time. But I could always find him conducting the band at basketball games twice a week. Ten years after leaving, he contacted me to finish up his degree and after a rough period seemed to be on a good career track. Taking on a time-consuming and enjoyable task year after year had prevented him from doing enough to complete his degree. A little balance would have put him on a viable career track much earlier.

None of these distractions are trivial. In fact, all of them can be helpful in your child's career mission. Having fun helps students find out what they like to do and how to balance work and play. Learning as a general mission builds the capacity for continuous self-improvement, and the knowledge gained may come in handy in a variety of life and job situations (at the very least, it will help with dinner conversation). Working on projects to improve society is a way to develop skills and also to demonstrate to future employers that you work for the good of the company, not just a paycheck.

There is an even more important reason why students should seek balance in their college lives: Work in the twenty-first century is interlaced with people's private lives like never before. The traditional nine-to-five job is disappearing and more people are working from their homes via the Internet. They bring work home, but the workplace is also an arena for social interaction. I'm not just talking about happy hour on Friday, but sporting events and community-service projects.

In addition, special interests and talents that may begin as hobbies sometimes turn into jobs. A book by Marci Alboher called *One Person/ Multiple Careers: A New Model for Work/Life Success* describes how people are developing multiple vocations based on their interests. This "slasher" pattern is likely to become more pronounced among college graduates as the variety of opportunities expands.[2]

Finally, work has to be meaningful. As Teddy Roosevelt said, "The best prize that life offers is the chance to work hard at work worth doing." Finding out what is worth doing requires students to figure out what they really value, and that's a result of the whole range of experiences they can have in college.

Balance is good as long as preparing for a satisfying career has a major place in your child's college life. Too many students put it at the bottom of their priority lists, figuring that they'll worry about it when they're seniors.

That's what happened to Jane, a bright and serious student, who came to Syracuse University ready to undertake every challenge but also to "take advantage of the best years of her life" (advice she had received from her parents). From her junior year in high school to her senior year in college, everything was a blur. She did well academically, performed a lot of community service, went to Spain for a semester because she "really wanted to learn Spanish," pledged a sorority, had great spring breaks, completed two majors, and maintained a 3.5 GPA. But by senior year, she had no idea what she wanted to do careerwise. She had some skills, but nothing that would distinguish her from the herd. Her summers were spent either relaxing or earning money to pay some of her expenses for the next year. She worked in retail sales. When I asked her if she was interested in retail sales as a career, she looked at me like I was crazy. When I talked to her about career interests, she could only bemoan her lack of direction.

Will Jane end up in a homeless shelter? Not likely, so don't panic if your child and Jane have something in common. Will she wander between jobs for a couple of years and be even more confused and frustrated than she was her senior year? Most likely! Will she settle for retail sales even though she seems to hate that idea? I wouldn't be surprised. And who knows? She could become the president of Saks Fifth Avenue someday. But if she had devoted time and energy to more skill-based courses, explored internships, and taken a leadership position in her sorority or some student organization, she would have been better prepared for the transition from student to professional.

Recognizing that your child will have several worthwhile missions in college is important because, well, that's the reality. It might be best if career preparation was his top priority, but my advice is to settle for career preparation as one of his top priorities.

Having your children focus at least part of their energies on career preparation is no easy task. You need to approach the topic consciously, strategically, and consistently because, as you already know, you don't have a lot of control.

What Parents Can Do

As discussed in Part One of this book, you want to encourage your children to:

Develop skills
Build character
Explore careers

To get your child to focus on these goals as he chooses his course work, student activities, jobs, and internships, you can employ a variety of strategies. With your advice, he should develop a specific plan for his four years in college. Remind him of these goals in conversations about his choice of college, his choice of courses and majors, and his choice of summer and part-time jobs.

Strategy #1: Monitor for focus. You may not be able to do much about how well your child focuses on his career mission in college. But you can keep tabs on his focus. I have listed some attitudes and behaviors that will help you:

1. Good Career-Mission Focus
   - Gets a summer internship between freshman and sophomore years and starts looking even before the freshman year begins
   - Checks to see how courses and experiences help prepare for and explore careers
   - Gets a summer internship each summer in college
   - Goes to the career center during freshman year
   - Chooses a major by sophomore year and sticks to it
   - Takes courses to develop specific skills he needs to strengthen
   - Selects jobs that will build skill and character
   - Selects student activities that will build skill and character
   - Maintains at least a 3.0 GPA
   - Can at any time and any place tell you not only how many credits he has and how many he needs to graduate, but also what requirements he has yet to complete and when he will complete them
2. Bad Career-Mission Focus
   - Plans to stop by the career center second semester of senior year to see if he should prepare a resume
   - Likes to play a lot
   - Sees learning for the sake of learning as his only purpose
   - Does not seem to care about flunking out
   - Has a GPA near or below a 2.0
   - Worries only about high grades and amassing more credits, majors, and minors
   - Does not ever have a summer job or internship to explore careers and develop skills
   - Does not do the best he can do, except when it comes to having a good time
   - Is frequently tardy with one or more of the following: paying bills, registering, buying books, selecting a major
   - Can't tell you how many credits he has completed or how many he needs to graduate
   - Shows signs of an obsession with one student activity
   - Works more hours than is needed to pay essential bills

Strategy #2: Avoid the "best years of your life" phrase. Parents sometimes unwittingly encourage their children to sacrifice career objectives for enjoying their college years. The usual phrase is that college is the "best years of their lives." This phrase sends the wrong signal. The truth is, as parents, we don't want our children to have their "best years" in their late teens and early twenties. That would mean that it was downhill after that. We want our children to have lives that become richer and more fulfilling every year as they grow more and more into themselves. Moderation between living in the moment and living for the future is the best way to ensure that the best will always be yet to come.

Telling your child that his college years will be the best years of his life implies that he should enjoy himself before he's "saddled" with a job and family responsibilities. But you should not present career and family responsibilities negatively. To me, it seems like another way to say, "Stay away from adulthood as long as you can." Unfortunately, employers prefer to hire adults. Don't inadvertently teach your child to avoid responsibility.

Besides, how could roommate problems, money shortages, test and paper anxieties, the crazy behavior of professors, a very uncertain future, and lousy food be the recipe for the best time of your life? Sure, it will be fun; it will be memorable, but I think it's safe to say that most students go to college to make every year better than the last. A rewarding career is one of the keys to a happy future, so suggesting that the college experience should be entirely about living in the moment is bad advice.

Some parents fear that their children are overstressed by school, work, or career exploration. If your child's anxiety is unmanageable, of course he should take a break. But living only in the moment leads to more, not less, stress in the long run. Helping your child focus on career preparation with a reasonable amount of energy is the best path.

Strategy #3: Ask questions to point the way. Asking questions is much better than expressing your own judgment or opinion. Even if the answer is "I just want to have fun," don't be discouraged or react strongly. Raising questions rather than giving directions is more likely to place crucial ideas in your child's own agenda. A harangue from you is likely to be counterproductive. As Dale Carnegie said, "The only way to get the best of an argument is to avoid it."[3]

If you see your child heading into a career area that you think will not be best for him, be happy he is at least thinking about the future. Don't rain on his parade; if the career is wrong, he'll figure it out himself. In any case, it is his future, not yours. Always recognize the possibility that you could be wrong. I see no problem in pointing out the risks and downsides of a career you think is not right for him. Forcing him to deal with negative information is a good thing. If it crushes his dream and drive, it may be that he didn't have the commitment to stick it out. If it makes him rebel and try hard just to show you he can do it, that's not a bad thing either.

If Junior announces that he wants to spend the summer playing with a rock band he and his college buddies started because he wants to see if he can have a career in entertainment, don't panic. Take a walk around the block and then turn it into a career-development exercise. Suggest he keep good receipts, pay attention to marketing, and assess each performance. It could be a great career-development experience. Plus, the more supportive you are, the more your child will be willing to try out your suggestions.

I speak from experience here. One of my students was part of a band throughout college. He would tell me how his band was doing well because it did a massive mailing and practiced a lot. He was amused by other student bands because they did very little serious marketing and then wondered why they rarely got hired. This student is now getting a Ph.D. and is headed for a college presidency if he really chooses academia. The organizational and marketing skills he developed to promote his band will serve him well.

Getting your child to stay focused on preparing for a satisfying career from the beginning to the end of her college experience is both vital and difficult. You will need to encourage and enhance the notion from the first day you discuss college until graduation day and even after.

Strategy #4: Don't be afraid to pull the financial plug. This discussion so far assumes that your child has a certain level of maturity that will help you encourage him to pursue the three goals. But, in many cases, immaturity is a major roadblock to a college experience worth the investment.

If you decide your child is too immature to focus on career preparation, you can do something about it here and now. You can threaten to stop providing any financial support. Faced with this threat, your child may suddenly mature overnight.

If the threat of pulling financial support doesn't work, you need to make good on the threat. A year or two of trying to earn a living will help him realize that college opens up more possibilities for a successful career than working up through the ranks as a high school graduate. It may also help him find something he likes, which will encourage him to pursue a college program that is more appealing than the one he was in. Conversely, it could lead to an unexpected career option and success. As I mentioned earlier, this happened to one of my sons, who went from mail room clerk to a manager of insurance underwriters without setting foot in college again.

Useful Resources

Helping Your First-Year College Student Succeed: A Guide for Parents, by Richard Mullendore and Cathie Hatch, in conjunction with the National Orientation Directors Association. Copies of this book may be ordered from the National

Resource Center for the First-Year Experience & Students in Transition, University of South Carolina, 1629 Pendleton Street, Columbia, South Carolina 29208. Telephone: 803-777-6229. It is especially helpful to those parents sending their first student off to college.

My Freshman Year: What a Professor Learned by Becoming a Student, by Rebekah Nathan (Ithaca, NY: Cornell University Press, 2005). Written by an anthropology professor who went undercover as a student for a year, this book provides a glimpse of the social and academic life at Northern Arizona University.

Ready or Not, Here Life Comes, by Dr. Mel Levine (New York: Simon & Schuster, 2005). This widely published author is a professor of pediatrics at the University of North Carolina Medical School and is director of its Clinical Center for the Study of Development and Learning. His book will help parents understand why today's teenagers and young adults have trouble focusing and planning their futures.

Notes

1. Dr. Mel Levine, *Ready or Not, Here Life Comes* (New York: Simon & Schuster, 2005).

2. Marci Alboher, *One Person/Multiple Careers: A New Model for Work/Life Success* (New York: Warner Business, 2007).

3. Dale Carnegie, *How to Win Friends and Influence People* (New York: Pocket Books, 1982), p. iii.

The Goldilocks Principle

"God grant me the serenity
To accept the things I cannot change,
The courage to change the things I can,
And the wisdom to know the difference."

—Reinhold Niebuhr

Goldilocks broke into the home of the three bears and selected porridge, a chair, and a bed that were "just right"—not too hot or hard and not too cold or soft. You need to follow the Goldilocks Principle when guiding your child through her college career. This chapter will help you figure out what mixture of hands on and hands off is just right for your child.

Your relationship with your child, his career mission, and his college experience is best approached by thinking of yourself as an investor and your child as the principal of the business that is the target of your investment. There are plenty of other dimensions to your relationship with your child leading up to and during the college years. This chapter isolates career preparation. When it comes to helping your child make the transition to a self-supporting and satisfying adult, the investor model makes the most sense.

No doubt you will more or less agree with the Goldilocks Principle advocated in this chapter. At an intellectual level, how could you disagree with the need to pursue a moderate path between micromanaging and a hands-off approach? But agreeing in principle and actually taking a moderate approach are two different things. Emotions get in the way. I recognize that it is difficult to approach your relationship with your child as if you were a cold, calculating investor.

Much has been written about the parent-child relationship in the transition to adulthood. The books I refer to at the end of this chapter provide comprehensive advice. The "parents office" at your child's college can be a great resource as well. Staff members can answer questions and troubleshoot for you. They usually hold events during opening weekend and on parents' weekend that provide guidance and information. If nothing else, going to these events will connect you with parents who are going through what you're going through. Finally, many independent educational consultants are willing and able, for a fee, to help you work with your child on the entire range of decisions relating to college. Too many parents turn to these consultants for the wrong reasons (i.e., getting into the most prestigious school possible). Those parents who hire consultants to give their children expertise and counseling on college, program, and activity selection get more than their money's worth when it comes to helping a child prepare for and find a rewarding career.

I will not attempt to provide you with a perspective on how to work with your child on all the aspects of a college education. This chapter provides only an investor's perspective on how to help your investment reach its full career potential. However, you may find the Goldilocks Principle has other applications.

What is the right balance for you as an investor in your child's college education? You have to decide that for yourself. The general rule is "a little hands on and a lot of hands off." Too much of either is not likely to result in a career-ready college graduate. Just the right mixture will ensure that your child will want to come home for visits but won't move home to avoid destitution.

The problem with my advice, as I am sure you've already realized, is that what was hot and cold for Goldilocks might not feel the same to you. "Just right" is a moving target that depends on you, your child, and the circumstances. In fact, finding the right mix is why I placed the Serenity Prayer at the beginning of this chapter. You can't change your child if he doesn't want to be changed. Pick your battles carefully, but also have the courage to take action if you are convinced a change is needed.

There is no cookie-cutter formula to apply when deciding whether to make a big deal out of dropping from a B+ to a B average or whether to just say something like, "As long as you are doing the best you can, I am satisfied." The best I can do is to provide general guidelines and observations. In helping you find just the right mixture of hot and cold for you and your child, I will violate a basic rule of good instruction. Instead of telling you what to do, I will have to tell you what not to do. You may be familiar with the reality show *What Not to Wear*, in which the hosts transform people who dress poorly into trendy fashion savants. The bulk of the show is negative, as the title implies, but in the end the people learn how to dress themselves. Hopefully, this will work for you.

Don't Be Too Hot

Sometimes businesses can get away with a high-pressure management philosophy. The president of a very successful small corporation (worth $25 million) told me that he follows the "didja do it" philosophy of management. He would pester his managers to see if they did what they said they were going to do. His micromanagement approach worked for him as the owner of the business. However, the "didja do it" approach will not work for you as a parent because, whether you like it or not, you are not the owner of your child.

I tell my students that they can't remove risk from their lives. The future is uncertain and with uncertainty comes the risk of negative consequences as well as opportunities for rewards. Your child understands this when she sees you demonstrate rational behavior. If she asks, "Which internship [or which course] should I take?" don't offer an opinion. Instead, say, "You need to make that decision, not me," and then add, "List the benefits and costs of each, and I bet it will become obvious to you which choice will be better." Resist the inclination to tell her what she should do or even what you would do.

A career counselor from a midwestern university e-mailed me the following message. You can see by the style that there is more than a little frustration here.

> A father calls me, [along with] about three professors, regularly to talk about the obvious. Well, actually *he* does all the talking about how wonderful and attractive his daughter is and "is she going to be okay? Is she going to get an internship?" Get my crystal ball! The thing is, the daughter is delightful and will be just fine on her own. Without the meddling father!

College administrators call this father a "helicopter parent." Plenty has been written about the hovering parents of today's college children. Blame the cell phone, e-mail, our hypercompetitive society, and the child-as-trophy parenting philosophy.

For some parents, the hovering doesn't even stop with graduation. A manager of recruiting at a major multinational corporation described to me how the mother of a child who received a job offer from his company called the next day to ask for a higher salary for her child. This is not an isolated event. Recruiters report that parents actually come to their children's job interviews.

Helicopter parents are way too hot. High levels of fear and anxiety become excessively controlling reasons why helicopter parents exist.

If they can't control their children directly, helicopter parents try to control others to prevent negative consequences for their children. A newspaper article titled "Maybe It's Mom Who Needs the Wake-Up Call" describes a mother who called a college official and asked that the official put in a wake-up call to her son's dorm room because he tends to oversleep.[1]

Excessive micromanaging is the single biggest mistake you can make "supporting" your children in college. Some attention to what your child is doing is expected, especially during the application process and first year, but turn over responsibility to your child as soon as possible. The college experience should help children become functional adults who can pursue satisfying careers on their own. The sooner you can remove yourself from the day-to-day details, the better.

Sometimes it's difficult for parents to realize they are micromanaging

A Parent's Comment on Technology and Helicopter Parents

It has become too easy for parents and their kids to communicate. Cell phones, e-mail, instant messaging. Whenever either has a question or concern, they shoot it off in an e-mail or call. Overcommunication has affected students' ability to think on their own and make their own decisions. It's also allowed for overly protective parents to be parents 24/7, even when the kids are thousands of miles away. In my generation, we were lucky to touch base every week or two via phone or a written letter. There was no asking mommy or daddy in real time; we were much more autonomous. Recruiters at top companies like GE are looking for employees that have self-confidence, the ability to think on their own two feet, and can make decisions and take action without checking every move with an authority.

—Steve Canale, corporate recruitment director at General Electric and parent of two recent college students excessively. So here's a list of telltale signs, presented in order from "a little too hot" to "scalding."

Level 1: A Little Too Hot

- More than two phone calls a week on average after the first month
- Too many calls from your child asking, "What should I do?"
- Nagging in the spirit of "didja do it" on a variety of small points, such as paying the laundry-service bill (Yes, it's true; many college students don't do their own laundry.)

Level one consists of communications between you and your child, where you are constantly nagging her to take care of her own business. The ideal state is that your child will do whatever is necessary without a peep from you. This includes mailing registration forms on time, preparing a resume to get an internship, going to class, or doing homework without parental reminders.

Some micromanaging, whether invited by your child or not, is common and will be tolerated by most children as only an annoyance, but you don't want to reach level one. If you find yourself at this stage, it's time to exercise some self-restraint because these behaviors could lead to levels two or three, which are guaranteed to prevent your child from pursuing her career mission.

Level 2: Too Hot

- Checking your child's class schedule to see if she is completing requirements
- Asking your child if she handed her paper in on time or studied enough for a specific test
- Threatening to withdraw financial support if your child has a GPA below 3.0 (but take action when it is heading below 2.5)
- Threatening to withdraw financial support if your child does not pursue a major that you think will lead to a viable career path

The first two behaviors show a lack of trust in your child's ability to take responsibility for her own education. Lack of trust can be a self-fulfilling prophecy. If parents don't trust their own kids to do what they know they should do, who will? In addition, students may stop listening to parents about small things and then totally tune out important information about their future. In any case, if you keep hovering, how will you know if your child is developing the personal responsibility she will need to do what needs to be done?

You may have good reason for your lack of confidence in your child's level of personal responsibility. If your lack of trust is well founded, you need to have a serious talk about the possibility of taking a year off. If you're not prepared to have that conversation, don't check up on your child. At some point, either your child will acquire the necessary responsibility, or you will be ready to have that conversation.

The last two behaviors move from nagging to threats from your inherent source of power: money. Threaten your child only as a last resort. Threats are hard to implement, and they raise questions about your credibility and create hard feelings. As Benjamin Franklin said, "They who threaten are afraid." Threats should only be used as a last resort. Make sure your threats are based on cool calculations designed to change behavior rather than an expression of your anxiety and frustration. Aside from their limited effectiveness, threats teach the wrong thing. They reinforce the idea that your child is still in a child's position when the purpose of a college education is for him to become an adult responsible for himself.

This is not to say that threats should never be used. They make sense if your child has a GPA below 2.5 and it looks like she may dip below 2.0.

The final item on my list of what not to do is to make threats about the choice of a major. Although the country-western song "Mammas Don't Let Your Babies Grow Up to Be Cowboys" probably offers good advice, it's okay to let your child grow up to be an art or English-literature major. Your child's major doesn't matter to employers; skills and character do. Besides, what you enjoy and what your child enjoys may be completely different. So although you should help your child explore different career paths and majors, she needs to be the one to make the ultimate decision.

College graduates don't usually go into fields related to their majors. The vast majority of jobs don't require specific majors. Unless your child is aiming for a specific technical profession like accounting, engineering, or architecture, the major doesn't make a difference. In addition, people change careers many times throughout their lives.

Choosing a major that your child likes increases the chance she will finish on time. She knows what she likes and what she can do. Forcing her into something that she doesn't like or that she believes is beyond her ability is going to prolong the time she spends getting a degree. Your child is better off getting the degree as quickly as possible. The best way to learn and deal with the real career world is to be in it.

Making threats over a choice of major is also an extreme form of micromanaging. Your child, not you, is going to classes and doing the work. For you to tell her what to take would be like telling her to eat her spinach. It may have been okay when she was nine years old (but probably not worth the battle), but it's very harmful and definitely not worth the stress now that she's nineteen.

Level 3: Scalding

- Writing your child's college application essays
- Doing your child's papers
- Fighting your child's academic battles over grades or requirements

At level three, the micromanaging becomes scalding because it's so intrusive that it places your child back in elementary school. This level of micromanaging is rare, but it is in my observation, unfortunately, becoming more common.

Every April, I run a scholarship competition and conference at the Maxwell School of Citizenship and Public Affairs for high school seniors who will begin attending Syracuse University in the fall. The competition requires a six-page paper submitted ahead of time and then conference participation in which students deliberate on their policy ideas with one another in small groups. The scholarship money, distributed to twenty-five winners, totals more than $200,000, which means there are a lot of anxious parents hoping for lower tuition costs.

While the competitors are in their small-group exercises on the day of the competition, I meet with parents to discuss the paper and the competition. Every year a parent will stand up in front of 150 other parents and say something like, "We had trouble getting information on the topic." Before I can say, "What do you mean 'we'?" another parent will say, "I didn't help my son write the paper because that defeats the purpose of the citizenship conference." This exchange clearly demonstrates the tension between extreme micromanagers and parents who want their children to learn through the consequences of their own actions.

The shocking thing about this little exchange is that some parents think it's okay to do their children's homework for them. If they didn't, how could they stand up in front of a group of strangers and say, "We did the paper"? As noted in chapter 2, the widespread cheating in high school, estimated to be 60 percent, already threatens the honesty of today's students. Parents should not contribute to that pattern.

The mother who objected to another parent cowriting her child's paper is a great model of the Goldilocks Principle. She mentioned that she put considerable pressure on her child to take part in the scholarship competition, not just for the money but also for the college experience. Once she "convinced" her child to do it, she offered encouragement but, unlike the micromanaging parent, she did not offer to serve as a research assistant. She left her child alone to rise or fall on his own merit.

This is not an isolated incident. A fellow faculty member told me that he caught a student plagiarizing something off the Web. The student's defense was that his grandmother regularly proofs and edits his papers (a scalding behavior already) and that she must have found something on the Web and put it in his paper without telling him. I wonder if the student even read the paper he submitted as his own work.

Where would I put proofreading by the parent? I think it's okay for parents to provide some proofreading assistance after their child has already done the proofreading and the parents can see the changes. It's not okay for your child to hand you a big fat mess and say, "Fix it please." He may do the same thing to his boss one day.

A few years ago a student told me that his roommate's parents did all of the roommate's papers. The student was not surprised because he also saw the parents of his friends in high school writing their college application essays.

If you proofread, edit, or cheat in any other way for your child, you are causing serious damage. I shouldn't have to explain why this type of intervention is wrong any more than I should have to tell you why cold-blooded murder is wrong. But just in case you need some perspective, think about what this teaches your child about honesty and good character. Employers rate honesty as a top characteristic in their search for employees, according to surveys. Parents who help their children cheat are not just keeping their children from developing skills; they are teaching them to be dishonest. We already have enough of that in today's workplace.

Another form of scalding micromanaging is when parents call college officials to fight their children's battles on academic matters. It could be to fight a grade or to convince the admissions office that it made a mistake in rejecting their child. I'm not talking about intervening in personal problems that could lead to life-threatening situations; I'm talking about meddling in academic decisions that are the domain of faculty and administrators.

Every couple of years, I get such a phone call from a parent, usually a father. He always has the same arguments: His child is a good kid, his child works really hard, or his child is going through some stressful times. These are "give-my-child-a-break" arguments. I'm a sympathetic guy, so maybe someday I'll get talked into it, but so far I've resisted. If appropriate, I end the conversation with the suggestion that the student still has a chance for a B. If that fails, I ask the parent if he thinks it would be fair to the other students if I gave his son a higher grade. Some parents insist there was a grading mistake or the grading was unfair. I call that the "incompetent professor" argument and frequently will ask the father if he thinks I'm incompetent. That usually ends the conversation one way or another. The father either backs down or says, "Hell yes."

Parents who do such things are hurting their children in two different ways. First, if your child doesn't fight her own battles, the professors or administrators can't really know if they're serving the child or the parent. Second, the parent is acting without all the facts and could create more work for his or her child, not to mention bad feelings toward the child by administrators and faculty members. I received an e-mail from the dean one day telling me a parent had complained that I was lowering his child's grade because the child had to miss a class for a religious holiday. It turns out that the child didn't even know the parent was calling, but he did know that my policy was to allow students to miss the class as long as they made it up. So there was poor communication between child and parent surrounding the event.

The point here is that as a parent you can't possibly have a complete understanding of what has happened, because you weren't there. You are not the student; your child is. In addition, your child may not be telling you the truth. An administrator of a tutoring program told me how a parent called about a peer tutor the administrator provided to a low-performing student. The parent said the tutor was incompetent and that was why his son failed the midterm despite his extensive studying. The tutor told the administrator that she had seen the son drunk the night before the exam. I would believe the tutor.

Most parents are at least polite, but some parents are not so pleasant. They become abusive verbally and may even use four-letter words, which I'm sure they never learned in college. Fortunately, most of these parental interventions are done over the phone or through e-mail, so the risk of physical danger is low. But parents who take on their children's academic battles are embarrassing themselves and their children even if they don't try to burn down the administration building.

Calling college officials on behalf of your children for academic decisions is bad for a second reason. You are sending a signal to your child that you need to protect her interests just like when you put sunblock on her when she was six years old. Your intervention can only diminish your children's ability to take on the responsibility necessary to pursue successful careers. In addition, it will give your child the impression that you will fight all of her battles, and she can just sit back and relax.

I want to offer a cautionary note here about staying out of your child's battles with faculty and administrators. Although your first step should be to let your child fight her own battles, keep a close watch on academic, administrative, or financial problems your child may have with her college. Although most college faculty and staff know better, they sometimes look at students as objects or cash cows rather than people. So, if you see your child fighting her own battle and getting nowhere, a call might be advised. Don't do it before making sure that she has taken all the steps she can.

For example, if she has talked to the professor and gets no satisfaction, she needs to talk to the department chairperson. If she says that she doesn't have time or will just drop it, do not do it for her. Deciding when to fight or give up is critical to both character development and problem solving. If she exhausts all remedies, you may want to intervene.

Your first step should be to call someone in the parents office to find out what procedures to follow, whom to call, and in what order. Sometimes the staff may make the call. As a general rule, staff and faculty, including the president or chancellor of the college, are frightened when parents call, so they will accept your call. Whether they listen or not is up to you. Your approach should be respectful. Don't back them against the wall. The best strategy is to apologize for calling and to say that you just want to make sure that your child's story is correct and that you would appreciate someone taking a look at the situation.

Excessive micromanaging will do more harm than good in your children's preparation for satisfying careers once they graduate from college. The more you practice it the less likely your child will be to take responsibility for her own education and her own life. She will be dependent on you to the point that she cannot function without your approval. She will listen to you even knowing that you do not have all the facts. She will be hesitant to take risks that could enhance her skills or help her explore a variety of careers. That is not what employers want in their new hires.

Don't Be Too Cold

Extreme looseness usually takes the form of "I will pay for your college education and it is up to you to use the experience wisely." This kind of statement makes the dangerous assumption that the student is capable of the self-discipline to succeed with no oversight from you.

Here are a number of reasons why a totally hands-off approach is not advised:

- Sixty percent of students attending college do not graduate in four years.

- Even if your child does graduate in four years, you could be paying additional tuition bills for summer school to make up for poor performance or not taking required courses.

- Responsible children can periodically become irresponsible, especially if a creepy boyfriend or girlfriend or just sketchy friends come into the picture.

- It's not good for a parent's health to see a child making little progress toward a degree while paying $40,000 a year.

Your hands-off stand means you may not even be able to monitor your child's progress toward a degree and you may be in for a big, unpleasant surprise. One parent told me that unbeknownst to her and her husband, her son did not attend classes the first semester but instead developed an irreversible drug habit.

Children are always on the lookout for attention. They have this funny way of seeing it as a symbol of love. How tight you should be depends on your children's past performance, but there should be a minimum level. I suggest five minimum requirements:

1. An explicit agreement with your child that one of her top missions in college is to prepare for a career by developing her skills, building her character, and exploring career options
2. An explicit agreement that your child will make available all critical information about finances, grades, and progression toward a degree
3. An agreed-on annual plan for how she will develop skills and explore careers before college begins
4. An agreement that it's okay for you to provide suggestions and advice but not okay to provide commands and demands
5. A plan of action if your child's GPA falls below 2.0

Following these five guidelines will help ensure a shared mission and will foster a serious respect for your financial sacrifices. It will promote a healthy and positive relationship during college and in addition will provide a solid basis for a satisfying, lifelong adult relationship. It will allow you to put in your "two cents" on all kinds of topics because you will be someone who advises rather than nags and commands.

The trick is to get your children to seriously think about your advice regardless of whether they follow it. Being the major financier of your child's education gives you some initial leverage, but you don't want to provide commands on that basis. It's much better if your child sees you as a resource for advice and encouragement.

However, you should switch to a more direct approach if your child's GPA approaches 2.0. Taking action over grades substantially above 2.0 is seriously harmful micromanaging, but if your child is on the path to flunking out, you will need to increase your monitoring at the very least. Serious threats about not paying for college may be necessary, especially if the poor performance continues beyond one semester.

Make your threat in a cool and calculated way. Worrying that your child may not graduate will predispose you to behave in an emotional way. Showing that your position is a rational calculation based on your financial investment will teach everyone a valuable lesson.

Just the Right Mixture

How can you tell if you have the correct balance between micromanaging and laissez-faire? If I could give you a general answer, I would not have had to spend the last few pages on what not to do. The relationship between you and your college student is too fluid and varied to warrant specific instructions. At the end of this chapter there is a list of questions to ask yourself, and they will allow you to adjust as the process evolves. The best overall advice is to keep your eye on the three goals of skills development, character building, and career exploration as you watch your child travel the college path.

What Parents Can Do

The Goldilocks Principle recognizes that your relationship with your child is undergoing a dynamic shift during the teen years. The size of the change is magnified by the college preparation and college years. Basically, you are halfway between a relationship with a child and a relationship with an adult. Although this book does not address much of that relationship, you may want to read some books on parenting to deal with it. Here are some strategies that will help you manage the relationship as it relates to college.

Strategy #1: Each week, record how many "didja do it" questions you asked your child about anything related to college. The ideal number is zero. Anything over ten is approaching the micromanaging danger zone. For example, calling to check if your child got her paper in on time is a no-no. Kick the habit by having no "didja do it" days and then weeks.

Strategy #2: Attend orientation sessions at the parents office and contact its staff if you have questions or think that your child is having problems, academic or otherwise. Even if you have no questions, check out the parents-office website, and when you're on campus, just stop by and pick up brochures. This way if you need help, you will have some familiarity with the people and policies.

Strategy #3: Require your child to provide you with information. This includes grade reports, bills, and information about activities pertaining to skill development and career exploration; your child should know that she should give you these resources without you asking for them every semester. Chapter 6 provides an ambitious approach to getting this information by having your child create a plan that she updates yearly.

Strategy #4: Monitor grades and use praise or guilt. If your child's GPA gets above a 2.5, say no more than, "I'm proud of you for doing your best." If it is not his "best," the guilt will make it his best the next time. Dale Carnegie talks about the need to give people a fine reputation to live up to. The "just do your best" phrase is an effective way to do it. Also, provide as much honest praise as you can for the grades and for other things your child does in college. Too much praise never hurts if it is an honest appreciation for a job well done.

Strategy #5: Take action if your child's grades dip below 2.5 and are heading below 2.0. Discuss taking a year off, and make threats if necessary. Be proactive on declining grades.

Strategy #6: As parents, form a united front. Reach an agreement with your spouse on what you both think is a comfortable and effective combination of hot and cold. If you are arguing over your child's college decisions, you need to reach an agreement with each other. There will always be differences. Don't let your child exploit them. Both you and your spouse have the same mission—to coach your child to use her college experience well.

Strategy #7: Use Dale Carnegie at every opportunity. Study and practice Dale Carnegie's principles, discussed in *How to Win Friends and Influence People*. His explanations on the importance of praise, enthusiasm, smiling, talking about the other person's interests, and avoiding arguments can help you maintain the appropriate tight-loose relationship. It can also help you role model the character you hope your child will exhibit in his everyday relationships with others. The Dale Carnegie principles will help you implement the six previous strategies effectively.

Strategy #8: Show your love and your commitment to your child's happiness. The advice throughout this chapter represents a rational and calculating approach to your relationship with your child. However, Gail Benedict, a parent of one of my students, sent me the following quote about how important showing your love is. She wrote, "First and foremost, we trusted our daughter and gave her unconditional love. Believing that self-confidence had to be verified by those closest to a child, we made this wish.

> Wherever you may go, however you may be,
> Know always our love will surround you.
> Wherever in time, however you find your way
> The beacon of our love will shine through you."

Useful Resources

The Launching Years: Strategies for Parenting from Senior Year to College Life, by Laura S. Kastner and Jennifer Wyatt (New York: Three Rivers Press, 2002). A short book that gives an accurate picture of what you and your child will be going through. It provides a perspective on how to come up with just the right combination between hot and cold through the eyes of two Ph.D.'s who have been through the process with their own children.

Letting Go: A Parent's Guide to Understanding the College Years, by Karen Levin Coburn and Madge Lawrence Treeger (New York: Harper Perennial, 1997). Written in a lively style, this frequently cited book discusses how parents deal with a child's departure for college and the first couple of years.

When Your Kid Goes to College: A Parents' Survival Guide, by Carol Barkin (New York: Avon Books, 1999). This is a short guide with lots of specific, nitty-gritty examples on things parents should expect of their children and themselves.

Notes

1. Mary Haupt, "Maybe It's Mom Who Needs the Wake-Up Call," *Binghamton Press & Sun Bulletin*, February 27, 2006.

A Plan Is a Beautiful Thing

"Make to do lists. You can't achieve dreams if you don't have a plan to get there."

—Penelope Trunk, writer and columnist

The trouble with Goldilocks was she had no plan, and that almost made her into a meal for three angry bears. She was like my Westie, reacting to whatever was in front of her. Without a plan, your child could find a viable career path after graduation, but he would be one of the lucky ones. His odds of success would improve substantially if he approached his college education committed to the three goals: develop his skills, build character, and explore career alternatives. Lack of planning may not only lead to permanent residence in your home after graduation; it could also delay or even prevent graduation.

As an investor in your child's college education, help him develop a plan before he goes off to college. He might resist, but stick to your guns. A well-developed plan serves not only the investor, but also the business. The same is true for you as an investor in your child's education. You should also revise the plan yearly in light of progress or lack thereof.

Planning activities can help you build a healthy relationship with your child with respect to her college education. Conversations in June or July before her freshman year will put her on the right path toward a successful career.

Access to Information

Collecting and examining crucial information is the foundation for any investment and the key to a successful plan. Like investors, you need precise and current information.

Some aspects of career preparation, such as skill development and character building, cannot be as easily measured. But you should encourage your child to regularly do some kind of self-assessment.

You can measure finances and degree progress, however. Information received directly from the college, especially on grades and degree progress, is an absolute necessity. This may seem obvious, but there is a possible roadblock.

Believe it or not, your child can refuse to supply you with information on his grades or degree progress. Even if you pay all of the bills, the U.S. government says you have no right to information from the college about your child's college education.

If this is your first experience with a child going to college, you may be surprised to find out that the law is not on your side. The Family Educational Rights and Privacy Act of 1974, also known as FERPA or the Buckley Amendment, limits what administrators are permitted to tell parents without the student's consent.[1] Your child can check a box instructing the college not to send grade information home. FERPA also precludes you from having conversations on the phone with university faculty and administrators without the permission of your child.

You should establish at the outset that you are to receive all information as a condition of your financial support. Require your child to give you access to her information about courses and grades on the college website. Establishing this as a nonnegotiable requirement as early as possible will save you a lot of trouble in the future.

This suggestion assumes that your child is willing to accept your financial investment as part of a contractual arrangement. He could refuse to give you access to the information and then you would be faced with a difficult choice. I would hope you make the right one and say, "No information, no tuition." You need to fight this battle before he goes to college. Access to information is access to power. If you get into a power struggle over this question, you will have serious problems down the road on many college and nonrelated subjects.

It may appear to be an unreasonably authoritarian position on your part. You might even see it as a form of micromanaging. The Goldilocks Principle calls for you to be neither too hot nor too cold. Getting information is not micromanaging. You might be afraid that if you demand information, your child will think you don't trust him. You could initially mention it and expect cooperation. If you don't get the access, persist even if your child says, "Don't you trust me?" or, "How do you expect me to grow up if you demand information about my business?" Such responses would show that your child wants independence, which is good. But paying the tuition isn't a gift; it's a business deal and business means having access to costs and performance.

The more you express the investment-like nature of your support through your words and deeds, the more likely your child will understand that her major missions in college are to develop skills, build character, and explore different career paths.

What Parents Can Do

Instead of providing a list of strategies you might follow, as I have done throughout the book, I suggest only one strategy here: Encourage your child to create a plan for his four years of experiences during college. Assuming you have reached an agreement on access to information, you are ready to help your child develop a document that might be called "A Plan for Career Success Through College." The document should not be a long term paper. People in jobs other than academics don't read term papers. Instead, it should follow a clear format and comprise the following five components:

1. The mission statement
2. Skills and character development
3. Finances
4. Career Exploration
5. Degree progress and grades

The plan should be in a digital format to help you keep a record of plans and achievements each year. Consequently, the planning will also promote continual evaluation of how well your child is preparing for a career.

The remainder of this chapter provides an explanation for each of the five components. I briefly describe and provide a format for each component. You can download a template from http://sites.maxwell.syr.edu/do gooddowell. Save the template as a Word file and revise and add to it each year.

In addition to guiding your child through her college experience, this exercise will provide practice for almost all of the thirty-eight skills from the list in chapter 1, especially those related to evaluating policies and problem solving.

In the spirit of honest disclosure, I have to tell you that all four students who read this chapter said that this will never happen. They say that your child will not create such a plan and you will not have the desire and capability to make him do it. I take this criticism to mean "I would never do this." Fair enough. Students who are serious enough to have read a draft of this book for me may not have to do it. They are planners and in effect do something like this in an informal way. Would they have benefited from creating a plan? Of course they would have. What about the students who are not planners, who are marginal in terms of their maturity and organizational abilities to use college to pursue careers? They would be helped even more by this process.

The bottom line is that completing and updating a plan would be helpful. If not done in actual practice, it should be done in spirit. It represents a template that you can use to guide conversations and to consider things that your child should be thinking about. When you read through the planning document and you say to yourself, "My kid will never do this," think of using it as a source of prompts for a series of conversations rather than as a strategic plan for a large corporation.

The resistance you will encounter from your child will be primarily based on the competing demands on her time. Going through the steps and writing down the ideas will be viewed as busywork and a waste of time. However, in addition to "I have more important things to do," another more sinister reason may be operating here. Planning means that you have to make decisions about an uncertain future. Your child will probably resist making a plan on the grounds that he doesn't know what's going to happen. Don't be surprised by this response, because the idea of planning amid uncertainty is new to teenagers and, unfortunately, some adults. Explain that a plan is like pie crust—made to be broken and adjusted as things change. Emphasize that it serves as a set of milestones and benchmarks to indicate progress or lack of it, and that it is not a contract; it is a clear statement of intentions.

1. The Mission Statement

The plan should start out with a clear mission statement like this: "To develop skills, build character, and explore different career paths during my years at college."

If your child is firmly committed to using her four years to prepare for a specific career such as a lawyer, journalist, engineer, accountant, or doctor, she could add a phrase such as "general professional skills and basic technical skills required for [chosen field]." Leave the section referring to career paths alone because she should look at related fields as well as the many jobs within the specific field she has chosen.

If your child wants to add noncareer skills and goals, she can list them as "other goals." Such goals might be travel abroad, gain in-depth knowledge of a certain field, get into graduate school, make the world a better place, or learn the art of wine tasting. Listing the other goals is important so your child gets these other interests in the open. It will help her come up with ways to pursue those interests while focusing her efforts on skills, character, and career exploration.

2. Skills and Character

I suggest you start with the list of ten categories of thirty-eight skills presented in chapter 1 as the basis for assessing general professional skills and character. Your child may want to add or subtract some from the list, which is fine. Just make sure the list is explicit and detailed. If he's relatively sure he wants to pursue a specific technical field, some of the basic skills of that field could be included. For example, if he wants to become an architect, he might add "skills in drafting."

You can use the next document as a starting point to assess where your child is now. He should plan to be able to honestly give himself a five on all areas by the time he graduates.

SKILL AND CHARACTER SELF-ASSESSMENT INVENTORY

Use the following questionnaire to indicate your current skill level and your plan for the next twelve months to develop these skills. For each skill listed, circle your current level according to the 1–5 scale. Under the question, write down your plan for improving your skills.

1 = Have no skill, not even sure I understand the item
2 = Understand the meaning of the item and have some idea of how I might do it
3 = Have some experience and competence in exercising the skill
4 = Have exercised the skills in a competent way on several occasions
5 = Feel confident that I can exercise the skills on topics where I have the necessary knowledge

Skills

Establishing a Work Ethic
1   2   3   4   5
Plan:

Developing Physical Skills
1   2   3   4   5
Plan:

Communicating Verbally
1   2   3   4   5
Plan:

Communicating in Writing
1   2   3   4   5
Plan:

Working Directly with People
1   2   3   4   5
Plan:

Influencing People
1   2   3   4   5
Plan:

Gathering Information
1   2   3   4   5
Plan:

Using Quantitative Tools
1   2   3   4   5
Plan:

Asking and Answering the Right Questions
1   2   3   4   5
Plan:

Solving Problems
1   2   3   4   5
Plan:

3. Career Exploration

As discussed in chapter 3, career exploration requires experience supple-
mented by research and instruction from the career-services staff. It also
starts very early in a child's life. For this reason, your child's plan should
contain a section where he can set goals for experiences and education or

research. The plan should include experiences outside the classroom, a reading list, aptitude testing, and professional guidance. Use the Career-Exploration worksheet.

CAREER EXPLORATION

List each experience you plan to have for each year of college. Remember, the plan should change over time. List the month and year you expect to start and complete. Comment on each activity's relevance with respect to a career field. Only those courses that clearly help in exploring a career should be included. Keeping this document as detailed and up-to-date as possible will help you produce a great resume and prepare for an even better interview when you apply for internships, jobs, and graduate school.

Books You Have Read and Instruction You Have Received, Most Recent First

Experience	Planned Date	Career-Exploration Relevance

Meetings with and Use of Career Services

Experience	Planned Date	Career-Exploration Relevance

Work and Internship Experience (Most Recent First)

Experience	Planned Date	Career-Exploration Relevance

College Activities (Most Recent First)

Experience	Planned Date	Career-Exploration Relevance

Academic Courses (Most Recent First)
Experience   Planned Date   Career-Exploration Relevance

4. Finances

The plan must identify projected sources of funding as well as projected expenditures. This form has a place for your child's cash contribution. As noted in chapter 2, your child should have some skin in the game. List your child's contribution, your investment, and financial aid from the college and update the list each year before the fall semester. This record will also document the percentage your child puts into her college education and will provide details if asked on an interview. See the Sources and Uses of Funds worksheet for the suggested format.

SOURCES AND USES OF FUNDS

Annual Financial Budget for	20__	20__	20__	20__
Costs				
Tuition				
Room and Board				
Other Charges				
Books				
Travel Costs				
Spending Money				
10% Contingency Fund				
Total:				
Source of Funds				
Student's Own Savings				
Student's Job During School Year				
Parents				
Other Family				
Scholarships				
Grants				
Loans				
Total:				
Balance:				

Running List of Aid
Scholarships

Grants

Loans

---

5. Degree Progress

Failing to graduate (or graduate on time) is not the end of the world, but the chances of this happening will be greatly reduced if your child plans early. The plan must focus on both passing the required courses on time and maintaining the program's required GPA, which in most programs must be above 2.0 to allow for graduation. I will have more to say about this topic in chapter 14, but at this point, the agreement should be that your child will complete the Degree Progress Report and update it each semester and will graduate on time. This worksheet will help this happen.

DEGREE PROGRESS REPORT

COURSES TAKEN/PLANNED	GRADE	RELEVANCE* (G, M, E, N)

List of Accepted College Credits Earned
in High School

Semester 1

    Semester GPA: _____ Cumulative GPA: _____
Semester 2

    Semester GPA: _____ Cumulative GPA: _____
Semester 3

Semester GPA: _____   Cumulative GPA: _____
Semester 4

Semester GPA: _____   Cumulative GPA: _____
Semester 5

Semester GPA: _____   Cumulative GPA: _____
Semester 6

Semester GPA: _____   Cumulative GPA: _____
Semester 7

Semester GPA: _____   Cumulative GPA: _____
Semester 8

Semester GPA: _____   Cumulative GPA: _____

*Relevance Key: G = General Degree Requirements; M = Major Degree Requirements; E = Electives; N = Does Not Count Toward the Degree

---

Useful Resources

No items appear here because reading about how to plan too often serves as an excuse not to plan. Your child is going to resist the planning activities suggested in this chapter. Giving her additional information will delay and prevent the necessary planning. The worksheets in this chapter are available on http://sites.maxwell.syr.edu/dogooddowell.

Note

1.   The Family Educational Rights and Privacy Act (FERPA), 20 U.S.C. § 1232g; 34 CFR Part 99.

PART THREE

The High School Years as Career Preparation

The four chapters in this section show why the high school years should be more about skills, character, and career exploration, and less about playing the admissions game.

Is Your Child College Material?

"Diligence is the mother of good luck."

—Benjamin Franklin

Asking the question, "Is your child college material?" is like asking, "Does your child deserve to live the American dream?" What parents would deprive their children of that opportunity?

Part of the angst surrounding this question is that going to college has become the premier measure of success for most high school administrators and for politicians who say they want to remedy the horrible academic performance of youth living in poverty. "College for all" has become the "solution" to widespread inequality in our society. Telling students that they are not ready for college is like telling them they are destined to a life of poverty.

This college-for-all mantra generates enormous social pressure on parents to want college educations for their children. And why shouldn't they? Government statistics show college graduates earn twice as much on average over their lifetimes as students with only high school diplomas. Many parents shoot even higher because the statistics also show that, on average, people with advanced degrees earn twice as much as people with undergraduate degrees.

The emotions are so high that questioning whether a child is college material is virtually taboo, not just for many parents but for teachers and guidance counselors. Don't respond to the hysteria. Keep an open mind to help your child pursue a viable career path.

The Wrong Message

The "college for all" attitude contributes to the hopelessly naive view that your child can be anything she wants to be. If your daughter is slow and uncoordinated, she will not be a tennis superstar despite what the sneaker companies tell her. Sometimes people do succeed against all odds, but they became what they had the capacity to be, not simply what they wanted to be.

The "be anything you want to be" attitude can have devastating effects as students spend time and money (and even accumulate huge debt) in college programs that they have little chance of completing. One student who was recruited into an engineering program at Syracuse University kept failing midlevel math courses even though she was trying very hard to pass. She was about to try for the third time when I suggested that she enroll in our program that emphasized quantitative skills for business, government, and nonprofits but did not require calculus. She became an A student, graduated, and is now completing a master's of public administration program. I shudder to think what would have happened to her if she had continued to fill the quota for a program that was suggesting she try again, regardless of what was best for her.

Students who complete their degrees sometimes do not use their college experience in a career-savvy way. I know many students who have graduated by the skin of their teeth and who majored in a liberal arts program only to return as full-time employees to their summer or part-time jobs in retail sales—at the same level they worked at when they were in college. They blame the college for not preparing them for a better start on their careers. The decisions they made about what programs to enter and what experiences to get are the actual primary culprits.

Another downside to the "be anything you want to be" syndrome is that giving up is not an option. Students can't be happy with themselves if they fail after being told, "You can do it." For example, consider a student who can't pass organic chemistry after several tries, but her parents are still telling her she can be a doctor. To try again and again would be like beating a dead horse, and dead horses can't have a good self-image.

For this reason, I tell my students to "be all you can be." Do your best every time, and you can be satisfied with yourself. It makes more sense than wishful thinking. Telling your child to be all she can be is both enthusiastically optimistic and realistic.

Overselling Traditional Four-Year Undergraduate Programs

The "college for all" attitude implies that everyone should attend a traditional four-year college program when there are better options for many, if not the majority, of high school students. Too often, parents view community colleges (which enroll 38 percent of all college students) only as a low-cost step to a four-year degree rather than a place offering many two-year and shorter certificate programs that can lead to well-paying jobs and viable careers. The attitude also diminishes the value of two-year and part-time programs offered by for-profit technical schools.

Four-year programs include a lot of unfocused course work justified as mind expansion under the category of liberal arts or general studies. About 40 percent of students choose such programs. Many do so because they are not ready to commit to one of the professional school options like business, engineering, education, social work, or communications. The 60 percent in the professional schools and programs also take many liberal arts requirements, ranging from 20 to 60 percent of their course work. Many students are not interested in what they see as doing high school all over again. More important, many students are not good at the advanced, overly abstract, and theoretical work offered in most of these courses. Liberal arts and general studies courses are rarely hands-on and become increasingly abstract as students advance. Most two-year and all certificate programs allow students to escape from these requirements.

I'm not saying that some of these liberal arts or general studies courses have no value to the student preparing for a career. Liberal arts and general studies courses can help students develop many of the thirty-eight skills listed in chapter 1. Defenders of these programs talk about writing and critical-thinking skills with some validity. However, for students who want a more technical education and are not able to jump through some of the requirements, a four-year program may not be for them.

Don't let the prestige factor of going to college prevent your children from exploring options other than traditional four-year undergraduate programs. Community colleges, online programs such as the University of Phoenix, and schools that are very career oriented such as Capitol College in Maryland (which prepares students for electrical-engineering technology jobs like circuit analysis and digital design for the aerospace industry) or Johnson and Wales (a business, technical, and culinary school) do not get on the radar screen for many students. Some of these more technical programs may lead to a desired career faster and cheaper.

Advantages of Going Directly into the Workforce

"College for all" expresses an undeserved negative attitude toward going into the workforce right after high school. Whether students go into a field where there is apprentice training through the unions or start in an entry-level position in manufacturing or customer service, they have significant opportunities if they have the skills and character employers want. I once met a regional manager for an upscale restaurant. He started as a dishwasher, became a cook, then a store manager, and now is the boss for ten other store managers in his region. The president of the company started the same way.

Don't forget the armed services as an option right out of high school. With all the violent conflicts that threaten American troops around the world, it's not an option most parents would encourage. However, the benefits for career development are enormous. Most important, many employers give preference to people with military experience and not just because they want to be patriotic. A business manager from Merck, a major pharmaceutical manufacturer, once said that when he screens resumes submitted in response to a newspaper advertisement, no more than one in ten candidates is hireable. When he works with military headhunters, the number of employable candidates rises to about seven in ten.[1] If your child considers the option, the benefits may outweigh the risks.

According to a Bureau of Labor Statistics economist, "Between 2004 and 2014, job openings for workers who are entering their occupation for the first time and who don't have a bachelor's degree are expected to total roughly 40 million. That's more than twice the number of job openings for 4-year college graduates."[2]

Working in one of these 40 million jobs could lead directly to a career path with no additional education leading to a degree, or more likely a few courses or training programs here or there. It can also give your child a chance to focus and start college part-time. Many of my most successful students at Syracuse University have done just that.

About 28 percent of all adults in the United States have college degrees.[3] The remaining 72 percent are not in a permanent state of misery and poverty. Although their incomes over a lifetime are on average half of what they would be if they had a college degree, they don't live in their parents' basements or end up on welfare. If your child drops out, she can finish college part-time while advancing in her chosen career field. If she never graduates, she can join the ranks of Bob Costas and Bill Gates, both of whom started college but never finished.

The largest employment sector by far is small business. Entrepreneurship generates jobs. Small businesses are not so bureaucratized as to demand a college degree unless it's for a job that requires a credential. There's plenty of room for job and income growth. Young people in and out of college start businesses and prosper all the time. Colleges are increasingly offering programs in entrepreneurship, but the necessary ingredients in the vast majority of success stories are skills and character.

Not being college material carries a stigma that can push your child in the wrong direction. If a student is interested in carpentry, nursing, police work, graphic arts, or starting a business, she may suppress or delay this ambition just to get a college degree. One of my colleagues who taught college and had a Ph.D. quit his job even though he had tenure. He wanted to paint houses and do carpentry work. He is as happy as a lark now. The same thing happened, as I mentioned in chapter 3, to one of my sons-in-law. He graduated from college, took several jobs open only to college graduates, and now is much happier in a career as a house painter. It takes a strong teenager to resist the college-for-all mythology, but that strong teenager may be sparing herself tens of thousands of dollars of debt and years of her life lost.

The drive to get a college degree can be a deeply held personal goal for some students. Some people define getting a college degree as a life goal. They may want to be the first in their families to get the degree. The college degree is an ornament or milestone that the student wants. Students driven by this desire don't always graduate, and even if they do, the cost may be devastating.

Some people also consider a degree as a way to move to different levels in their careers. But perhaps if they put that energy into their existing vocational opportunities, they would be better off. I also see people use the dream of getting a college degree as an excuse for not doing their best in their current positions.

I'm not suggesting that teenagers give up dreams of a college education. I am suggesting they be thoughtful about viable options. If a teenager is marginally qualified for a four-year college, is committed to hard work, and is focused on developing her capacity for a satisfying career, she should give it a chance. However, if her school and test records are weak and/or she lacks the maturity and focus to succeed, she needs to go into the workforce, where she can discover her strengths and a focus that only comes through age and experience.

It makes more sense for your child to go into the workforce before going to college if she is not ready or able to make the college investment pay off. She can see where her job takes her.

Your child should see this first job as more than a holding pattern until she is ready for college. Seeing a job as a stopgap measure is likely to reduce your child's efforts to be the best she can be in that job. She'll fail to develop the skills and character critical to her success even if she does go to college.

Work experience can transform a person in ways more schooling can't. For example, Ronny J. Coleman, who is the director of business development at a company called Emergency Services Consulting, Inc., never graduated from high school because he was a self-described juvenile delinquent. But his teenage joyride ended when he found himself in front of a judge for driving a hot rod 107 miles per hour in a 35-mile-per-hour zone. The judge said, "Join the Marines or go to jail." He made the rational choice and learned how to handle explosives in the Marines. When he left the Marines, he joined a fire department and became chief at 31 years of age. Over the next thirty years, he got his associate's degree, his bachelor's degree, and a master's degree to build his credentials.[4] Skills, character, and smart career decisions worked for him, and he is having a grand old time.

Young adults who are not college material can waste time and a lot of money avoiding the workforce by getting into college or community college by the skin of their teeth. According to published research, students who take vocational programs in high school earn 8 to 9 percent more than those who take academic or college-prep programs. Even going to community college is not a low-risk choice, because 86 percent fail to get a degree.[5]

It Is Easy to Get into Some Colleges; It's Not So Easy to Graduate

Every high school graduate (and even some who don't graduate from high school) can get into some four-year college. It's no big deal to get into college, just as it's no big deal to go into a supermarket and buy cough drops; college is just more expensive. But graduating from college is a much bigger deal, and it will only happen if your child has the capacity to do so.

Just because Harvard accepts a very small percentage of its applicants doesn't mean the vast majority of schools do. In fact, there are plenty of empty spaces in colleges below the top 100. Only 20 to 30 percent of all four-year colleges and universities attract enough applicants to be able to discriminate.[6] In fall 2004, 91 percent of freshmen said they went to either their first-choice (70 percent) or second-choice (21 percent) schools.[7] The U.S. Department of Education estimates that 400,000 students enroll in college each year without even graduating from high school. Students having trouble getting into a four-year college can go to a community college and perform well enough to go to a four-year school. In cases where a student has not mastered the three R's, the student may spend a year or two in remedial courses. But he will get into college if he persists. Or, to put it another way, some colleges will take any eighteen-year-old in America.

You'll get little help from your high school if your child is not suited for the traditional four-year undergraduate program. Most guidance counselors encourage everyone to go to four-year colleges because they don't want to be hassled or fired for suggesting alternatives. They are even afraid to tell a student with a B+ average that she's not getting into Harvard. Few parents see realistic advice as well meaning. The rest will attribute it to a personality disorder, incompetence, or (if the counselor is white and the student is not) racism. School boards measure success by the number of students who go to college, which makes for overwhelming pressure on guidance counselors to push college. Many school board members are not even satisfied with high percentages; they live to brag about Ivy League admissions.

Many more students go to four-year schools than are ready for it. Most experts agree that students would be better off going to college after they have a firm grasp on why they are going and what it takes to succeed. This comes with maturity. If you decide your child needs a few years to mature before you cough up the $100,000+ for a college education, you are more likely to be pleased with the results of the education. But don't be misled. Those years between high school and college need to be for maturity, exploration, and discovery—not consumed by the search for the best beer, casino, or beach.

Going to college doesn't mean graduating from college. Less than 50 percent of college students graduate in four years, and about 55 percent graduate in six years, according to the most recent reports by the Department of Education.[8] Remember, many students still incur substantial debt even though they have no degree to show for it. Parents should seriously consider whether their child has the capacity to graduate.

What Parents Can Do

Predicting whether your child will benefit careerwise from a college experience requires you to assess a complex set of factors. Here are some to consider:

Maturity
Intelligence
Educational background
College and program
Mental and physical health (a big one frequently ignored)
Addictions to drugs, alcohol, gambling
Luck
Finances
The U.S. economy
World events

The following strategies will help you and your child decide if she is ready to take the risks associated with going to college either right after high school graduation, a few years later, or perhaps never.

Strategy #1: Change the question. Let's play a little semantics game here. The first important step in answering the question, "Is your child college material?" is to change the question. Replace the word *college* with the phrase *postsecondary education* and add *at this point in time*. So the question is, "Is your child postsecondary education material at this point in time?"

Just asking the revised question will help you and your child explore options and search for a good fit. It will also introduce the idea that waiting to go to a postsecondary program might make a lot of sense. Many students choose that option, and those who eventually end up in college say it was a good decision. The risk and fear is that once out of school, your child may never want to go back. Delaying college for a different kind of learning experience is a big risk, but so is going into college directly out of high school.

In looking at all postsecondary opportunities, have your child explore some community-college options. For example, I frequently meet students who are good at and like fixing software problems. They often decide to enter computer-engineering programs at four-year schools, even though they are not so good at mathematics and abstraction. A two-year program in electronic engineering would be the best path for them initially. Success there might then lead to a four-year program or not. It could also lead to founding a company worth millions or moving from the technical field to general sales or management. In many fields, a job as an apprentice might work better than going to college.

Strategy #2: Raise the question. Raising the question about whether your child is ready to enter some postsecondary education program will jump-start the process of applying to college. The application process should be more about self-exploration and less about winning the application game. In raising the question, you are sending a clear signal that you are willing to see your child go directly into the workforce or to choose a nontraditional college option. You may think it's counterintuitive to communicate this open-mindedness about attending college, especially if your child is showing little enthusiasm. But, this signal tells your child that he must earn your confidence in order for you to make the investment.

Concerned with his son's poor performance in high school, a father I know said, "If you keep this up, you will not go to college and I will be saving a lot of money." The son became agitated and said—apparently in shock—"I want to go to college." The father said, "I'm not really interested in spending the money so you can have a four-year party." The son improved his high school work enough to get into a four-year school and graduated with only a couple of anxious moments.

The key to the father's action was not the threat itself. Parents are always making threats. The crucial factor was that the son realized that his father did not see college as a critical part of his future. To be credible on the subject of succeeding in college, you have to deal from a position of strength. Desperately seeking a college education for your child places you in a position of weakness and is a recipe for disaster.

Parents who show no fear that their children might not go to college may shock their children. They have been led to believe that going to college is their right, one of the many entitlements they enjoy. Realizing that their parents hold the financial strings and want to see a payoff provides the power base to implement many of the suggestions provided throughout this book.

Strategy #3: Don't overvalue brainpower. Thomas Edison said that "genius is 1 percent inspiration and 99 percent perspiration." The inventor of the lightbulb and the founder of General Electric might have a point. The tests that I use in deciding if any given high school student is going to develop the skills and character employers want and explore careers through college has a little bit to do with brains and a lot to do with work ethic.

To have a reasonable chance of gaining skills and career perspectives from a college education, your children should be able to read, write, and do math at least at the tenth-grade level. If students do not have basic reading and number literacy, most college programs will be out of their reach. Some technical programs may work, but solid reading and number skills are a requirement.

How can you make a reasonable judgment about basic intellectual capability? Look at grades and look at SAT or ACT scores. These are imperfect measures, but they provide some useful information.

High school grades provide only a rough approximation. Students with a B average or above are likely to be reading at grade level and therefore might have the basic skills needed to benefit from a college education. This assumption might not be true for schools in disadvantaged areas, if my experience and most of the research is any indicator. For now, let's just make the assumption that below a B average is not a good sign.

However, students with C, D, and F averages may also read at grade level. They could just be lazy or distracted. This raises the obvious point that grades are a reflection of basic intelligence plus hard work. You never know which it is or whether it's both. Use grades in high school as an indicator of minimum competence. A GPA below 3.0 is a warning sign that college work, especially in traditional four-year programs, may be beyond your child's reach or at least require remediation in college. This could lead to added expenses and more years in college.

If you take the time out to get to know your children, then the answer to the "lazy" question should not be hard. If your child comes home from school and plays video games and watches TV all day but then scores a 2200 on the SAT, I am sure he is able to read, write, and do math. If your child works hard, comes home every day, sits at his desk, and concentrates but still isn't maintaining above a B−, then we have a problem. The first thing you should do is use the school or an outside service to see if your child has a learning disability. Hard work and professional help correct many learning disabilities.

Because grades give such cloudy information, most college admission officers use standardized tests like the SATs and ACTs. Performance on these tests is a reasonable predictor of success in completing college requirements and therefore should not be readily dismissed. Performance below the fortieth percentile may be a sign that your child will have trouble passing college-level courses.

The questions on the tests have little to do with life skills or career development. If you ask an auto mechanic, I am sure he can tell you how to change a flat tire and explain all of the terminology associated with the car. But asking that same mechanic how the use of imagery influences an author's short description of why butterflies are beautiful is useless.

Studies on the relationship between these tests and college graduation are not conclusive, but then again few statistical tests are. Some studies suggest that the scores are a partial predictor. Some of my most successful students careerwise were in the fiftieth percentile and they had no trouble maintaining GPAs above 3.0, but my experience also suggests that on the whole, general performance on these tests tracks closely to academic performance.

You can get a preview as early as the tenth grade, when PSATs and ACTs appear on the horizon. Low performance in these pretests should send up a red flag. Encourage your child to prepare better for the next test. Although I'm not a big fan of commercial test-preparation programs, you may want to have your child try a few sessions.

Test scores are not always critical for getting into college. Some colleges, highly ranked and otherwise, do not require test scores. Plenty of colleges will take students in the fortieth percentile or below and even some, as already mentioned, will take anyone who has a pulse. The real test is not getting into college; it's graduating in a timely matter and, even more important, using college to pursue the three goals of skills development, character building, and career exploration.

Strategy #4: Give more weight to work ethic and focus than brains. Although brainpower is important, work ethic and focus are much more important. Angela L. Duckworth and Martin E. P. Seligman published research suggesting that self-discipline can predict academic achievement better than traditional standardized tests.[9] Students who can't defer gratification long enough to do their homework and show up for class awake are not college material and are not going to have career success unless they change.

I have seen some students with weak reading and math skills graduate from college and pursue satisfying careers because they worked very hard in a consistent way. I have also seen even more very bright students who are lazy and distracted fail out of college and take years to get on a viable career path.

In assessing work ethic and focus, be on guard for alcohol, drug, and gambling addictions. If your child has had these addictions in high school, don't assume that college will eliminate them. Help your child deal with these addictions, even if it means waiting to go to college.

Employers prefer hard workers over brainy workers. Hard workers continuously improve themselves, which means they can and will learn. Experience, hard work, and focus make the less intellectually facile look bright, and the lazy and unfocused but intellectually strong look stupid. Experience is the best teacher. As a whole, corporate America spends more money on training its employees than colleges spend educating students. If an employer hires someone who has character and reasonable reading and quantitative skills, the employer can help the employee get all the other skills he needs for success.

Let's face it: Many students are just not ready for college when they graduate from high school. Some may never be ready for the four-year commitment. As a parent, you need to realize that this is not the end of the world; in fact, it could lead to a successful path for your child without the costs of college.

Once you reach a conclusion about whether your child is ready for a postsecondary education opportunity after graduating from high school, you need to act on it. If you decide the odds are 50-50 that your child is ready, the most prudent course is to suggest a community college, work, or other structured experience after high school. If the odds are less than 50 percent that your child is ready, refuse to provide the financial support. This action alone may change your child's direction. If not, a year or two in the workforce might do the same. Or, he could become such a valued employee at a job he likes that eventually he could reach the standard of living he desires.

Useful Resources

Beyond College for All: Career Paths for the Forgotten Half, by James Rosenbaum (New York: Russell Sage Foundation, 2001). This is a formal and heavy-duty scholarly book, and unless you are into that stuff, don't bother with it. However, if you want some convincing evidence on how careers can happen without a college degree and how students who are not ready for college will do better economically if they don't go, this book is for you.

Success Without College: Why Your Child May Not Have to Go to College Right Now—and May Not Have to Go at All, by Linda Lee (New York: Broadway Books, 2001). A journalist and novelist, Lee originally wrote an article called "What's the Rush? Why College Can Wait" and got so much mail that she wrote this book. The book presents stories of successful students as well as statistics demonstrating that waiting a while or not going to college at all does not mean economic failure. The most valuable feature is a set of questions that will help parents assess how their children will benefit from college. This is a must-read book for all parents, not because it will convince them not to send their child to college, but because it will place a college education in the proper perspective.

Notes

1. David Moniz, "In Quest for Workers, Firms Search Ranks of US Military," *Christian Science Monitor,* August 26, 1999.

2. Olivia Crosby and Roger Moncarz, "The 2004–14 Job Outlook for People Who Don't Have a Bachelor's Degree," *Occupational Outlook Quarterly,* Fall 2006, vol. 50, no. 3, p. 29.

3. U.S. Census Bureau, "Census Bureau Data Underscore Value of College Degree," press release, October 26, 2006.

4. Ronny J. Coleman, e-mail to author, November 21, 2006.

5. James Rosenbaum, *Beyond College for All: Career Paths for the Forgotten Half* (New York: Russell Sage Foundation, 2001), p. 84.

6. Dick Teresi and Janet MacFadyen, "Hard Knocks," *Forbes Magazine,* September 16, 2002, p. 103.

7. *The Chronicle of Higher Education,* Almanac Issue 2005–2006, p. 18.

8. *The Chronicle of Higher Education,* Almanac Issue 2006–2007, p. 14.

9. Jay Matthews, "Self-Discipline May Beat Smarts as Key to Success," *The Washington Post,* January 17, 2006, p. A10.

Get College Credits in High School

"The early bird catches the worm."

—William Camden

More than three million high school students in the United States earn some type of college credit each year.[1] Encourage your child to take at least two such courses or as many as she can fit in her schedule. A growing number of high schools offer several options for college credit. As we will see, some are better than others.

Getting college credit during the high school years makes a lot of sense from almost every perspective. This is a situation where the benefits clearly outweigh the costs. Let's look at the two major costs first.

The first cost is financial. In most cases there are charges ranging from $80 to take an Advanced Placement test to $300 for a three-credit course. But even at $300, the cost is less than 20 percent of what you would pay at a private university.

The second cost is time. This is more complicated. Courses that generate college credit are more time-consuming and difficult. They therefore create more stress for students, especially those who take on too much. Capable students may overload themselves and create stress that's not really necessary.

Moreover, students who are not serious or not prepared to take advanced courses could have a bad experience, which might convince them prematurely that they aren't interested in college. Many students will take these courses but will not earn college credit if they do not get high-enough scores on the examinations. In some cases, if the course is needed for high school graduation and your child does not pass it, she may have to go to summer school to graduate from high school. For example, the introductory course for my policy studies majors is offered in fifty high schools in the Northeast, and some of those schools offer it to fulfill graduation requirements. Each year, a few students fail the course, primarily because of laziness (commonly known as senioritis), and then have to go to summer school to graduate.

But a bad experience may have positive consequences if it serves as a wake-up call that college is not high school. A student may realize that he needs to work much harder when he gets to college, or he may figure out that traditional academic programs are not for him. Better he realize this during his senior year in high school than his first year in college.

The benefits of taking college-credit courses in high school far outweigh the costs. Here are the benefits, roughly in rank order:

- It saves significant amounts of money if it allows students to graduate from college early or stay on track to graduate on time.

- It creates a strong college application because most admissions officers like to see challenging courses on the student's transcript.

- It allows students to avoid freshman courses that may be overcrowded, full of warmed-over high school material, or of no interest.

- It creates de facto tracking by placing students in high school classes with better teachers and stronger peers. Because of scheduling constraints, this will shape the entire high school schedule.

- It allows students to take lighter course loads while in college.

- It provides a "college-level" experience to challenge and test students and introduces students to the types of material covered in college.

These benefits are not uniform for all college courses offered in high school. The most important difference is the transferability of the credits. Different colleges have different policies: some refuse to accept any transfer credits; some accept all such credits; most are somewhere in between. Some colleges will not apply the credits toward a degree but will permit students to take higher-level courses in the same subject. However, even if the credits don't transfer, there are many other benefits. As we will see in the discussion of the four different college-credit programs, some options in general have more benefits than others.

Some critics, especially higher-education officials, are lukewarm about earning college credit in high school. They have legitimate concerns about the quality of the programs, especially in terms of the oversight and training of the high school teachers offering the programs. They are also correctly concerned that students learn from their peers, and high school peers are not as beneficial as college peers.

Although these criticisms have some validity, college credit in high school programs still makes good sense. In many cases, the high school courses are better in educational quality than college courses. Getting the credit gives the student more freedom of course choice in college, and the possibility of early graduation far outweighs the concerns.

Most political leaders are strong advocates of earning college credit in high school. They see it as a way of countering the high cost of a college education while raising standards in high schools. High school rating systems usually include the number of college-credit options in the high school. There will be more options in the future, and parents should encourage their children to take advantage of them

Options for College Credit in High School

This introduction to the kinds of college-credit options available is brief not only because it would take a book as big as this one to provide a comprehensive discussion, but because they are changing all the time. Also, as a parent, you can only worry about the options available to your child. In most cases you will have more than one option. Your child should weigh the costs and benefits of each carefully. Here are the four options:

1. Advanced Placement (AP)
2. College-Level Examination Program (CLEP)
3. International Baccalaureate (IB)
4. Dual/concurrent enrollment

Advanced Placement (AP)

The Advanced Placement program is the most well-known and widely accepted program available to high school students. The College Board (which offers the program) provides syllabi and training to high school teachers who teach AP courses. Students sign up to take the AP examination at a cost of $80. The student's performance on the AP exam determines the amount of the college credit or advanced standing she earns. Test scores range from zero to five; five is the highest score. Colleges vary on what scores will count for credit. Some will take a three for most subjects, but most require a four and a few require a five.

An important consideration with respect to AP courses is how well students do on the exam. Credit is awarded only on test performance. About 59 percent of AP test takers earned a three or better in 2005, and 33 percent earned a four, which colleges increasingly require.[2] Although there are no definitive statistics on what percentage of students actually get the credit, these two numbers suggest it is around 40 percent.

College-Level Examination Program (CLEP)

The College-Level Examination Program is commonly referred to as CLEP. Unlike AP, CLEP is purely an examination program. It assumes that the college student will have obtained the education needed to pass the examination through job training, advanced/honors high school course work, life experiences, and language proficiency.

Currently, thirty-five examinations are available in five subject areas: business, science and mathematics, history and social sciences, foreign languages, and composition and literature. Exams are ninety minutes in length with the exception of English composition and are composed primarily of multiple-choice and fill-in-the-blank questions. Sometimes there are optional essays, which are graded by the institution your child plans to attend.

CLEP exams cost $55, compared with $80 for AP exams. Students take CLEP exams at one of 1,300 test centers across the country; the majority of centers are on college campuses. Recently CLEP instituted computer-based testing. As a result, students receive their score reports immediately after completing the exam (if no essays are required).

CLEP materials offer the following statement: "Currently, about 2,900 colleges grant either credit or advanced standing for successful completion of a CLEP exam." However, the standards and rewards vary greatly among colleges. A 2003 study found that the minimum acceptable scores varied from 35 to 75 and that the number of credits granted varied between three and fifteen per examination. Some schools grant students exemptions from mandatory, introductory courses but not credits toward degree completion. Prior to registering for an exam, have your child contact the schools that he or she is considering applying to and find out their policies on CLEP credit. Most often this information is in a college's course catalog or on its website.

This requires effort by your child, because less than half of schools provide this information with admission or orientation materials.

CLEP study guides are available and your child's high school may offer classes that prepare students for CLEP exams. For example, many high schools already have a foreign-language requirement. This course work alone may adequately prepare your child for a CLEP exam.

For more information on CLEP, to register for an exam, to find the nearest test center, or to find the colleges and universities that accept CLEP for credit or advanced standing, visit the official College Board website at www.collegeboard.com.

In principle, the CLEP approach makes a lot of sense. In practice, however, I have never met a student at Syracuse University who actually received college credits with CLEP, and I have met at least one who did well on the test but did not receive credit. Syracuse University's College of Arts and Sciences sees less than one request a year for CLEP credits.

International Baccalaureate (IB)

Recently, the International Baccalaureate Diploma program has grown tremendously (but from a very low base) in American high schools. It's a comprehensive and classical liberal arts program created and administered by the International Baccalaureate Organization (IBO) in Geneva, Switzerland. IB was developed to accommodate students whose parents move around a lot; the program gave their children consistent course work. The program statement says that IB "embodies a philosophy that centers on developing critical thinking, global perspectives, intercultural understanding, and responsible citizenship." The following description is an excerpt from the literature provided by the IBO:

"High schools that offer an IB curriculum must receive authorization from the IBO and teachers are trained by attending special institutes held throughout the world. Currently, the program is offered at over 1,300 schools in 114 countries."

Students in the IB program take courses in six different subject areas and must complete comprehensive examinations in each area. Three to four of the six subjects may be studied at the "higher level," considered equivalent to college work. The exams are scored on a scale of one to seven, and students typically must attain a score of five or higher on a higher-level exam to earn college credit for their work. Like other advanced programs, each college has its own policies about granting credit for IB. Students who successfully complete the program receive an IB diploma. Students who do not complete all of the diploma-program requirements are awarded certificates for the examinations completed.

Dual/Concurrent Enrollment

The title for these programs is difficult to understand because it's so general. It refers to programs offered to high school students but managed and credentialed by a college. The availability of dual- or concurrent-enrollment programs depends upon agreements made between high schools and postsecondary institutions. This means that procedures vary greatly from program to program. The National Center for Education Statistics collected information on these programs, which can provide a starting point for you and your child.

Dual/concurrent programs include college classes taught in your child's high school or at a local college campus. Traditional programs have expanded to also include new distance-learning and online courses. In 2002 and 2003, about 680,000 high school students took college-level courses through dual-enrollment programs, and approximately 70 percent of public high schools offered dual-enrollment courses.

The majority of dual-enrollment students take courses offered by public, two-year postsecondary institutions, such as local community colleges.

Where Do Students Take Classes?

- Eighty percent of postsecondary institutions that offer dual-enrollment courses encourage high school students to attend class on the college campus.
- Fifty-five percent offer college-level courses to high school students on high school campuses during regular school hours.
- Twelve percent of participating institutions offer courses at some other location, such as a vocational or technical school.

Either high school teachers or college professors teach the courses, depending on the location of the classes. Most colleges require a high school teacher who leads a college-level class to have the same qualifications as the professors who teach the material on the college campus.

When deciding whom to admit, most institutions consider the student's GPA and some require admissions testing. However, the majority of colleges report that admissions standards for high school students differ from those for regular college students. Tuition for dual-enrollment programs can come from the school district, the state, or the college offering the program, but parents usually pay a significant amount.

Credit is awarded at the completion of the course. The majority of dual-enrollment programs offer students credit at both the high school and college level for each successfully completed course. Most students choose to take just one or two dual-enrollment classes during their junior and senior years. Some programs offer an opportunity for high school students to enroll full-time at a university. Whether part-time or full-time, participation in these courses gives your child an experience with college-level course work and a competitive edge in admissions. In addition, it can save you money! But always check whether the schools your child might attend accept dual-enrollment credits. Even though your child is taking college classes, they may not be accepted universally. Because most students take courses at local community colleges, some four-year universities will not accept these credits.

Examples of Large Dual-Enrollment Programs

- **Syracuse University Project Advance (SUPA).** Classes are taught during the regular school day within high school classrooms; they are offered in New York, New Jersey, Maine, Michigan, and Massachusetts. http://supa.syr.edu/.

- **Running Start.** Began in Washington in 1990; tuition is paid by the school, and the books and class fees are paid by the student. runningstart@ospi.wednet.edu.

Which Approach Is Best?

Before I comment on this question, I have to reveal a conflict of interest. Syracuse University Project Advance has offered my freshman course, Public Affairs 101: Introduction to the Analysis of Public Policy, to more than fifty schools in the Northeast since the mid-1980s. Students take the course in their high schools from teachers whom I train for a week in the summer and then meet with twice a year in a workshop to introduce curriculum changes. Many of the changes come from the suggestions of the teachers; they become college faculty members and they deliver the instruction just as well. We give common assignments and grade through an agreed-upon set of grading guidelines. My staff grades the final assignments to ensure uniform standards. About ten different Syracuse University courses are offered using a similar format. Faculty members visit the high school classes each semester to assess how the students are doing.

My experience influenced my comments about the relative strengths of the four approaches. They are also colored by what teachers tell me about the programs. Ultimately, you will need to judge for yourself.

But to evaluate the merits of each program, it's important to determine which of the options has:

- The best educational quality
- The lowest cost
- The highest rate of credit transfer

Question #1: Which of the four has the best educational quality?

Except for the CLEP option, they all depend on the quality of the teacher or college instructor—and that can vary greatly. With the heavy emphasis on the test, the AP approach inevitably requires teaching to the test, something that does not encourage the kinds of skills employers want. The CLEP appears to be a result of what the student happened to take. The IB program is more integrated and requires active learning, but the curriculum shows the biases inherent in the classical liberal arts approach to education. Only 35 percent of all college graduates come from liberal arts programs. IB is clearly superior to AP and CLEP, but the goals are academic rather than career oriented.

As far as dual-enrollment programs go, the quality can vary. Some colleges send a booklet and some tests to the teachers but provide no specialized training or quality control. The quality depends then on the teacher, and there is no reason to assume that the program adds much value to the educational experience.

Other programs, like the one at Syracuse, require ongoing professional development for the teachers. These programs tend to be of better quality, but it still depends on the teachers. If the children attend college classes on the college campus as if they were college students, the quality is as good as the institution and may be the best option.

The best bet for quality and career relevance is the dual-enrollment approach, for two reasons. First, the college offering the credit has some control over the content and materials if the program is well run. Second, there's a greater variety of offerings and some courses are likely to be more career focused than those offered through AP and IB.

The conclusion I reach is that "educational quality" should not be much of a consideration.

Question #2: Which of the four has the lowest cost?

The IB program is usually completely supported by the school district, so is "free" to your child.

Unless the school system absorbs all costs, the next least expensive are CLEP and AP. Cost is always a consideration but so is the chance of reward. In this case, the AP and CLEP programs have a high risk of no return. Only about a third of the students get high-enough scores on the tests to have a chance to earn credit. Dual-enrollment programs that do charge are likely to be the most expensive. For example, the cost of a three-credit course offered through SUPA is $275. This is less than a third of the normal charge but more than three times as much as AP.

Question #3: Which of the four transfers most easily?

The answer to this question varies by college. Most community colleges accept most of the credits, and generally the more highly rated the college in *U.S.News & World Report*, the stingier the college is in giving credit. For the SUPA program, about 90 percent of students who earn Syracuse University credit through the program get credit at the college they attend. If they attend Syracuse University, not only do they get all the credits, but their GPAs start with their high school work. This can be good or bad for the student, depending on how she did in the courses.

State governments and the federal government have been pressuring colleges to have more liberal credit-acceptance policies. A college typically discloses its acceptance policies in its general course catalog. Headings to look for include:

- Credit by Examination
- Advanced Placement/Advanced Standing
- External Degree Program

Some colleges limit the number of outside credits accepted toward degree completion, but they may grant exemptions from requirements. The minimum score required to qualify for credit differs from exam to exam.

In my experience, students with IB credits have a fight on their hands. College officials love the concept of IB, especially liberal arts faculty and staff, but they don't know exactly how to translate it into course credit. The confusion may lessen as more IB students go to college, but don't count on it for your children. It might get worked out for their children. Despite the growth in the number of schools offering IB, relatively few students complete these programs.

What Parents Can Do

Although you should encourage your child to participate in one or more of these types of programs, he is faced with many choices. I'll provide some general advice to help in making decisions. As is the case with other advice in this book, the more students research and understand their options the better. You should not take on the responsibility of making the decision yourself. Instead, follow these strategies.

Strategy #1: Encourage your child to seriously consider college-credit options in high school. For all of the reasons discussed at the beginning of the chapter, your child should look into these options. If he refuses or gives you a hard time, take that as a warning sign about maturity. He may eventually decide not to take any of the options, but if so, you need a reasoned explanation from him.

Strategy #2: Let your child make the decision. High school students who take college-credit courses are likely to participate in many activities. They have learned to do well without doing too much academic work in most cases. Well-taught college-level courses in high school are much tougher than other courses. You don't want your child overcommitted because he expected more of the same. Your child should indicate what trade-offs he is making to take on this extra work. High school students should take no more than two college-level courses a semester.

If your child is not maintaining at least a B average in high school, you should be hesitant to encourage him to take college-credit courses. The pay-offs of having some advance credit before college are great, but they are not absolutely vital to success in college. Many students take AP courses but then never take the test or get a high-enough score to get college credit.

Strategy #3: Before you put down the money or allow your child to take a college-credit course in high school, require a reasonable defense of the decision. Ask your child to defend his decision with respect to the three criteria of "quality, cost, and transferability." Although he can be specific about cost, he can only speculate on quality and transferability. Thoughtful speculation is better than a wild and uninformed guess.

Strategy #4: Encourage your child to choose courses likely to be core requirements in college. This suggestion may sound negative, but I make it for three reasons. First, most colleges require freshman writing courses and survey courses in science, the humanities, and the social sciences. The class size for these courses tends to be enormous and the professors have to present material to a wide range of students. In any case, most students complain that this is high school all over again. If your child can remove himself from this experience, he will be better off.

Second, skipping the required freshman courses will allow your child to take higher-level courses. In my experience, higher-level courses are more interesting to students; better taught; and, oh yes, easier. The freshman courses are used to "weed out" students.

Third, these options are designed primarily to help your child get on with his college requirements, not to give him an early taste of college. Each faculty member is so different; it will not be a representative taste.

Useful Resources

The College Board website (www.collegeboard.com) provides more information on AP courses and the colleges and universities that accept AP examinations for credit or advanced standing.

The International Baccalaureate Diploma program website (www.ibo.org) offers more information on the IB program.

The National Alliance of Concurrent Enrollment Partnerships website (nacep .org) provides more information on dual-enrollment programs.

Notes

1. National Center for Education Statistics, "Dual Enrollment of High School Students at Postsecondary Institutions: 2002–03" and "Dual Credit and Exam-Based Courses in U.S. Public High Schools: 2002–03". Available at http://nces.ed.gov/pubsearch/pubsin fo.asp?pubid=2005008 and http://nces.ed.gov/pubsearch/pubsinfo.asp?pubid=2005009.

2. College Board, "AP Exam 2005 National Summary Report." Available at http://www .collegeboard.com/student/testing/ap/exgrd_sum/2005.html.

The Application Process as a Career-Development Test

"It is good to have an end to journey toward; but it is the journey that matters, in the end."

—Ursula K. Le Guin

If what I have said in chapters 7 and 8 is correct, the most important aspect of applying to college from the perspective of skill development, character building, and career exploration is not finding and getting into the perfect place. There are plenty of good places where your child can develop skills, build character, and explore careers. Other factors, such as proximity to home or wanting to be by the ocean, may legitimately be more important to your child.

The most critical aspect by far is the application process itself. As Le Guin says, it is the journey. You and your child should look at the application process as a learning experience for your child and an opportunity for you to assess whether your investment will pay off. Wanting you to invest in his "business," your child should convince you that you will get the payoff you desire. The application process provides your child the opportunity to sell you on the investment, and you get the opportunity to reach a sound decision. Your child's behavior during the application process is an indicator of things to come.

If your child is already in college, this discussion could still be useful. Think back to what your child did during the college-application process.

Did he show work ethic and focus on using college to prepare for a satisfying career? If your child is on the right path in college now, you probably saw healthy behaviors in high school. If your child is not committed to the career mission, you might reflect back and see that a lack of maturity and career focus was in the cards. Thinking about the application process will help you devise a strategy to encourage a more serious approach to developing skills and exploring careers.

If you're working with a child in high school, encourage him to look at the application process as an opportunity for learning and self-evaluation. A high school student who conducts the application process the right way will be developing and exhibiting skills, building character, and exploring careers in ways that will make him a great hire when he graduates from college.

The application process consists of four stages, and your child's performance in each can be instructive for you and him.

1. High school course selection and college-prep test taking
2. Initial scanning activities
3. Narrowing down the choices
4. Making the decision

I will now describe each stage in detail and suggest what your child should be doing to win you over to the idea that your investment will pay off.

Stage 1: High School Course Selection and College-Prep Test Taking

Although you may not think of this as part of the application process, it is. Children who select more difficult courses and courses that carry college credit are demonstrating a desire to go to college in a tangible way. They are taking on more work and showing a focus on the future.

Your child's score on standardized testing is one indicator, but his attitude toward testing is another. If your child chooses to do any of the following, he is showing you the work ethic and focus that will make your investment in him pay off:

- Takes the pretests (e.g., PSATs)
- Uses practice opportunities provided by the school or does practice exercises on the computer or from a book

- Goes to bed early the night before the test and shows up ten minutes early to the test

- Doesn't wait until the last possible opportunity to take the test

Note, I said "chooses to do." Parents frequently are successful in forcing their children to do any of the items listed above. If you find yourself doing that, recognize that this is an indicator of your child having either a poor attitude toward a college education, a lack of time-management skills, or both. Take a hard look at your planned investment in your child's college education or at least have a very serious talk with your child—as early as the tenth grade.

Watch out for overkill. Taking too many honors and college-level courses and spending money on professional test training are not good signs. Enrolling in college test-preparation programs from outside vendors like Kaplan may make sense for students who have trouble with breaking 1000 on the SAT, but trying to go from a 1300 to a 1400 is obsessing over getting into a stretch college and a sign of misunderstanding what the mission is. Hopefully, the competition bug will not produce these stressful behaviors.

Stage 2: Initial Scanning Activities

Your child will be barraged by information from colleges seeking your dollars as early as the tenth grade. How he handles the information blitz will provide a clue to how he will deal with the overwhelming number of choices and options he will face when he goes to college. Does he develop a system for triage so that as time goes on, more and more material gets put into the trash can? Does he look at the prospects for career development in an area that he might have some interest in when judging the material? Does he disregard information about the programs for learning and career development and instead concentrate on the physical facilities and options for fun?

In addition to scanning the material he receives in the mail, does your child search the Web and collect information on schools that do not contact him? Does he attend college night at school? Does he use computer programs and advice from guidance counselors and adult contacts who can help him see what kinds of programs might fit his interests and talents?

Private colleges spend on average $2,400 and public colleges spend $750 on promotional material for every student they register, so your child will need to develop a critical approach to the promotional material.[1] You may be tempted to micromanage your child's scanning process by reviewing the material and offering opinions. If so, go to a movie. Your child will learn more by trying to figure it out without your help. If he tries to discuss the information with you, listen carefully and gently suggest he think about how what he is reading may affect his future. If you are going to offer any advice, give him a bunch of file folders and suggest that he label them for each college and place material in them. That is about as far as you should go. Remember the Goldilocks Principle: The less micromanaging and the gentler the advice the better.

Your main goal here is to observe and coach your child's behavior in problem solving and information gathering. If your child understands that the information needs to be managed and then he actually manages it, be happy. If he can't seem to scan and organize the information because he is either too lazy or unfocused, be worried.

Stage 3: Narrowing Down the Choices

Your child should begin the second stage of the triage process sometime before the end of the first semester of the junior year, because he will want to visit campuses in the spring and summer. Let's say he has twenty prospects in folders. By December of his junior year, he should narrow the number of schools down to between two and six.

Selecting just one college shows impatience with the process, an inability to explore options required for any kind of problem solving, and possibly a lack of work ethic. More than six shows an inability to focus and make choices. It could also mean that he's not willing to spend the time to decide which colleges to throw out. It's like not writing a shorter letter because you didn't have the time. The ability to narrow down choices is required for good decision making and time management. Moreover, your child should only visit the colleges on his short list because more than six becomes expensive and time-consuming.

The two-to-six rule is only a general guideline. There may be good reasons to look at just one college. For instance, your child might be admitted to West Point, which is free, prestigious, and focused on careers. Your child might also get a full ride at a top-200 school. If your child wants to do more serious study and visit more than six schools, you will need to make that judgment, not your child. Just watch out for laziness and lack of focus. College visits are a great opportunity for you to teach and encourage skills development, character building, and career exploration. They also are a way to miss high school classes and have a vacation.

Stage 4: Making the Decision

The amount and quality of research your child does on the short list of schools may be the most important piece of evidence you can use to decide if your investment will pay off. Your child should thoroughly examine each of the topics described in chapter 10 with respect to each college on the short list. Prior to each visit, he should collect information to answer some of those questions. During the visits, your child should probe in areas that need more investigation.

Your child's research strategy should be to gain information from many sources, through both reading materials and talking to people with different perspectives. These sources are in chapter 10. The more he studies, the better you should feel that he is on the right track to a successful college career.

Written material and admissions representatives are trying to make a sale and will present information as positively as possible. Students and alumni are the best sources of information as long as your child can get a cross section of opinions. If these people are handpicked by the admissions office, they may not be representative but they may still provide information if your child listens carefully and critically.

These discussions of how to conduct the application process as a learning activity may make sense, but as Emily Pecachek says in the sidebar, don't think it will be an easy sell.

Too many high school students wrongly believe that the college application process is only about getting into and choosing a "prestigious college." Having been told since elementary school that success in life is based on their ability to jump through academic hoops, they approach the application process like they approach their tasks in school. Success is defined as winning high grades; actually learning something isn't the concern. Applying to college for most children is too much about winning and self-validation, and too little about looking for the right fit.

Finding the right fit isn't difficult because developing skills, building character, and exploring career options has more to do with your child's focus and commitment than where she goes to school. Winning a place at some exclusive college is the wrong prize at the end of the application process.

Most people judge colleges based on rankings, the media, and peers. But the truth is that prestige is in the eye of the beholder. For all too many high school students, a prestigious college is one that they think may deny them admission.

As a faculty member, I've been bemused to hear students talking about admission to Syracuse University. Students who come from wealthy suburban school districts or private schools frequently say that Syracuse was not their top choice. They refer to it as a "safety school," that is, a school to be admitted to in case they don't get into an Ivy League school. Students from

. . . .

A Student Voice: Why the Advice in This Chapter Will Be Difficult to Follow!

A lot of good kids (me included) would have failed your "ready for college" tests. That's probably because, especially at competitive high schools, teachers, coaches, and classmates are always pushing you to do so much that it's very easy for high achievers to lose perspective and become obsessed with the present. Remember, up until this point in their lives, kids don't have to make a lot of choices. The school district or their parents have decided where they go to school. Mom and Dad probably got them started in activities as little kids and they've continued in those activities ever since. We're used to focusing on sixth grade, knowing that seventh grade will come on its own. Making the transition to college takes a whole new mentality, and parents have to help their children understand that. Basically, your kid is used to thinking, if I do a good job on what I'm doing right now, I'll be okay. Parents need to help them realize that part of being an adult is learning to do a good job on your work at the present while planning for the future.

—Emily Pecachek, a 2006 graduate of Syracuse University, looking back on the application process

. . . .

rural and blue-collar areas see Syracuse as highly prestigious and are forever thankful that the university let them in.

With colleges investing more than ever in public relations, students can use a lot of different criteria to claim their school is "prestigious." It provides many ways to "win." Even so, students and parents buy ratings books and magazines and fret over the right choice based on the search for status.

The bottom line is that many high school students don't see the application process as a test of their ability to find a proper fit. They see it as a game to win. But it's also a stressful game that does little for your child's career mission and, at best, can only give a fleeting sense of self-validation. At worst, it can create an unnecessary scar he'll carry with him for a long time.

People who obsess over extrinsic rewards often seek a designer-label college degree. Students who have self-confidence derived from ability, not from ornaments they wear, are students who will successfully use college to develop their careers.

What Parents Can Do

If your child gets an A+ on the four stages of the application-process audition, he will have demonstrated most of the thirty-eight skills listed in chapter 1 and demonstrated character by treating the process as the serious and expensive enterprise that it is. The irony is that the A+ means that perhaps he is already prepared for a satisfying career and doesn't need college, unless he plans to enroll in a technical program. More realistically, it means that he will choose a college from which he can graduate with advanced experiences and more opportunities for experience-based learning.

The college search is time-consuming. If your child does a great job on this, he is already showing the skills and character employers want. If he makes a reasonable effort, he's probably worth the investment. If he's too lazy or unfocused to make an effort, think about withholding your investment.

Strategy #1: Apply the Goldilocks Principle in the process. Your role in this process will be limited by the Goldilocks Principle described in chapter 5. You should have a discussion with your child early in the process, probably the tenth grade, to set the ground rules that college is a serious investment and you will be watching how your child completes the process. Make it clear that you are looking for hard work in getting and organizing information and making decisions along the way. Offer to discuss these decisions and activities with your child all along the way. Select some dates or milestones using the suggested schedule in figure 9-1, and provide some soft reminders. The more you have to ask, "Didja do it?" the weaker the performance of your child. Remember that it's not the end of the world if your child doesn't go to college, and don't fail to communicate that to your child.

Strategy #2: See the application process as a test of your relationship with your child about college. Do not, under any circumstances, make excuses to yourself if your child fails to exhibit at least a minimum level of responsibility. I've met parents who run around the university interviewing professors because their child is "too busy" to do it himself. One time I gently suggested to a parent that the child should be talking to me and not the parent. Apparently, I was not gentle enough because she threw a little tantrum and left the office. I wonder if that parent completed her son's college application because Johnny was too preoccupied.

So actually, the application process is not only a test for your child; it's also a test for you and your relationship with him about the college process. As Aristotle says, "excellence is a habit," and if you get into a habit of doing your child's work, that is clearly not excellence.

Strategy #3: Suggest a timetable for the application process. Figure 9-1 provides a general timetable that you should encourage your child to follow. This is a general timetable, and you can adjust it if your child plans to apply for early admission or to take a year off. Some students apply for early admission in the fall of their senior year and a few do so in their junior year. There's a lot of controversy over this practice. It settles things early, but it may be premature. As long as the decision to take early admission is not based on a strategy motivated by the competition bug, it doesn't make much difference either way.

Figure 9-1. A timetable for the application process.

	9th F	9th S	10th F	10th S	11th F	11th S	12th F	12th S
Stage 1: H.S. Course Selection and College Prep Test Taking	▬	▬	▬	▬				
Stage 2: Initial Scanning Activities				▬	▬			
Stage 3: Narrowing Down the Choices						▬	▬	
Stage 4: Making the Decision							▬	▬

Useful Resources

Most of the books and websites on college admissions are too much about winning the admissions game and too little about finding the right fit. They may do more harm than good in helping your child make the application process a learning experience. These books focus on the process.

Countdown to College: 21 To Do Lists for High School: Step-By-Step Strategies for 9th, 10th, 11th and 12th Graders, by Valerie Pierce and Cheryl Rilly (Partners Pub Group Inc., 2006). This book will help your child approach the college process systematically throughout high school with concise suggestions.

Applying to College: A Planning Guide (Lifeworks Guide), by Casey Watts (Perseus Publishing, 2003). This book emphasizes fit more than competition.

Note

1. Amy Rainey, "Private Colleges Spent Far More Than Public Ones on Student Recruiting in Past Year, Study Shows," *The Chronicle of Higher Education,* March 3, 2006.

CHAPTER **10**

Choosing a College Based on Career Mission

"I don't care to belong to any club that will accept me as a member."

—Groucho Marx

Too many high school students wrongly believe that the college application process is only about getting into and choosing a "prestigious college." Having been told since elementary school that success in life is based on their ability to jump through academic hoops, they approach the application process like they approach their tasks in school. Success is defined as winning high grades; actually learning something isn't the concern. Applying to college for most children is too much about winning and self-validation, and too little about looking for the right fit.

As I will discuss in this chapter, choosing a college can be based on many factors. One of those factors should be to find the right fit where your child can develop skills and character and explore careers. Fortunately, this is not a difficult task, because the career mission has more to do with your child's focus and commitment than where she goes to school. Winning a place at some exclusive college is the wrong prize at the end of the application process.

Most people judge colleges based on rankings, the media, and peers. But the truth is that prestige is in the eye of the beholder. Groucho's quip operates here. For all too many high school students, a prestigious college is one that they think may deny them admission.

Some Basic Choices

Hopefully, your child is ready to choose a college based on something other than perceived prestige. The choice is difficult because there are so many criteria that are subjective and for which there is only scanty information. I have listed ten, but your child may be using more.

1. Location
2. Proximity to friends and family
3. Specific extracurricular activities like sports or music programs
4. Facilities like residence halls, student union, and library
5. Academic programs
6. Opportunities for career preparation
7. Cost
8. Size of the school
9. Job-placement rate
10. Makeup of the student population

All these factors and many more may be considered. Any one of them can be the primary criterion as long as pursuing the three goals of developing skills, building character, and exploring careers are a main focus also.

Career preparation doesn't have to be the main criterion, because it can be pursued regardless of which college your child chooses; she can place herself on a direct path to career success no matter where she goes. In the case of technical programs like nursing, engineering, and physical therapy, the college must have the program and the necessary accreditation. Other than that, where your child goes to college is far less important for career preparation than what she does when she gets there.

This chapter will help you help your child assess the relative strengths and weaknesses of college choices with respect to career preparation even though that is only one of the criteria she should use in making the choice. This chapter is not a substitute for serious study and counseling from school, career coaches, or educational coaches. Your goal should be to help your child find a match between her capabilities and interests and the opportunities available on a particular campus.

There are three basic distinctions you will need to keep in mind in thinking about your child's choice of college. They are:

1. **Two-Year Versus Four-Year Programs.** The former are usually called community colleges or junior colleges. Two-year colleges are sometimes called associate-degree institutions, and the four-year institutions are sometimes called baccalaureate-degree institutions.

2. Public Versus Nonprofit Private and For-Profit Private. Public universities are usually funded by the states, although some cities and the federal government fund a few. Nonprofit private colleges and universities are funded primarily from tuition and endowments. For-profit institutions are expected to turn a profit for their investors and provide an increasingly wide range of programs.

3. Technical Versus General. Technical colleges provide training in specific technical fields like engineering or nursing; general institutions provide liberal arts degrees but also may have many technical programs, which they call "professional."

This discussion provides only a general perspective and some questions to ask. Your child should review one of the references provided at the end of this chapter to obtain more information.

Two-Year vs. Four-Year Programs

The most important distinction by far is between two- and four-year programs. Statistics compiled by the U.S. Department of Education reveal the following breakdown for fall 2004:

- Eleven million, or 61 percent, of full-time students are in four-year schools.
- Seven million, or 38 percent, of full-time students are in two-year schools.
- Half a million, or 1 percent, of full-time students are in post-secondary institutions that offer programs shorter than two years.
- For full-time and part-time students, the split between two- and four-year schools is about 50-50.

It makes a lot of sense to seriously explore both two- and four-year programs. Unfortunately, although the options are almost infinite, information about four-year programs is more abundant. The media and high school counselors concentrate on four-year programs, and four-year colleges spend a lot more money on selling their programs than two-year schools do. Even if your child is set on a four-year school, she should explore what two-year schools have to offer. Looking at community colleges will help in three different ways:

1. It will confirm her choice of a four-year college.

2. It will help her look at more options within the four-year college.
3. She will seriously consider a two-year college when she hadn't given it much thought.

Four-year colleges have more general academic programs and two-year colleges have more specific programs. But this rule is frequently broken. Four-year colleges can have very specific and technical programs, especially if their leaders are worried about enrollment. Two-year colleges often provide general academic programs for students who want to enroll in four-year schools later.

The next list shows the programs offered at Onondaga Community College (OCC), which is in the Syracuse area. It should give you a good idea of the range of options offered by community colleges nationwide. However, other community colleges could offer a very different set of options. Encourage your child to look into the programs offered at the nearby community college if it makes sense for him to stay at home. Increasingly, two-year colleges are opening residence halls, which means your child could get out of town if he wants an experience away.

Programs at Onondaga Community College

(A.A. = Two-year associate of arts; A.S. = Two-year associate of science; A.A.S. = Two-year applied associate of science)

Accounting, A.A.S.
Adolescence Education, A.A.
Apprentice Training: Building
    Trades, A.A.S.
Apprentice Training: Electrical
    Trades, A.A.S.
Architectural Technology, A.A.S.
Art, A.A.S.
Automotive Technology, A.A.S.
Business Administration, A.S.
Business Technology, A.A.S.
Childhood Education, A.A.
Computer Engineering Technology,
    A.A.S.
Computer Information Systems,
    A.A.S.
Computer Science, A.S.

Criminal Justice, A.S./A.A.S.
Electrical Engineering Technology,
    A.A.S.
Electronic Media Communication,
    A.A.S.
Emergency Management, A.A.S.
Engineering Science, A.S.
Environmental Technology—
    GeoScience, A.A.S.
Fire Protection, A.A.S.
Food Service/Restaurant
    Management, A.A.S.
General Studies, A.A.
Health Information Technology,
    A.A.S.
Hotel Technology, A.A.S.

Humanities and Social Sciences, A.A.
Human Services, A.S.
Interior Design, A.A.S.
Labor Studies, A.S.
Math and Science, A.A. or A.S.
Mechanical Technology, A.A.S.
Music, A.A.S.
Nursing, A.A.S.
Photography, A.S.
Physical Therapist Assistant, A.A.S.
Recreational Leadership, A.S.
Respiratory Care, A.A.S.
Telecommunications Technology, A.A.S.

List of Certificates

Early Child Care
Fire Protection
Hotel Front Office
Microcomputer Troubleshooting and Maintenance
Professional Cooking
Public Safety
Surgical Technology
Web Technology

Here is a list of four-year programs at Syracuse University for comparison purposes only. You can see a lot of overlap but fewer technical programs than at the community college.

Four-Year Programs Offered at Syracuse University

Accounting
Advertising
Advertising design
Aerospace engineering
Architecture (first professional degree)
Arts and Sciences BA/BS
Art education
Art photography
Art video
Broadcast journalism
Ceramics
Chemical engineering
Child and family studies
Civil engineering
Communications and rhetorical studies
Communications design
Computer art
Computer science
Design/technical theater
Drama (acting)
Education
Engineering
Environmental design (interiors)
Environmental engineering
Fashion design
Fiber arts/material studies
Film
Health and exercise science
Health and wellness
Hospitality management
Illustration
Industrial and interaction design (five years)
Information management and technology
Interior design

Jewelry and metalsmithing
Management
Marketing management
Music
Newspaper
Nutrition
Painting
Performance (organ, percussion,
    piano, strings, voice, and wind
    instruments)

Photography
Physical education
Printmaking
Retail management
Sport management
Stage management
Technical theater
Television, radio, and film
Textile design

The trade-offs between a two-year and four-year college depend on what programs your child may want to follow. If she wants a four-year degree, she could select a two-year program and then transfer. The main advantages of going to a two-year program first are saving money and perhaps receiving more personal attention in the classroom. The savings can be substantial. The full sticker price for one semester's tuition at OCC is $1,605; Syracuse University is $14,410; and State University of New York–Binghamton is $2,175. Grants and scholarships may lower the difference. Some students actually pay less at private four-year colleges than at public ones. The cost of community college is almost always lower than that of the four-year schools, even with larger grants from those schools. That's part of why community-college enrollment has grown considerably over the last decade.

The main disadvantage of going to a community college with the intention of transferring to a four-year school is the need to adjust to a new school after transferring. Many four-year schools have agreements about accepting community-college credit, but the process is far from hassle free. I'll discuss the trade-offs of this path in more detail in chapter 13. If your child is considering a more technical field, a community college might be a better choice unless a four-year degree is required to work in that field.

There are also important cultural differences. The number one mission of two-year colleges is serving the educational needs of their students whereas four-year colleges have that as one of their missions. In addition to the hands-on nature of many of the programs, the quality of them may be better than that of the first two years of a four-year school.

At a community college, students are taught by professors rather than by teaching assistants. Classes tend to be small and there are many support services. From an educational-quality point of view, however, the student body is less likely to be well prepared academically, which may mean that classes are not as "hard" as they would be at a four-year institution. If your child transfers, he may find the four-year institutions more challenging, which may or may not mean more educational.

General vs. Technical Programs

Your child must also choose between a general program of studies at a liberal arts college and a technical program offered either at a community college or at a four-year professional school. The distinction isn't as sharp as it might appear. In professional schools your child can take very general programs, and in liberal arts programs your child can minor or double major in a technical field or go to graduate school in a technical field.

There are two basic reasons why skills and character are so important regardless of whether your child is in a technical or general program. The first is that high school career goals are fleeting. Students realize that they don't have the ability or the will to complete a program in engineering, for example, or they realize that they enjoy sales or teaching. The typical student changes majors three times. Having general skills will allow your child to transition easily from a technical career to a career that requires a technical competence that can be learned on the job.

The second reason general professional skills are important for any technical field is that the first rung of the career ladder uses technical skills, but climbing the career ladder requires general professional skills. Engineering managers don't want to hire graduates who can't write, communicate, or deal with complicated software programs. Your child may be great at writing contracts as a lawyer, but she is going nowhere in the law firm and will never be a partner if she can't develop and maintain good client relations. Technical jobs can lead to higher-paying positions in management only if your child has the range of thirty-eight skills listed in chapter 1.

If your child plans to pursue technical training, whether it's engineering or physical therapy, she must have general professional skills in addition to technical skills.

So she must look at colleges with both skill areas in mind. Traditional four-year programs try to accommodate everyone, but if your child has a specialized interest, you may suggest that she look into specialized programs offered at two-year institutions. For example, she may have an interest in working as an administrator for a company. A two-year program would work. This wouldn't prevent her from moving to a four-year program, but it opens up other options. A student who likes numbers could get a two-year degree in business administration, then start as an administrative assistant and take care of budgets. She may find she likes the work, wants a more analytical and higher-paying position, and can go back to school for an accounting degree. If she did well in that program, her initial administrative training and experience would increase her value to the accounting firms and make her a better hire.

Another reason why the differences between technical and general programs are not as great as you might think is that all careers require professional skills that can be developed regardless of the major. Students graduating from a technical program like engineering may end up in a management or sales job where a broader set of professional or soft skills is important. Conversely, I know many students with liberal arts degrees who found themselves in computer programming jobs and had to learn on the job or get brief training.

The choice between a general and technical program is probably the most perplexing. I've tried to show that it's not as stark as it appears, because colleges are allowing students to mix the programs to some degree and because most technical programs require a general or liberal arts education. It is still a difficult choice with a variety of implications. This is a place where professional help can be most valuable. Career and college counselors can provide a great deal of information about educational and career choices and help your child decide how specialized a path she wants to take. It's better for your child to face this question before going to college. Facing the question does not mean she will come up with the correct answer, but it will be an important step in career exploration.

The biggest downside to choosing any of these options is that if your child decides it's not for her, especially after the first year, she may have to spend extra time in college to complete her new degree. That's another reason why your child should seriously explore the choice while in high school.

Technical education is almost always hands-on, and general or liberal arts education tends not to be. If your child is truly undecided, a general or liberal arts education makes sense, but she should explore a technical minor like business or communications. Pure liberal arts majors change their majors and careers more often and frequently go to graduate school because they can't figure out what else to do. Other ways to make a general education more career friendly are provided in Part Five of this book.

Public vs. Private Four-Year Institutions

Because the majority of two-year institutions are public, this section will discuss only four-year institutions. Public colleges receive a significant percentage of their funds from the government, usually at the state level.

About six million students attend public institutions, compared with three million private-school students. Both private and public institutions have a large range of programs and, depending on the institution, can each be academically strong or weak. In general, the tuition at public institutions is much less than at private institutions because the government heavily subsidizes the tuition. However, state support seems to be waning, so the subsidies may change over time. Don't just compare sticker prices. In 2004–2005, private four-year colleges provided a 33.5 percent discount, public four-year colleges provided a 14.7 percent discount, and two-year colleges provided a 12.5 percent discount. Both merit and need-based aid are part of the discount. There is a noticeable upward trend in merit aid.[1]

As far as the quality of the programs goes, it's difficult to generalize. Private institutions do not have a clear edge over public institutions. This shouldn't be surprising if you accept that skills and character (not the pedigree of the degree) are what counts. Large state universities have honors programs to allow the academically gifted to get the same kind of education that they might get at an Ivy League school.

The one difference I've seen is that students at public institutions have a more difficult time getting the courses they need to graduate on time. With a high student-to-teacher ratio, your child is more likely to spend an extra semester at a public college than a private one. The four-year graduation rate for private colleges is 52 percent, but it is 24 percent for public institutions.[2] However, public colleges take many more students who need remedial help and have fewer financial resources than private schools, and this may be even more important in accounting for the difference in graduation rate. Careful planning and persistence in getting into necessary courses should minimize this risk.

Professional Skills and Character

Whether your child is on a technical-career path or is completely undecided, she should choose a college that will help her develop the skills and character that employers want. She should also choose a school that will help her explore careers. Opportunities to do these things exist at most colleges, but whether she gets these experiences is ultimately up to her. Students can pursue the activities described in Part Five of this book in most colleges. However, some colleges are better than others.

Your child should find answers to these questions before selecting a college:

■ **How will size and location affect your child's ability to gain skills and explore careers?** Any college can help students develop the skills they need to succeed in the workforce, but some schools have advantages. Most students will have better opportunities to develop their skills and explore careers if the school is less than thirty miles from a metropolitan area of no less than 250,000 people, because they will have more internship opportunities. There will be more instructors with real-world experience and networking connections in key classes. Larger institutions (over 10,000 students) have a greater variety of job-oriented programs and more opportunities to learn outside the classroom. Another factor is specialized location. If your child has some of the following careers in mind, he might want to choose a more appropriate location:

- Financial services: New York or Chicago
- Computers: Silicon Valley, Seattle, or Austin, Texas
- Government service: Washington, D.C. or any state capitol
- Entertainment/film industry: Los Angeles, New York, Vancouver, or Toronto

The mix of employers around the university is also important, especially if they are open to interns or are growing. But this guideline is a general rule. Going to college anywhere can also lead to jobs in those areas.

■ **How can your child tell if the institution or the program she chooses has made career services a high priority?** Most colleges invest money in career services, but some put more resources in than others. To check this out, students should ask six questions:

1. How many full-time and part-time professional (not graduate assistant) staff members are there in the career-services offices?
2. What software programs (such as eChoices, Discover, or SIGI Plus) have been purchased for student use?
3. What are the placement rates for new college graduates in the fields I may want to pursue? As part of this question, find out what fields graduates enter.
4. Do business recruiters visit this school, and what do they think about the graduates of this school?
5. How involved are alumni in the career-exploration process?
6. What are some of the negative aspects of this school's career-placement activities?

Carefully evaluate negative comments by students. Too many students see the career-services office as an employment agency and want the work done for them. However, not all career-services operations are as good as they could be. They are frequently understaffed and depend too much on student employees. Most serve their students well.

■ **Are the computer facilities in clusters and/or classrooms?** Given the large impact that computers have on many of the skills employers want, students should make sure that the institutions have adequate computer facilities and electronic classrooms. Although students need to bring their own computers to college, they will also need to use the institution's facilities for special software that is integrated into the course work. Adequate cluster facilities mean not standing in line during crunch times to use a computer.

■ **What kind of support is there for active learning (such as projects and simulations), internships, and community service?** Giving credit for experiences in the real world is a great indicator that the college is skills focused. Your child should see if there are offices and staff available to help students get these experiences and find out if fieldwork is a requirement for the programs she is interested in. She should look for co-op programs, where students spend a semester or more off campus in an internship or job as part of the degree requirement. Being able to do off-campus work and still gain credits toward a degree is important whether we are talking about studying abroad or spending a semester at a state capitol. Programs that require fieldwork as part of the academic program are also worth further investigation.

I have tried to narrow down the questions that are most important for your children. More detailed information on college and program selection appears in *10 Things Employers Want You to Learn in College.*

What Parents Can Do

Watching your child go through the college selection process can be nerve-racking, but it doesn't have to be. Here are several strategies to help your child benefit from the application process and make a good decision:

Strategy #1: Do all you can to reduce stress over the decision. The advice provided in this chapter and in 9 and 10 is designed to help you help your child approach the decision in a rational and calculating way. The three most important ideas are:

1. Don't make it a competition to get into a stretch school.
2. Treat the application process as a learning opportunity.

3. Emphasize that what your child does with her college education is more important than where she goes to college.

You need to balance helping your child seriously think about her choice of college with not looking for the perfect choice. She will know whether it is a good choice only after she attends the college.

Strategy #2: Follow the Goldilocks Principle—except when it comes to money. The hot-cold balance in your approach to your child's college experience described in chapter 5 applies to the college-decision process. Provide counsel and watch how seriously your child gathers and organizes information about her choices. Be loose except for the question of money. If you are paying the bulk of tuition, you should have a strong say in how many colleges you visit and what college your child selects. To not set limits on financial questions sends a whole series of messages that can slow your child's progress in being career ready after college. Allow your child to explore schools that are more expensive than you would prefer. She may realize their programs are not worth the extra cost. Furthermore, the expensive colleges may give more aid and the less-expensive colleges may give less aid than you initially thought.

Strategy #3: Encourage a careful analysis of the information. The more your child is careful about collecting and analyzing information the better. There are three steps that can help your child collect and analyze information. Encourage your child to spend time studying options (and be very encouraged about her career future if she does).

1. **Get multiple sources of information.** By asking the same questions several times of different sources, your child will have a better base on which to make her choice. Use the following sources:
    - Study guides like *America's Best Colleges* for basic information about different colleges. Pay special attention to graduation rates. They tell you a lot about the student body.
    - Program descriptions.
    - Admissions representatives.
    - Faculty in the programs you are thinking about attending.
    - Students from those same programs.
    Although the various rating books tend to oversell highly selective schools, they are worth purchasing for your child to study. They provide excellent counsel on how to approach the process. The ratings may be useful, but the exploration process stimulated by these books is more valuable.

2. **Help your child explore what is important and rate her priorities.**
   One of the biggest problems in making complex decisions is unclear
   thinking about what is most and least important. Your child needs
   to make a list of her priorities in selecting a college and rate them. I
   suggest she do that with the items listed in figure 10-1. People who
   can't rate what is important to them think everything is important
   and can't manage their time worth a lick.

3. **Provide a framework like the rating system in figure 10-1.** With
   good information and ranked priorities, your child can look at the
   pros and cons of each school she is considering and decide which
   choice is best. You can do this informally in your everyday conversations, but it would be much better if your child actually used the
   table in figure 10-1. The table is available on my website in a Word
   document so she can make a copy for each school she rates. The

Figure 10-1. College rating sheet.

Rating for_____ (Name of College)

Factors	Positive (1–3)	–	Negative (1–3)	= Sum	×	Importance (1–3)	= Score
Location		–		=	×		=
Friends/family		–		=	×		=
Activities		–		=	×		=
Facilities		–		=	×		=
Subject		–		=	×		=
Cost		–		=	×		=
Size		–		=	×		=
Job-placement rate		–		=	×		=
Makeup of student body		–		=	×		=
Other Factor		–		=	×		=
Other Factor		–		=	×		=
Totals		–		=	×		=

Key:
Importance: 3 = High; 2 = Moderate; 1 = Low
Positive: 3 = High; 2 = Moderate; 1 = Low
Negative: 3 = High; 2 = Moderate; 1 = Low

(Available at http://sites.maxwell.syr.edu/dogooddowell.)

number at the end of the table is a summary for the rating. Filling out the table for several schools would be time-consuming, so your child may want to wait until she has narrowed her choices down to two or three. If your child actually used the table, not only would it help her make a more rational decision, it would also be a very good sign that she is serious about her career mission in college and has a positive approach to preparing for a very successful college experience. Most of the students who read a draft of this book said that they would never do this. Like other tables in the book, you can use it as a discussion base.

Useful Resources

Cool Colleges: For the Hyper-Intelligent, Self-Directed, Late Blooming, and Just Plain Different, by Donald Asher (Toronto: Ten Speed Press, 2000). This book describes schools and programs that the author says will provide a better intellectual experience. The author admits a strong bias toward small liberal arts schools, but he also favors colleges that provide hands-on activities. Even if you are not interested in any of the schools discussed in the book, it will help you to get a better perspective as you look at schools you are interested in.

Fiske Guide to Colleges 2007, by Edward B. Fiske (Naperville, IL: Sourcebooks, Inc., 2006). A widely used general screening guide, this book has a checklist to help you decide between a small and a large college and between a liberal arts school and a university with several professional schools.

Peterson's Two-Year Colleges 2007 (New York: Thomson Peterson's, 2006).

Peterson's Four-Year Colleges 2007 (New York: Thomson Peterson's, 2006).

Colleges That Change Lives: 40 Schools You Should Know About Even if You're Not a Straight-A Student, by Loren Pope (New York: Penguin, 2000).

They Teach That in College? A Resource Guide to More Than 75 Interesting College Majors and Programs and *They Teach That in Community College? A Resource Guide to 70 Interesting College Majors and Programs* are both published by College & Career Press in Chicago. These two books provide descriptions of nontraditional programs that may spark an interest in your child. If nothing else, they will show the variety of programs available.

"America's Best Colleges 2007," *U.S.News & World Report.* Published every fall, this publication provides rankings for hundreds of colleges and universities on a variety of dimensions.

The Best 361 Colleges, 2007 Edition, by Princeton Review (Princeton, NJ: Princeton Review, 2006).

Parents' Guide to College Life: 181 Straight Answers on Everything You Can Expect Over the Next Four Years, by Robin Raskin (Princeton, NJ: Princeton Review, 2006).

Notes

1. Doug Lederman, "Documenting the Shift to Merit," Insidehighered.com, September 12, 2006. Available at http://www.insidehighered.com/news/2006/09/12/discounting.

2. U.S. Department of Education National Center for Education Statistics, "1993/03 Baccalaureate and Beyond Longitudinal Study Methodology Report." Available at http://nces.ed.gov/pubsearch/pubsinfo.asp?pubid=2006166.

PART FOUR

Academics: The 50-50 Principle

A college education is more than passing the courses required for the degree, but academics can play a significant role in career preparation. This section will help your child separate the wheat from the chaff.

CHAPTER 11

The Limits of Academic Course Work

Two possible definitions of academic: *"very learned but inexperienced in practical matters"; "having no practical or useful significance."*

—Merriam-Webster's Collegiate Dictionary

Think of how the terms *it's academic* or *ivory tower* are used as negatives in our everyday speech and even by faculty members outside of the earshot of the public and their students. When it comes to gaining skills, building character, and exploring career, the academic course work your child will take in college is not enough.

In my senior year at Johns Hopkins completing my undergraduate degree in the social sciences, I passed the written examination for the Foreign Service and had my oral examination in front of three high-powered State Department officials. During the interview, one of the three said, "I see you've had a lot of political science courses, so could you tell me what the Pendleton Act was." I had never heard of this act even though it established the modern civil service. I said I didn't know, but being a twenty-year-old show-off on the defensive I countered with, "Ask me about Thomas Hobbes or John Locke." I naïvely thought stuff these English philosophers said was the mainstay of knowledge about politics because that's what we studied in my courses. They responded that they weren't interested in political philosophy. They asked me if I knew anything about the civil service. Actually, at the time I had no idea what the civil service was so there was silence. They told me to come back in a few years when I had more experience.

As long as classes have to do with reading textbooks, listening to lectures, and taking highly structured tests, the courses will emphasize theory and deemphasize application. They will be about the professional scholarship, not about experience in the field.

To illustrate, a lot of students take courses in psychology because they are inherently interested in why people behave the way they do and they would like to improve their own social skills. They are introduced to the field of psychology as a scientific discipline. This means learning a lot of definitions (like the term *cognitive dissonance*) and studying what different scholars have had to say about various concepts. Studies of rats and surveys of college students used to generalize about all human behavior will provide the "scientific" evidence. This basic introduction to the discipline of psychology has about as much value to those seeking to improve their human relationships as a book on how to swim.

However, most students get no experience in human relations in psychology courses and get no hint of what a practicing psychologist might do. Those students who have a passion to understand and help people frequently get tired of the academic psychology courses even though they may complete the major. There's no question that from a career-development perspective, your child will be much better off taking the Dale Carnegie introductory course in human relations, where they practice oral communications and apply principles of getting along with people, rather than taking Psychology 101.

From your children's point of view, this gap between their desire for career preparation and the faculty's theory and abstract knowledge can be confusing at best and discouraging at worst. It is not that academic course work provides no value with respect to skills, character, and career exploration. It does, but not nearly enough.

On average, formal course work teaches at most 50 percent of what your child will need for his career. Most college graduates say 50 percent is far too high, but I find it useful to give the academics the benefit of the doubt. For brevity's sake, I will call this the 50-50 Principle throughout the remainder of the book.

A longtime director of career services, Robert Oliva presents a story in the sidebar about his experiences in working with the faculty. As he notes, things have improved especially outside the arts and sciences faculty, but it is still a struggle. While Oliva's story shows some progress, remember he is talking about the economics department of a public college that caters to blue-collar families. While college administrators recognize the importance of career support for their students, they rarely find faculty who want to integrate that perspective into their course work.

The Titles of Professors

Professor titles are sometimes bewildering, so here's a quick introduction. Ultimately, your child will find that the title doesn't mean much in preparing for a career. A full professor or a part-time lecturer can provide what your child needs regardless of title. It's the luck of the draw. The titles are not especially good predictors of the quality of teaching your child will receive with respect to his career, but they will help your child have some understanding.

What Career-Service Providers Are Up Against

As a member of the career services staff in 1985, my role was to reach out to faculty and increase their awareness of our efforts at student career preparation. Arriving at the first departmental meeting I was ready to speak about the variety of career-related communication and organizational skills students needed to master by the time they graduated. As I began speaking, I heard rustling to my right. I ignored it. As I proceeded, a professor to my left put his newspaper down and glared. I glanced at the professor nearest to me to see him shaking his head as if to say "No, no, no!" I then uttered the fateful words: "The corporate and business sectors look for students with highly developed communication skills." I don't recall uttering another word. Jeering and frantic bellowing broke out: "Capitalist dupe." I was literally booed out of the room.

Fast forward to 2006. I am teaching a course for that same department on Business Leadership and being evaluated by the chair of the department. After finishing my lecture/discussion on leadership skills, the chair approaches me and says I am providing crucial information and inspiration to the students. He thanks me for my efforts. My evaluation comes back with the highest rating. Department chairs routinely ask me for data supporting the career relevance of their major. Things do change. I am now the director of a state-of-the-art career-development center in that same college that nearly booed me out of town.

—Robert Oliva, Director, Magner Center for
Career Development and Internships, Brooklyn College

Two practices affect the titles of professors. The first is tenure. Tenure means professors cannot be fired unless they do something very immoral or fail to meet their basic contractual obligations. For professors at teaching-oriented colleges, this means there is a lot of pressure on them to teach well. At research-oriented colleges and universities, the overwhelming pressure is to do research, and teaching sometimes suffers. Once they get tenure, some professors turn more of their efforts to teaching but in general the pattern set early in their career continues.

The other important consideration is the role of the Ph.D. in faculty selection. A Ph.D. takes on average about seven years of graduate work to complete. It's a requirement to teach at the assistant, associate, and professor levels in most arts and science departments. Teaching jobs at many professional schools also require Ph.D.'s.

Ph.D. programs are almost always about research and almost never about teaching. Fortunately, most people go into Ph.D. programs because they want to teach. Some potentially gifted and dedicated teachers don't survive, but many do despite the overemphasis of research in their Ph.D. programs. The bottom line here is that the Ph.D. is no guarantee of a good teacher. It may not even be a guarantee of a teacher well versed in the subject matter, because new hires are asked to teach courses that are introductory and that cover topics they may have never studied.

■ **Professors with Some Kind of Fancy Name Attached.** The fancy name might include the words *distinguished* or *university professor* or even *distinguished university professor*. If the word *research* is in the title rather than *teaching*, your child should also be wary unless she too wants to be a career academic. If *teaching* is in the title, your child can assume the professor cares about students and does a good job.

■ **Professors Without Some Kind of Fancy Name Attached.** Also known as full professors, they have maintained high-enough standards in research, publication, or other kinds of creative work to move up the faculty food chain. They may or may not be effective teachers.

■ **Associate Professors.** These professors are usually faculty members who have tenure and need to build a bigger publication record to become full professors. A person at this level for more than five years may have trouble publishing articles and books. If your child is lucky, an associate professor in that position "too long" may have decided to devote more time to teaching.

■ **Assistant Professors.** These professors are usually untenured individuals who have Ph.D.'s or significant work experience in a professional school. If they are in this position for more than five years, you can assume they are having trouble publishing enough to get promoted and may be on their way out. Such an assistant professor may be devoting a lot of time and energy to teaching, which would be good for your child but not so good for future students, because he or she will not be around for very long.

■ **Instructors or Lecturers.** These people usually have not finished their Ph.D. dissertations (they are also known as ABD, or "all but dissertation"). In my experience, these are usually good teachers whose dedication to teaching may stand in the way of completing the dissertation. The term is also sometimes used for part-time teachers and some full-time teachers not on a tenure track.

■ **Adjunct or Part-Time Instructors.** These are freelancers who teach a few courses when there is a large demand and the tenure-track teachers don't want to cover the class. If the department administration is competent, these professors are usually good. They would get fired if they weren't. Parents and students sometimes wrongly think these instructors are not as good as professors higher up the food chain. Nothing could be further from the truth. They may have more experience outside of academia and connections to help your child with internships and jobs.

■ **Teaching Assistants (TAs).** These are graduate students working on their Ph.D.'s. They may teach discussion sessions of large lecture courses or they may have courses of their own. Their quality varies at least as much as tenure-track professors'. The one advantage is that the TA is likely to be young and enthusiastic and will really want your child to succeed. A universal problem with TAs is that English may not be their first language. Many graduate students in American universities, particularly in the science, engineering, and mathematics areas, are from overseas, so this happens a lot in universities with Ph.D. programs. How would you like to take an introductory Spanish course with an instructor who is a twenty-two-year-old from China and is also trying to learn English? It could work, but odds are not in your child's favor.

The only conclusion you can reach from these generalizations is that titles don't tell your child very much about the caring and competence of the professor. A higher ranking doesn't mean better teaching. Your child is better off asking the opinion of peers, advisers, and the professors she knows and trusts than to look at titles. She should also not be afraid to drop a course if she runs into a professor she has trouble understanding for whatever reason. She needs to give the professor a fair chance but also needs to take action to make the most out of her education.

A Pretty Dismal Record

It should not be surprising that undergraduate education in the United States is in the hot seat, and not just because of skyrocketing costs. Widespread evidence suggests that higher-education institutions are not preparing students for the workforce, financial management of their own lives, or citizenship.

Criticism from Government

With college costs rising 10 percent per year, politicians, primarily at the federal level, have been asking for the last five years, "What do you get from a college education?" In 2006, a special commission on higher education known as the Spellings Commission convened to decide what to do about the poor performance of higher-education institutions. As complaints and criticism mount, the higher-education lobby works hard to maintain and increase federal funding and to stop any attempt to require that colleges be accountable for actually educating students. Because the pressure is coming from both Democrats and Republicans, which is rare in the current political climate, we can assume that where there's smoke there's fire.

Criticism from Business

Additional evidence can be found in what businesspeople have to say about college graduates. As Daniel Langenberg wrote in an article in the *Chronicle of Higher Education* in 1997, "If we listen to those who employ our graduates or to educators in graduate and professional schools, we hear that an enormous chasm exists between what higher education claims it is doing and what it has actually achieved."[1]

Employers see the college degree as a measure of persistence and maturity, and some competence in the three *R*'s. But they want more out of their new employees, and they have learned through bitter experience they can't trust a college degree to tell them whether or not a job candidate has the people, communication, teamwork, and problem-solving skills essential to a successful career. If your child relies on his course work alone to demonstrate her competence in areas like teamwork and problem solving, she will be heading straight back to your house after graduation.

Despite the consensus on the importance of these professional abilities, many college graduates lack them, according to a 1999 report by the Business Higher-Education Forum and studies of the Collegiate Employment Research Institute at Michigan State University. Corporate-recruiting managers confirm that students may have technical skills, but they tend not to have essential "soft skills."

If colleges did a better job of preparing graduates for jobs, corporations wouldn't have to spend so much money on training employees. Total employee training is estimated to cost between $318 and $417 billion annually, "more than the combined budgets of all higher education institutions in the United States."[2]

Research Shows College Graduates Lack Basic Literacy Skills

Studies show that an alarming number of college graduates lack simple skills in searching for and using information and in identifying and performing simple computations. If you want to see what the tests look like and examples of what the researchers call "prose, document and quantitative literacy" go to the National Assessment of Adult Literacy on the National Center for Education Statistics website. Only between 25 and 31 percent of college graduates are considered to be proficient in all three types of literacy. A U.S. Department of Education study indicates that the performance is getting worse over time.[3]

This lack of literacy directly impacts American business. According to an article appearing in the *New York Times*, The National Commission on Writing concluded that as much as $3.1 billion is spent annually on remedial writing training. With e-mail becoming the prime source of communication among employees, the article states, "Millions of inscrutable e-mail messages are clogging corporate computers by setting off requests for clarification."[4]

What Parents Can Do

Parents who want their children to be prepared for a career can help them separate the wheat from the chaff in their academic course work. These strategies will help:

Strategy #1: Raise awareness without generating resistance. Your child may already be aware from his high school education that academic programs rarely hit their mark and that perhaps over the long run, courses may be less useful than they appear. If so, he may not be surprised that academics in college are an extension of high school, at least for the first two years. Although he will have some initial disappointment, he must be ready to pay his dues if he wants that degree.

However, many students I work with are not ready for more of the same. Some students try to take upper-level courses that seem appropriate to their career interests despite prodigious efforts by administrators to keep that from happening. They opt to take the lower-level and general education courses in the summer or find themselves in freshman classes during their senior year. Others become so frustrated that they don't do well academically or drop out of college.

Basically, your job as a parent is to help your child "suck it up." Freshman and sophomore general education courses, not just in liberal arts programs but also in undergraduate professional programs, are an educational "rite of passage." Point out that despite the seeming irrelevance and randomness of the classes, any course work will develop the following skills employers want from the experience:

- Being able to kick yourself in the butt to be enthusiastic about the course and do the best you can do
- Working with people by satisfying professors
- Paying attention to detail by doing the assignment asked for rather than the one you imagine is asked for
- Writing, editing, and proofing so your written work is outstanding
- Using Microsoft Word so you can do quality written work quickly
- Asking and answering the right questions, which has to do with figuring out what the professor is driving at and what will be on the test
- Problem solving by identifying the problem posed by the professor
- Time management by getting your papers in on time and coming to class on time
- One-on-one communications by meeting with the professor to exchange views
- Gathering information through the reading and research usually required for any course
- Keeping and using records required for assignments in many courses
- Building character by paying your dues

Strategy #2: Suggest skills courses. While every course can help your child develop the skills listed above, some courses can build additional general skills employers want. Offer advice when asked about course selection. If you have the opportunity to provide advice, suggest courses not by the specific content but by the way they are structured. Here are some things to be on the lookout for:

- Courses taught by faculty who worked in the career field associated with the course. This usually means adjunct faculty but not always.

- Courses requiring statistical analysis. Suggest intermediate-level social science courses or courses in professional programs like management where students play with data. Courses taught in mathematics departments rarely do that.

- Courses that serve real-world clients or are judged by real-world clients. Frequently faculty will involve their students in projects for a nonprofit, government agency, or business. Having to do a project for an organization in the real world will help students prepare for demanding clients. Programs like entrepreneurship frequently have contests judged by outsiders for the best business plan and can be taken by non–business majors.

- Courses that require a lot of writing. Writing for an outside individual rather than the professor is the best but any course requiring extensive writing is good to develop both research and writing skills. Courses requiring research papers, rather than brain dump in class exams, are also recommended.

- Skill-based computer courses like Excel, Access, and Web design. Computer courses are very important because they give your child skills that are in big demand. Courses where the students learn skills by producing a product are much better than those that just require tests and lab assignments.

- Courses that require fieldwork ranging from internship credit to a community service component. More and more colleges are requiring these community-based courses.

- Courses that require teamwork. Increasingly, professors use a team approach for assignments and projects; they provide an opportunity for students to practice what they will face in most work situations.

- A semester off campus either within the United States or abroad. These programs usually require activities outside the classroom such as internships for credit or fieldwork. In addition, the courses are usually less traditional and less time-consuming.

- Thesis-type experiences in honors programs or in department programs that require a senior thesis. A final written research paper can help with many skills even if the topic is academic and theoretical. Working with a thesis adviser and meeting the demands of the professors is excellent experience in preparing for supervisors in the world of work.

Courses that have some of these characteristics are less readily available in liberal arts program than in undergraduate professional school programs. That's one advantage of taking an undergraduate professional school program in business or communications even if you don't plan to go into those fields. However, liberal arts programs are increasingly adding academic experiences like those described above. Your child can always propose an independent study or experience-credit project with a professor in liberal arts if you can find one with mutual interests.

You might encounter resistance from your child to taking the kinds of courses described above. Courses that ask for the application of skills can be threatening because the questions are not so clear, and the answers are even less obvious. Even more significant, they can be time-consuming and result in a greater loss of control than traditional courses. Parents can help students understand that these more time-consuming courses will provide the skills essential to career success.

Strategy #3: Encourage your child to establish relationships with selected professors. Many students go through their entire college career without visiting a professor to ask questions and share ideas. I know because I never talked to one of my professors outside of class and hardly opened my mouth in class during my three years as an undergraduate at Johns Hopkins. As a student, approaching a professor is intimidating. If you can encourage your child to take the risk, you have made a great contribution to her skills and character development.

Help your child see that professors are human beings who have feelings. Most professors will try to present themselves as authoritative figures to be respected. Respecting someone because of his position or expertise means listening to what he says and assuming that he has a strong basis for the legitimacy of his view. However, respect should also come from the recognition that the person is a human being.

Strategy #4: Help your child understand the variety of roles professors can play in her career development. Too many students see professors only as classroom instructors. Here is a list of roles professors can play in their lives:

■ **Reference and Recommendation Writer.** If your child has any inclination to go to graduate school, she will need professors to write letters of recommendation. If your child is going into the job market, she can ask if a faculty member may be listed as a reference. Employers don't put a lot of stock in faculty recommendations except in technical fields, but they would like to see a professor as a reference. When approaching professors for recommendations, students should make it easy for them to do it by providing a resume, presenting some basic points that will show the professor has thought about the connection between the student and the program, and sending the request via e-mail so that the professor can lift some of the comments. Professors who write letters for students are usually in short supply and have many to do each semester all around the same time. The easier students make it, the better the letter will be.

■ **Teacher in Another Course.** Sometimes a professor just clicks with a student and the student will want to take additional courses with him or her. As part of the general philosophy of the great and varied feast that some professors think undergraduate education provides, some might advise against this practice. They would argue that the more opinions you hear the better. My view is that depth is always better than breadth. I advise that your children take as many courses as they can from professors they find helpful to their career mission or just plain interesting.

■ **Adviser on Future Course Work.** Professors have strong opinions about courses and other professors. However, your child should be careful to assess the biases of the professor. A theory-loving professor who is looking for prodigies might discourage your child from taking courses that are more applied. Some of the professors can be more objective if they are student oriented rather than subject-matter oriented. In any case, soliciting opinions can't hurt.

■ **Supervisor of Work, Either for Pay, for Credit, or as a Volunteer.** Professors may ask if anyone wants to help them on research or other projects. If your child is competent and has at least a mild interest in the topic, he should jump at the chance. It will give him an opportunity to develop many of the skills employers want, such as meeting the needs of a boss and taking responsibility. It could also lead to paying and for-credit positions that could be a high-powered activity with an additional cash bonus.

■ **Mentor.** Students frequently look to faculty for career advice. It is better if they go to the Career Services office, where there are professionals trained in career development and where they can help your child connect with an alumnus who is in the career your child wants to pursue. On occasion, some student-oriented professors may be able to provide valuable career advice depending on your child's career interests. This usually makes most sense for students who are thinking about an academic career. If a student is interested in a technical position like accounting, engineering, journalism, or acting, a professor who has actually worked in that capacity can be trusted more than someone who went straight to a Ph.D. program.

All of these roles can be important to your child's career mission in college, but advise your child not to depend too much on professors. Your child may have difficulty finding and connecting with faculty. Her main goal should be to find a couple of professors who will serve as references. Other than that, mentors and career advisers can be found in other places, as I will discuss in subsequent chapters.

Even if your child finds a professor or two who can provide advice, your child should take this advice with a critical mind. Just as your child should not depend on you as a parent to tell her what to do, she shouldn't let anyone else make decisions for her.

This will help them take full responsibility for what they decide to do. Employers want to hire people who can listen to advice but make their own decision and then stand behind it.

Useful Resources

Our Underachieving Colleges: A Candid Look at How Much Students Learn and Why They Should Be Learning More, by Derek Bok (Princeton, NJ: Princeton University Press, 2006). Written by a former president of Harvard, this book shows how colleges could do a much better job, not just in career preparation but in all kinds of learning.

College: The Undergraduate Experience, by Ernest L. Boyer (New York: Harper & Row, 1987). This book is the starting point for understanding the way in which colleges attempt to educate their students. It is critical of many undergraduate programs for their emphasis on specialized over general knowledge.

Notes

1. Daniel Langenberg, "Diplomas and Degrees Are Obsolescent," *The Chronicle of Higher Education*, September 12, 1997.

2. Employment Policy Foundation: Summary Findings of the American Workplace 2001, www.epf.org.

3. "Graduate but Not Literate," *Inside Higher Education News*, December 16, 2005, reporting on the U.S. Education Department's study entitled "The National Assessment of Adult Literacy."

4. Sam Dillon, "What Corporate America Cannot Build: A Sentence," *The New York Times*, December 7, 2004, p. A23.

CHAPTER 12

Beware of Academic Overachievement

"The main difference between a successful person and an unsuccessful person is that the successful person has had a lot more failures!"

—Louis Blair

Every semester, students who have high GPAs and several intended majors and minors seek me out because they're confused. They have no idea where they're headed once they graduate and don't know what majors and minors to declare. Having fallen hook, line, and sinker for the idea that college is a great intellectual feast, they're stuck in the academic buffet line.

Academic overachievers come in two basic varieties. The first type of overachiever is the student who really loves learning for its own sake. These students take as many courses as possible, trying to sample everything they can. I enjoy my conversations with them for their breadth of knowledge and wit. Some are quite interesting and impressive. However, for the most part, they're pretty confused, and their chatter reminds me of my Westie and his tendency to change his focus every couple of seconds.

The second and most common is the grade-grubber. They're usually premed or prelaw students who are concerned about getting into a top program after college. They think a 4.0 and a triple major will guarantee them admission to the best programs. They also know the Law School Admission Test (LSAT) and Medical College Admission Test (MCAT) will play a big role, so they worry a lot about these tests. Grade-grubbers exist in all fields because they are nervous about their career futures or they have a need to win.

High academic achievement is not in itself a bad thing. It only becomes a negative for students if they make decisions that prevent them from developing their skills, building character, and exploring careers. If they're planning on academic careers, the multiple-focus behavior is not so limiting. In fact, it's a strength because academics are in the business because they love to learn. However, most students tell me they have no interest in academia as a career. For them, high academic achievement is more ornamental than useful.

The Triple Major

Students who have three majors or minors are not necessarily in trouble if they pay attention to career exploration either in one of the majors or as an ensemble. For example, a student who majors in a foreign language, English literature (or whatever the college happens to call it), and geography could easily pursue a career mission if he had the proper approach. The student might choose a foreign language because he sees the need to use the language if he becomes a teacher or a businessperson. He could select English literature because he got hooked on it by a talented high school teacher and thinks maybe he wants to be a writer. He could see geography as a way to learn Geographic Information Systems, which he knows will instantly get him his first job. In addition, he can be sure to take a series of hands-on courses in his majors and elsewhere. For example, he might take a course where students work in teams to plan a new business or to improve the services of the local Boys & Girls Club. A couple of good summer internships, perhaps with a publishing company, to see if he would like to become a writer, or with a nonprofit in Washington, D.C. doing data crunching, could round out this student's career mission in college.

However, students who have the learn-everything-they-can-learn attitude rarely make decisions that will give them a chance to pursue their career missions in college. They talk a good game, but they have trouble avoiding courses that merely sound interesting. When they take that extra course, they are depriving themselves of the opportunities to develop skills and character outside of the classroom.

Don't think that these triple majors are always the cream of the crop academically. In my experience, they are truly overachievers because they are frequently reaching beyond their grasp. Many of them are incoherent in their conversations and writing. All too often, they're fuzzy thinkers who have come to believe in their own brilliance. I'm not saying they're C students, but they're not always A students. Some are in for a rude awakening three or four years down the line.

Students don't become overloaded academically just because they're eager to learn for the sake of learning; faculty members encourage it. Many faculty members see students as potential protégés and compete with other faculty members to get the students into their courses. Advisers, especially faculty advisers, encourage students to take all the opportunities the college has to offer. This is especially true for liberal-arts faculty members, who tend to favor breadth over depth. The students are flattered by the attention and have trouble resisting the pressure.

High GPAs from the Perspective of Employers and Graduate Schools

GPA is much less important to career success than people think. The view that a high GPA is a prerequisite to career success is a myth and like all myths can be dangerous if carried too far. A high GPA may be one key but certainly not the only key. A study by the National Association of Colleges and Employers (NACE) placed GPA as seventeenth on a list of twenty top skills and characteristics employers want.[1] A corporate recruiter sent me this note: "Our cutoff is 3.0 (on a scale where 4.0 is the top). A 3.2 is really looked at no differently from a 3.7."[2] Plenty of companies use 2.5 as a cutoff and some have no cutoff. Below a 3.0 may signal a lack of basic intelligence or, worse, a lack of work ethic. However, a 3.0 satisfies most employers, and some place no stock in the GPA at all. Very few are looking for a 3.8 or above.

A few employers have told me that they become suspicious of students with GPAs above 3.5 if the students don't show significant on-campus student activities and positive summer work experience. Employers recognize the limits of highly competitive grading curves and theoretical material learned for its own sake. Colleges demand a huge amount of content mastery measured through multiple-choice and brain-dump essay tests that don't necessarily measure problem-solving, decision-making, or people skills. When was the last time you or anyone you know had to write a thousand words in a couple of hours based on 2,000 pages of reading in your place of employment?

Even in fields like accounting, engineering, architecture, and information technology, many employers are just as interested in what corporate recruiters call "soft skills" like teamwork, one-on-one communications, and writing as they are in the technical skills. In recent years, recruiters and human-relations executives have talked about "emotional intelligence" and "social intelligence." Although the terms may seem strange to you, the idea is that students need book smarts and street smarts. To put it more starkly, academic geeks are not welcomed unless they demonstrate the entire skill set—something GPA hardly ever measures.

In technical fields, employers may view GPA as evidence of knowledge in the basics of the field. But employers are frequently disappointed when new hires with high GPAs don't seem to have mastered the basics. In any case, these firms also put new hires through a lot of initial training.

For all jobs, a high GPA is taken as an indicator that the student has some work ethic, focus, and maturity. It also means that the student is able to play the academic game and deal with a variety of "bosses" (professors). From experience, however, employers know that this is a limited indicator.

Some parents worry that their children will not be able to get into the best graduate schools with mediocre GPAs (usually defined as under 3.5). The truth is that graduate schools weigh the MCAT, LSAT, GRE, and GMAT scores over GPA anyway. Except for medical schools, your child will be able to find a graduate program that will admit him. The school may be less prestigious, but that doesn't mean the educational or career payoffs will be less.

Most graduate schools prefer to take students who have been in the workforce for a few years. Graduate schools seek students who have lived a little beyond college, because they have experience to share with other students. The more postcollegiate work experience a student brings to the table, the less important the GPA is in the final admission decision.

Reasons Why a High GPA Is Not Key to the Career Mission

Let's quickly look at some factors that make GPA not so critical to your child's college education as he develops skills, builds character, and explores careers. Understanding the dynamics here will also help you understand why a high GPA is not the primary determinant of career success.

One reason that GPA is less important than might be expected should be clear from the discussions throughout this book. If the 50-50 Principle is correct, then it's reasonable to assume that GPA is only as important as the course it measures. Most courses have only a marginal impact on skill development and career exploration. The most helpful courses from a career perspective are those that provide projects or fieldwork experience; these are frequently graded as pass-fail and don't go into the GPA calculation.

Courses that your child is likely to receive lower grades in are probably less relevant to skill development and career exploration. These courses are hurdles that students are required to jump. If you are getting ready to wage

World War III over a C+ in intermediate microeconomics, let it go. Just remember, Churchill almost flunked out of college, and the founder of FedEx received a C on the paper proposing the idea that revolutionized shipping and made him a legendary business leader.

Another reason GPA isn't crucial is that grades are arbitrary and have more to do with figuring out what the professor wants than with developing skills. Have you ever seriously thought about the grade curves used by professors, especially in large freshman and sophomore courses, which are frequently used to "weed out" students? A curve happens when the professor assigns grades by ranking the scores on a test and then giving a certain percentage of students an A or a B or a C, etc. As a student at Johns Hopkins University in the mid-1950s, I found that grade-grubbing premeds wrecked many courses. In the freshman psychology class, they did so well on the multiple-choice tests that approximately 75 percent of the class scored above 90 percent. Rather than use the normal guideline that a 90 is an A−, the instructor created a curve so that a score between 90 and 95 percent would yield a C. I know many professors who give tests where the highest grade is 40 percent; they adjust the grades so that 40 percent is an A. Professors who use this practice appear not to know what they are testing for or are unable to develop a test that measures it.

This discussion leads to a third reason the GPA is less important than you might think: grade inflation. For the last decade, grade inflation has become more than a favorite topic of conversation among college faculty members. Older faculty members always complain that new faculty members are too soft. Science faculty members are cross with social science and humanities faculty members because faculties in the "soft" fields grade too easy. The discussion has turned into a preoccupation of certain faculty members, who have become grade-inflation police. Stuart Rojstaczer, who retired from Duke University, created a website about the topic,[3] and others have written many books and articles about it.

Clearly, there is grade inflation. The average GPA at most colleges has risen steadily so that it now approaches 3.09 across the nation. The real question is, What is the impact of grade inflation on your child's career mission in college? The reduced pressure on grades may allow your child to work less on his academic course work. Less hard work is never good except if it allows students to devote more time on something more useful to them.

In terms of career preparation, however, grade inflation is good for several reasons.

First, most universities allow students to drop courses fairly late in the semester, resulting in higher GPAs. For instance, my freshman class is called "boot camp" by my successful graduates. Students have to submit five papers during the semester at about two-week intervals. If they get low grades back or fail to turn in papers on time, some drop the course. Most universities permit late drops, which gives students more flexibility in finding their interests and exploring their capabilities. This source of grade inflation is a test of character and persistence and therefore helps shape character.

Second, because undergraduates learn, on average, less than half of what they need to learn for their career missions from formal course work, higher grades give them some breathing room to undertake activities that will help them develop skills and build character. It also gives them more time to work so they can make their tuition payments.

Finally, grade inflation allows faculty members to provide apprentice opportunities (such as conducting laboratory research, reviewing literature, or starting a mentoring program for a local youth agency) to the best students. Students who complete these assignments usually get high grades and therefore contribute to grade inflation. In this case, a professor who gives a lot of high grades for specialized research work is providing his students a better, not a worse, education.

Grade inflation provides students with extra time and opportunities to have experiences that will count more. It allows students to escape the limits of formal schooling and take responsibility for their own education. However, grade inflation also means that employers are less trustful of high grades. They consider grade inflation a bad thing and a reason to devalue the GPA in assessing job and internship candidates.

Discounting GPAs can be okay because overvaluing them can have pernicious effects on the three goals of career preparation. First, it can lead to more hours spent in the library than in gaining useful experiences and skills from part-time employment or student activities. Second, students can get high grades by taking shortcuts, which deprive them of developing their skills and exploring careers. A hyper-grade-conscious student will pick easy and useless courses and will drop a course if he doesn't get an A on the first paper. The most successful people in the world also fail the most because they take the most risks to develop themselves. Third and most disturbing, grades can become a definition of the person. If grades are high, they create a sense of entitlement and arrogance that will not please employers. If grades are low, they can produce defensiveness and reduce self-confidence and independence. Finally, too much of a commitment to a high GPA is risk-averse behavior. None of these attributes are what employers want to see in their employees.

The bottom line is that students place too much importance on high GPAs. Assuming they are not about to fail out, GPA is just one indicator employers use to decide on whom to hire. Once the job starts, no one asks for GPA. If students obsess over their GPAs, they could ignore many opportunities to gain and demonstrate the skills and character employers want and to explore the careers they want to pursue.

What Parents Can Do

Parents should realize that grades are an important part of their children's academic experience. How they deal with grades can have a major impact. Too much pressure for high grades can lead your child to ignore her career mission, and too little interest may encourage her to slack off. As in much of the advice throughout this book, the Goldilocks Principle applies.

Strategy #1: Don't pressure your child if he's maintaining an average close to or above 3.0. I say this for several reasons. First, students usually perform at the level they are going to perform at anyway, so you are not likely to improve grades with pressure. Second, the time necessary to earn an A rather than a B could be better spent on skill development in a job as a dormitory resident adviser or fraternity treasurer. Third, it sends the wrong message that grades are more important than learning.

Some parents may place high GPA requirements on their children. Some use threats or sanctions because they believe high GPAs provide better career options. However, making an issue over high grades ignores the reality that getting your child on a successful career path is about skills, character, and career exploration and not grades.

Unless grades are heading below the 2.0 mark, a situation I will discuss in chapter 14, do not use threats to "encourage" your child to get higher grades. For example, it's not a good idea to threaten to pull financial support if your child doesn't make the dean's list. A GPA above 2.5 means your child is likely to graduate, and that should be your main concern with respect to grades. Even more important, you really don't know enough about the courses to decide whether two tenths of a point means anything.

I speak from experience on this. I had a student who was very bright and could easily have had a 3.8 GPA but he liked to party and was not engaged in his course work. In my freshman course, which he took as a sophomore, he received an A. I invited him to be a teaching assistant (TA) for the course the next semester, but he said he was going to take a leave of absence because his father said that if he didn't receive at least a 3.0, he was pulling the financial plug. I called the father and told him that I needed his son to be a TA and hoped that he would reconsider. Because this was the first good news the father had received about his son's college escapades, he was quite happy to give his child another semester. During the remaining two years, the student did well and graduated with a cumulative GPA well

above a 3.0. Today, he's a successful businessman and has at least one graduate degree from a selective MBA program, which he earned after working
for a few years.

The moral of the story is that the father really didn't know the specifics.
He was right to think that the student partied too much, but his overconcern
about his son's performance could have led to years of unnecessary trouble.

Strategy #2: Help your child overcome the stress he places on himself. Some
parents face the opposite problem when their child is much more grade
conscious than they are. For some students, the higher their GPAs, the more
they obsess over grades. These students avoid courses in which they might
get Cs and will drop courses if they're not doing well. Students with GPAs
above 3.5 are frequently afraid that their GPAs are too low. Even as seniors,
when they can't really get their GPAs much higher even if they get all As,
they'll continue to make decisions designed to raise their cumulative GPAs.
Apparently, they can't do the math. If after 90 credits a student has a 3.5
GPA and he gets all As for the last 30 credits, the student's GPA will only go
up to a 3.63.

I once gave a student a B+ in a junior-level course and he showed his
grade obsession by writing me to say that the B+ was going to ruin his life.
I suggested that if that were true, he didn't have much of a life. I didn't hear
from him again, but he was friendly at graduation and has done quite well
since then.

Occasionally, a student will write to tell me that he has a perfect 4.0
GPA after four semesters. I offer congratulations but then add that this
might not be such a blessing because the only thing the student can do is
maintain the same average or drop. Perfection is an illusion in life and the
sooner that students give it up, the better. They need to read the quote at
the beginning of this chapter.

I mention my remarks to these students because I think it would be just
as effective coming from a parent. Your guidance on the modest importance
of GPA and triple majors will build character and help your child focus on
the prize of preparing for a successful career.

You can't do a great deal for a hyper-grade-conscious child except to
make sure the pressure isn't coming from you. Your efforts will have a
marginal impact at this time in your child's life because the pattern was
probably set in early childhood and cemented in high school. Just don't
hassle your child about his grades or brag to your friends about his GPA
when he's around (feel free to brag when he's not within earshot). You can
have a discussion about the importance of other activities that will allow for

Thoughts on High GPAs

This is a very relevant chapter to my life. I was a straight-A student in high school with all honors and AP credits. I have received only a few A− grades in college; the rest are A's. The funny thing is, getting an A is just what I expect of myself. I do not even congratulate myself when I do it again year after year after year. I have grown so used to it that I sit in class thinking about what I can do to get an A. I do not think this is a bad approach, however. I think its shows a lot of exceptional qualities. At the same time, I think it is necessary that parents understand that hyper-grade-conscious students are usually confused about what they want. All I want is someone to say, "Asher, this is what you are doing with the rest of your life, now do it." It is hard to understand that I have the choice, because for so long I have changed and molded my abilities to each individual class and not so much for me as a person, but to please some professor.

—Asher Epstein, a college sophomore

career exploration or skill development, even if those activities slightly detract from grades.

Students who are hyper-grade-conscious and bloated with triple majors and minors and extra credits frequently have trouble in their senior years focusing on what their next step will be. They have been so busy with academic achievement that they haven't taken care of their career missions. These are usually the ones who end up in graduate school or backpacking through Europe trying to figure out the next move. It's not the end of the world if this happens; it will just cost more in time and money as they try to figure out what they want to do when they grow up.

Asher Epstein's observation (see the sidebar) on the impact of grade-grubbing provides added perspective. He wrote this as a first-semester sophomore. Two days after Asher wrote this, he sent me an e-mail expressing serious concern that he missed an A on a paper because he made a stupid clerical error. He wanted advice, maybe on whether to approach the instructor. I wrote back and suggested that this "failure" was good for him. He wrote and said, "Thanks, I needed that," especially because he agreed that grades had to be put in perspective. Yet he still had that knee-jerk reaction, which demonstrates how deeply ingrained the high-GPA myth dominated the thinking of such a thoughtful student.

Useful Resources

Professors' Guide to Getting Good Grades in College, by Lynn F. Jacobs and Jeremy S. Hyman (New York: HarperCollins, 2006). This book is in some ways a counterpoint to this chapter. The authors argue that students should go after good grades because it will improve their education. I would just like to see some balance. Grades should be a means to an end, not an end in themselves.

Notes

1.   National Association of Colleges and Employers (NACE), "Job Outlook 2005," January 20, 2005.

2.   Steve Canale, statement through e-mail, July 13, 2006.

3.   http://www.gradeinflation.com.

CHAPTER 13

Transferring Is Like Moving to a New House

"The grass is always greener on the other side of the fence."

—Anonymous

Students transfer to other schools after their first or second year of college because they think they are moving to a better place for one reason or another. Just like moving to a new house, transferring always creates more costs than expected. In some cases, the benefits outweigh the costs but in most cases it's a wash or worse with respect to career preparation.

Other factors usually trump the career mission.

Why Your Child May Transfer

According to a 2002 report by the U.S. Department of Education, close to a third of all college students transfer to another college before they obtain their degrees.[1] The percentage of transfers who never complete their degrees is even higher. No definitive study exists on why students transfer. Reasons usually cited in published sources and from interviews with students include the following:

- Variety of personal reasons, such as missing family or inability to deal with dorm life or boyfriend or girlfriend
- Using freshman year to prepare for a first-choice college
- Lack of fit socially

- Lack of fit academically
- Cheaper somewhere else
- Attended community college first

Transfer fever usually starts early, frequently before students leave for college. Those students who start to think about it before they even set foot on campus are most likely to be those who think they are not going to a college that is good enough for them (i.e., they've chosen a safety school). The typical pattern for freshmen is that they have doubts starting in October, start a discussion with their parents over Thanksgiving, select colleges to apply to between semesters, finish the second semester, and then go to a new college in the fall.

Upside and Downside

When looking at the relative benefits and costs of a transfer, there are many factors to consider, as the list above suggests. My goal in this chapter is to help you consider both the downsides and upsides of transferring only with respect to career preparation. Transferring to a new college may have nothing to do with preparation for a better career future. Family or romantic reasons may be the prime factor. Thinking about the career consequences should always be part of the assessment underlying the decision, no matter what the real reason is.

Transferring May Save Money

From a career perspective, transferring to a cheaper college may be a solid decision. Significantly higher costs may require more hours in part-time employment or summer work at a job that doesn't contribute to new skills and career exploration. Higher costs can also produce more debt after college, which could limit career options.

The financial factor can be a plus or a minus for the transfer student. Transferring to a school that charges less can save a lot of money. Many students who plan to get four-year degrees go to community college to save on tuition costs. Transferring from a private college that charges $30,000 a year to a public college that charges $10,000 or less is obviously a big savings. Prices vary substantially. In making those financial assessments, students need to factor in financial aid so they are comparing the "discounted" costs of both institutions.

However, there's a general rule about moving to a new house that also applies to moving to a new college: The new costs will be higher than expected. For starters, students who transfer rarely get credit for all the courses they took at the first institution. This may mean summer school or an extra semester.

Looking at the tuition or room-and-board price differentials, therefore, is not enough. Students need to look at all the added costs and expected savings to see if they are saving enough money to make the move worthwhile from a career perspective.

Degree Progress

Despite pressure from state and federal government for colleges to accept credit from other colleges, most transfer students lose some credits when they transfer. They may get credit for courses they thought would satisfy their core or their major requirements but find out that they only count as elective credit. If they already had enough elective credits to be on track for their degrees, this would mean that the credits are in effect lost. As a general rule, highly ranked colleges accept fewer transfer credits, so safety-school leavers can expect summer school, heavier course loads, or an extra semester.

Many community colleges have agreements with four-year colleges, especially public colleges, that an associate of arts (A.A.) degree satisfies the liberal-arts or general requirements of those colleges. Students who are transferring to four-year colleges after obtaining an A.A. should find a college that has such an agreement.

Aside from the question of how many credits will transfer, students also face considerable challenges in getting straight answers and clear commitments from colleges. Transfers are usually a relatively small group of students, perhaps less than 10 percent of new students in any year. They are susceptible to falling between the cracks at the new school. They may have to choose a major right away, and they may find it difficult to connect to an adviser who can really help.

The question of degree progress usually presents a downside to the transferring student. The best that can be hoped for is that your child will lose no credits in the transfer process. Unless the new college accepts some Advanced Placement credit where the old college did not, it is not likely to give the student more credits than your child earned.

Networks

From a career perspective, relationships with other students and with faculty and staff are critical for success. Peers tell one another about job leads and talk to one another about career goals. They also participate in student organizations and other activities that can be great learning experiences for career-savvy students. Key staff in the career-services office and advising programs can make a big difference in the connections students develop. Students can talk with alumni and recruiters at career fairs. Faculty members can provide advice on careers, particularly if they're in the professional schools and, in some cases, connections with employees and alumni. Faculty members can also write letters, which are important for graduate school applications. They can also be resume references.

Just as moving to a new house requires you to meet and establish good relationships with the new neighbors, students moving to new schools have to invest time and energy in connecting with peers, staff, and faculty members. Many people move into a neighborhood and when they leave five years later hardly know the neighbors. The same can happen with transfer students who basically have to break into existing social networks. It's not impossible and it's a very good exercise in human relations and character, but on the whole, networking presents another downside to transferring.

Academic Programs

Remembering that course work contributes only 50 percent of the experience needed for the career mission, you can see that differences among academic programs are usually insufficient to justify a transfer. Except for the relatively remote possibility that the new school has a technical or specific academic program that the original school did not have, odds are the new college's academic program is not appreciably better.

The term *better* is always ill defined by most students. First, the term is used as a substitute for the words *more prestigious*. The term is also used to mean that the student body of the intended school is smarter and more competitive. The environment is more challenging and therefore students will learn more. But as discussed previously, "prestige" might not help a student's career mission in college. It's nice in theory, but this idea ignores the fact that there is no evidence that students are better prepared for careers if they take harder classes.

The upside of transferring to get into a specific academic program could be that students have a better picture of what careers they may want to pursue, and they have seriously studied the placement rates, corporate recruiters' visits, and evaluations of students and alumni. They may also have decided that they want to live in specific cities or regions and decided that they have a better chance to pursue their careers in those locations. Careful thought and research from a career perspective can provide sound reasons to transfer.

What Parents Can Do

As a parent, you have even less influence over your child's decision to transfer than you had over her original college choice. Recognizing the Goldilocks Principle, you can't force your child to stay at her present college. But there are a few strategies you can pursue either to deter your child from transferring or to make sure that there is a sound basis for the transfer decision.

Strategy #1: An ounce of prevention is worth a pound of cure. During the first two weeks of any new school year, I usually find myself talking to a student who decided to transfer before she arrived on campus. Usually, she didn't get into her first-choice college. In some cases, it's more bizarre. I had a student who wanted to go to a D.C. school and was admitted to that school, but her parents wouldn't let her go because they didn't want her to go so far away, about 400 miles, from her home. Syracuse was 150 miles. The student would have been better off starting her college career in D.C.

Another student decided that he wanted to go into teaching and would go to a public university in his home state, which was on the West Coast. So he traveled all the way to Syracuse for nothing. It's possible that he changed his career interest between the time he submitted his deposit on May 1 and the time I spoke to him in September. But if that's the case, what's to stop him from changing his career interest and his transfer decision in the next four months?

My point is that if your child is making noise about transferring before she even gets to college, don't shrug your shoulders and say, "Well, maybe everything will work out and she'll come to her senses." Instead, suggest that she try to think this thing through or go to a local community college for a year.

If your child appears happy as she goes off to college, don't be surprised if she comes home at Thanksgiving thinking about transferring. If one out of three students transfers before graduating college, we can assume that at least 50 percent think about it at some point—usually in their freshman year.

Strategy #2: Keep the focus on careers in the decision-making process. Because there are many reasons for students to transfer and only a few have to do with career preparation, your child needs to decide if the other reasons are good enough for her to make the career focus secondary. If she does, then this strategy will not work. However, if your child is talking about prestige and academic programs, it's time for you to ask for serious research and thought over whether this is a good move careerwise. A trip to the intended school and a comparison between career services and career-development opportunities outside the classroom are very good ideas.

Strategy #3: Require a careful financial- and degree-progress analysis. A friend of mine was approached by his son, who had the safety-school problem with where he was during his freshman year. My friend said to the son, "We are paying for only four years of college for you, so if you decide to transfer and you can't graduate in four years, you will be paying for the fifth year." The son transferred and graduated in four years. Such a strong position could serve to deter a transfer but even if it doesn't, it will require your child to carefully study the financial as well as degree-progress consequences of her migratory behavior.

Strategy #4: Present options while staying in the initial college. Students have a lot of trouble realizing how short the four college years are. If they are at colleges where they aren't particularly happy, they may want to consider the following points about how much time is spent at college:

- Each academic semester is less than four months. That means students only spend three years on campus.
- Early graduation (by bringing in credits, going to summer school, or taking more credits each semester) can reduce that time.
- Two or three semesters can be taken off campus. Off-campus programs are a great resource for students' career mission.

These strategies assume that it's best for your child to stay put from a career perspective. There may be other legitimate reasons for a transfer. Having your child think hard about the upside and downside of the transfer increases the chances that it will not cost you more money, your child will graduate on time, and your child will be ready for a career at graduation. It's worth a try to follow these strategies because in almost every case, from a career perspective, transferring is not a good idea.

Useful Resources

How to Transfer to the College of Your Choice, by Eric Freedman (Berkeley, CA: Ten Speed Press, 2002). This book provides a solid discussion of reasons for transferring and how to go about it. It does not focus on career preparation, but it provides useful tips.

Note

1. Jeffrey R. Young, "Third of Students Transfer Before Gaining Degrees, Education Dept. Study Finds," *The Chronicle of Higher Education*, December 19, 2002.

CHAPTER 14

Graduation: Early, On Time, Late, or Never

"I have never let my schooling interfere with my education."

—Mark Twain

You may think it is normal for a college student in a four-year program to graduate in four years. Why would they call it a four-year program if that wasn't the case? But this is not the most likely scenario. More than 54 percent of students don't graduate in four years.

Your child can't be certain he will avoid the unpleasantness associated with late or never graduating because, as they say, "things happen." However, you can take steps once your child is in college to avoid the costs and anguish associated with extended college experiences or dropping out. You can also help your child make a rational decision about graduating early. From a career perspective, better early than on time, better on time than late, better sometime than never.

Should Your Child Graduate Early?

For your child's career-preparation mission, the answer to this question is almost always yes. The real question is how early.

■ **One Semester.** There is almost no downside to graduating a semester early, and the upside is saving money and getting started in a job early or having time to explore. Also, if students have one or two courses left, they can drop out and finish part-time, saving a lot of money.

■ **Two Semesters or One Academic Year.** From a career perspective, this is generally a good idea for the same reasons as graduating a semester early, especially if the student isn't having a lot of fun or is running out of money.

■ **More Than One Academic Year.** Students shouldn't graduate more than a year early unless they have some plan for what they're going to do afterward. Students who want to enter some kind of program or have a job lined up might want to consider this option.

Graduating early is generally a good idea, not just as a cost-reduction strategy but also because of the 50-50 Principle. Taking traditional classes is like reading a book on how to swim. The sooner your child swims in the ocean of reality the better.

College faculty and advisers will always advocate more schooling. Why wouldn't they? Remember, if learning for the sake of learning is the goal, the more the better. Hence, your child is not likely to get sound advice from them. In fact, you may be hearing a request for another year of college to learn more. From the perspective of developing skills, building character, and exploring careers, getting out of college as soon as possible makes more sense.

Like all general rules, there are costs and exceptions. Here are a few to ponder. If your child is switching into a technical field like accounting, then an extra semester or two might make sense. If your child is just not ready for the real world, an extra semester might seem like a good choice. I would only accept this argument if your child is so afraid about going into the real world that it might send him over the edge and back to your home forever. Some children just aren't ready.

The not-quite-ready-for-the-real-world child has better options than staying in school for more credits. Many programs like Teach for America, the Peace Corps, or AmeriCorps could fill two years and in some cases one year right out of college. Some of these programs have high entrance requirements but others do not. Many nonprofits would be happy to hire someone at $25,000 a year, and that can be an extremely valuable educational experience for your child. In addition, a year working for a temporary-employment agency would do more for skill development and career exploration than another year in school. These options will result in low salaries, but your child will be getting paid rather than paying for tuition yet again.

Another viewpoint students sometimes express is that staying an extra semester or two might help boost their GPAs so it would be easier to get into graduate school or impress employers. GPA is not important enough to admissions officers to be worth another $25,000 or $50,000. As I noted in chapter 12, if you do the math you'll see that another semester will not change a GPA very much. Moreover, most graduate schools are so eager to admit students that if your child can't find one, it is a pretty clear message that he needs to work for a while. Finally, the longer your child is in the workforce before applying to graduate school, the less important GPA is. For employers, a couple of decimal points on a GPA mean nothing.

Staying in school beyond the minimum number of credit hours needed to graduate doesn't make much sense with respect to developing skills and exploring careers. Prolonging academic course work would be like reading more than one book on how to swim. The real world will do much more for career exploration and skill development because it's a much more powerful teacher than formal schooling.

If for no other reason, I advocate getting a degree as quickly as possible for the sake of establishing normal sleeping patterns. College means the freedom to stay up all hours of the night and to sleep in. This turns into a lesson for the group of undergraduates I send to intern in a New York City high school every spring. They say it's a great learning experience but everyone also says that by the end of the week they're exhausted. Getting up at 6 A.M. to get on the subway by 7:30 A.M. to get to the school by 8 A.M. and then work until 5 P.M. (along with a possible evening or two a week) is much more time on the job than most college students spend. At the end of the week, they don't go partying. They hit the sack by 10 P.M. Graduating early means learning that work ethic and time management are very important in a successful career.

I offer the graduate-early advice as the most rational course, but many students like to graduate with their entering class and to spend their college time having some fun. Because my advice is always about preparing for a career, I don't include "fun" as an objective. However, as I was reminded by some students, fun can help in career development and skill building. Well, maybe a student needs another year or semester for that reason. As a parent, it's your call.

Reasons Why Students Graduate Late or Drop Out

Few students really have to worry about graduating early. Some students take longer to graduate or never graduate at all for the following nine reasons:

1. Can't do the course work
2. Won't do the course work
3. Takes the wrong courses
4. Delays choosing a program
5. Changes programs
6. Can't fit required courses into his or her schedule
7. Has financial problems
8. Has health problems
9. Has family pressures

I will briefly comment on each. The key to helping your child graduate on time is to share accurate and current information on degree progress. The plan described in chapter 6 is designed to help you both monitor degree progress.

Can't Do the Course Work

Your child may not be able to do the course work that his program requires. If you want your child to "be all he can be," you need to face this reality quickly. Students are put on academic probation if they score below a 2.0 GPA, and schools will eventually ask them to leave if it looks like they won't improve. If your child's GPA after the first two semesters is below a 2.0 and you're sure your child is putting in the hours, you have a strong indication that he just can't do the work. He may have learning disabilities or maybe he's in a major that's beyond his reach. The sooner you get help from on-campus advisers and administrators the better. These professionals can test for learning disabilities, provide tutors, and suggest better course options.

Won't Do the Course Work

The first-semester GPA is a great test of commitment to graduating from college on time. Assuming your child can do the work, a GPA at or below 2.0 is a sign that your child is not putting in the effort. Keep a close eye on GPA each semester if it goes below 2.5. Take strong action when academic probation is on the horizon.

Takes the Wrong Courses

How would you like to invest $150,000 in your child's college education and then be told that he's missing three credits and you are in for another $1,000? Students often wait until the last semester to go for a degree check, which is too late. They can't make course adjustments and are headed for summer school or an extra semester to graduate. The most common reason for this avoidance behavior is fear and loathing of the general or liberal arts requirements when they were freshmen.

This situation won't happen to your child if you put your foot down by requiring a degree check once a year. Require your child to show you the paperwork the administrator provides. Updating the planning document suggested in chapter 6 will help to avoid this costly mistake.

Delays Choosing a Program

One of the biggest sources of late graduation is failure to pick a major by the end of the sophomore year. In fact, at Syracuse University, students can't register for their junior year unless they have signed up for a major. Some financial aid is dependent on choosing a major.

Some students consider choosing a major to be crucial to their future, but they're wrong. Students change majors many times and most of them don't go into the fields they selected unless it's a technical field like accounting and engineering. The major isn't important for career development. It's the skills, character, and career exploration that count, which are best pursued through activities outside academia.

Students not doing well in majors such as chemistry or engineering may find themselves spending an extra semester or two in school if they don't make changes by the end of their sophomore year. Your child should be alert to this possibility and explore alternatives even as he continues in his chosen major during his freshman and sophomore years. Many of my most successful students are architecture, engineering, and premed dropouts.

The point is to be flexible and understand that choosing a major is not choosing a life.

Changes Programs

Changing programs may or may not be a good idea. If your child can't pass the courses in a technical field and is really trying, he should make a change. If your child wants to move to an entirely different field, for example, from a history major to an exercise-science major, that makes sense. However, if your child is close to completion in a liberal arts major like psychology and wants to move to another field within liberal arts like English, it doesn't make a lot of sense. He could take some courses in English, still complete the major in psychology, graduate on time, and then get a position in publishing to explore his interest in English.

A student of mine visited me during her junior year to tell me that she was transferring to another program, which would require her to spend an extra two semesters in school. She could have taken three or four courses in her current program and graduated on time. I tried to convince her to do that after I pointed out the cost and time savings, but I didn't persist because I realized that the decision had more to do with fear about going into the real world than academic preparation. Perhaps her decision was right, but not from a career-development perspective.

Parents should be ready for requests to stay in school longer than four years to take additional courses to change programs. There may be legitimate career reasons for such requests, such as moving from or to a technical program. Other than that, staying in college to change a major will not improve the skills most students need for successful careers. Except for technical fields, most jobs require general professional skills, which your child will have if he follows my advice about skills, character, and career preparation.

Can't Fit Required Courses into His or Her Schedule

Your child needs to be on the lookout for course sequences and closed courses. Sometimes, colleges are at fault for not having enough space for all their students. More often, the student is at fault for not planning carefully.

Your child should pay a lot of attention to both general and major requirements to make sure she'll graduate on time. For example, if she's required to take a two-course sequence in which the first course is offered in the fall and the second in the spring, she should get the sequence out of the way early just in case she wants to study abroad in the spring semester.

If your child is shut out of a course that could delay graduation and she did all of the right things like complete other requirements, encourage her to be aggressive about getting into the course. Before she goes up the chain of command, she should meet with the department's secretary or administrative assistant. This person's job is to solve student problems so that the higher levels are not occupied with such matters. If that does not work, she should approach a professor or department chairperson. A little persistence and strategic thinking usually pays off.

Has Financial Problems

Many financially strapped students face stress and long hours stocking shelves or waiting tables during the academic year. This can get in the way of progress toward a degree. Frequently, if the university doesn't receive payment on time, it wipes out the student's registration. The student then spends the first week missing class because he's trying to re-register. Financially strapped students, particularly if they aren't strong academically, often have a hard time keeping up (or, for students who have to re-register, catching up). These students should seriously consider colleges that are less expensive, and they should work out a regular payment schedule to keep on top of tuition bills. If payment can't be made that way, going part-time may lead to a degree faster than going full-time and dropping or failing half the courses.

If you're wondering how many hours your child can work per week and still go to school, most experts say no more than twenty. That number depends on how organized your child is, how efficient he is in doing schoolwork, and the number and type of courses he's taking.

Has Health Problems

Sending your child to college is like sending him to nursery school as far as catching illnesses goes except they don't send him home so you get sick too. I marvel at the variety of illnesses and ailments that beset students. Most of the time, poor health just adds stress or may cause withdrawal for a semester. Accurate knowledge about course work and degree progress can help you advise your child on what to do. Most professors will bend the rules on completing courses if the problems are serious enough and documented. If a health problem arises, encourage your child to finish up the courses even if it means lower grades.

Has Family Pressures

Family problems, like the death of a loved one, divorce, or serious illness, can also be very disruptive to your child's academic progress. Again, knowledge of academic progress may help you counsel your child.

In some cases, pressures to come home every weekend, to take on family responsibilities like babysitting, or to fly to Vail for a family ski vacation disrupt a student's academic performance. Your family priorities are important, but think twice about how these decisions affect your child's academic programs and career mission.

What Parents Can Do

Timing graduation raises many complicated questions. Adequate information and open conversation are essential to helping your child do the right thing. I can provide a few guidelines, but you will have to mostly follow the Goldilocks Principle: neither too loose, nor too tight, but just right. Try the following three strategies:

Strategy #1: Have your child indicate in the planning document when she expects to graduate. The key to graduating on time or early is using something like the Academic Credits and Grades worksheet in this chapter. Updating the plan every semester will help your child graduate on time or early. Even if your child doesn't prepare a formal plan, careful study of degree progress by looking at grade reports and other records each semester is a good idea. As I noted in chapter 6, your child will probably resist creating a planning document. This is especially true for students who are not doing well and are in danger of failing out.

Strategy #2: Arrange for the orderly communication of information about grades and degree progress from the school. Here is a list of the kind of information you and your child should share. The template presented in chapter 6 appears below it to refresh your memory. Be sure that you have settled with your child that you will have direct access to all her grade and financial information from the college.

■ **Advanced Credits.** Even before the first semester, you should be aware of whether your child is bringing along any advanced credits. As described in chapter 8, your child can earn and transfer a lot of credit in high school. Suggest to your child that she have the information sent to the college in a timely manner and to get in writing what credits have been accepted for what requirements. The College Board will send the information to the college, but double-checking is always a good idea. This is something worth the "didja do it" micromanaging, because students tend to assume the college staff will take care of it, and they usually do, but a proactive nudge from the student is good insurance.

■ **Courses and Grades During the First Semester.** Check into the courses your child is taking the first semester and how they fit into the degree requirements by asking your child to explain them. If you don't get a clear answer, ask your child to provide you with any worksheet he was given. Some colleges also send out midsemester grades, especially during the first semester, to alert students who are having trouble. The colleges have a vested interest in your child doing well. Find out if there are such reports at your child's school and, if so, get them. Your child should have already given the college permission to share information with you. As noted in chapter 6, colleges usually send the grades home unless your child instructs them not to. If suddenly the information isn't there three weeks after the end of each semester, you need to investigate.

■ **GPA Monitoring Each Semester.** Once grades for the first semester are in, see how far above 2.0 they are. Students tend to do poorly the first semester, but anything 2.5 or below may signify serious trouble ahead.

■ **Degree-Progress Monitoring.** You could try to master the degree requirements and conduct a degree-progress check yourself, but that's not your job. It falls in the category of a "too hot" form of micromanaging. A better plan is to get your child to show you the paperwork for his own degree-progress check. Each spring, students should visit their academic advisers or the staff members who record grades to update their progress.

■ **Make Sure They Graduate.** Look for a confirmation in the mail that says your child has graduated, or request an official transcript about two months after your child has graduated. I know many students who faked their degree completion, not just to their parents but their employers. Parents should not be fooled because they saw Junior dress in a robe and walk in the ceremony and even get a piece of paper from the dean. Colleges don't verify the completion of degree programs until one to six months after the event, so whatever is handed to your child is a meaningless piece of paper. A copy of the diploma should be the last item in your file.

Chapter 6 provides a worksheet called "Degree Progress Report" (p. 61) to monitor the degree progress of your child. Update it after each semester. If you don't use this worksheet, be sure to ask for a transcript or to check it online at least once a year.

Strategy #3: Take action if degree progress is slow. A student who has a GPA below 2.0 is usually put on probation; if the GPA stays below 2.0, the student is eventually asked to leave for a semester or longer or to go to a community college. The time to take action is before it drops below 2.0. Don't assume the college will take action. Most colleges give second, third, and fourth chances to students with GPAs below 2.0. A fourth chance could cost you $80,000, with no college degree in sight. Allowing your child to continue with such poor performance, even with the permission and encouragement of the college, isn't a good idea.

College administrators closely monitor progress toward a degree, and they take many steps to help your child meet the requirements in a timely manner. But students tend to either ignore or avoid degree requirements.

You should carefully review all information. These details will help you see if your child is progressing toward the degree and if the bills are being paid. The information also feeds into the annual plan described in chapter 6. The key component is progress toward a degree. If grades are heading below a 2.0 GPA or the number of credits is not adding up to thirty per year, ask your child about this pattern and start thinking about possible direct actions. Other than that, the information becomes part of the overall picture and is discussed in the context of the annual plan.

If your child is getting bad grades and it looks like the underlying cause is a lack of commitment, you will need to make some threats that may even include refusing to provide any more financial support. The balance between too much micromanaging and too much "hands off" is part of the Goldilocks Principle discussed in chapter 5. Each situation is unique. You will have to decide what is appropriate.

I see too many parents allow their children to prolong their stay in college in the hope that their children will straighten out. Many of these students would have been better off if they had taken full-time jobs rather than use the excuse of staying in college to have a good time. Many students have returned to college two or three years later and done exceptionally well. They tell me that they just weren't ready for college when they were nineteen years old. Others stay in the workforce and survive. It's not the end of your child's economic future if he doesn't graduate from college. If you realize that, you'll be able to guide your child with the wisdom of rational thought rather than the irrationality of blind panic.

Useful Resources

College Rules! How to Study, Survive and Succeed in College, by Sherrie L. Nist and Jodi Patrick Holschuh (Berkeley, CA: Ten Speed Press, 2002). In addition to its observations on professors, this book provides advice designed to help your child graduate on time and get good grades. Written in a clear style, it is one of the best I have seen.

PART FIVE

The Other 50 Percent

If the 50-50 Principle means that only 50 percent of preparation for a successful career in college happens through course work, the other 50 percent happens elsewhere. The opportunities are limitless.

CHAPTER 15

The College of Hard Knocks

"Experience is a hard teacher because she gives the test first, the lessons afterwards."

—Vernon Saunders

The phrase "school of hard knocks" usually refers to the real-world education people who don't go to college receive. But I see no reason why students can't attend two colleges—the one they get their formal degrees from and the one that gives them real-world experiences to develop skills, build character, and explore careers. Fortunately, both "colleges" exist in undergraduate education today. Unfortunately, parents and students give too much attention to the former and not enough to the latter.

George Foreman, former heavyweight champion, businessman extraordinaire, and entertaining sports commentator, is a great example of this. George writes, "Job Corps took me from the mean streets and out of a nightmare lifestyle into a mode where the most incredible of dreams came true."[1] Job Corps is one of the most successful federal programs of all time because it gives troubled youth a chance. This program puts teenagers and young adults in a camp, gives them job training, and sends them on their way. It helps them build character and develop skills to find new lives. They don't all make a fortune out of boxing and selling mufflers and grills, but they do find viable career paths.

The Job Corps program uses the same principle that I am suggesting for your child's college experience. Its "students" are given the opportunities to develop skills, build character, and explore careers. It combines classroom activities with hands-on learning.

I'm not saying you should try to get your child in the Job Corps. I am saying that your child should view a college education as four years of learning opportunities, at least 50 percent of which are not in the academic programs. The point about George Foreman is it took a formal education program like Job Corps to transform him. He had plenty of hard knocks before he entered the program, and the program was designed to give him formal training and more hard knocks. It worked for him and more than two million other graduates since its inception in 1964. Formal education is an intervention that sets the stage for a complete education. In itself, it's not enough.

No Pain, No Gain

The term *school of hard knocks* implies that painful experiences are a potent form of education. Although there's plenty of pain in the classroom, the difference between pain meted out by a professor through grades and the pain of a real-world experience is immense. If students misspell a word in a term paper, they may lose a point or two. They are not likely to get a lower grade in the course unless they keep making mistakes. However, if someone in the work world makes a clerical error in a project estimate to a customer, a piece of advertising for a business, a statistical table for a consulting company, or any other activity that requires attention to detail, that person could be fired or reprimanded. It will hit the pocketbook and the career hard. These things can happen even to the most meticulous, but employees who do this kind of thing more than once are likely to be looking for another job.

In college, students have internships, community-service positions, student groups, and many other activities where they will mess up. They will receive "knocks" that are not necessarily as hard as losing a job. But the knocks will be hard enough. They might include negative feedback from peers; a poor performance report; and, if the student is committed to excellence, a sick feeling in her stomach that will tell her she doesn't want to do such a thing ever again.

Students will also receive praise when they do the right thing, which will be much less fleeting than a higher grade or "good job" from their professors. The learning will be more intense, more character building, and more skill developing.

If during an internship a student has to prepare a report using Excel and bar graphs for the executive director of a nonprofit, for example, she will learn Excel and practical statistical analysis much better than if she takes a class in statistics. Her client will need a quality project. If the report is not good enough, the executive director will not use it. If the report is good enough, it will be used and the student may even be asked to attend the meeting where it's presented. In either case, the student will see the consequences of her work. She will suffer the pain of it not being used or enjoy the praise of playing in the major leagues. The depth and lasting effects of the pain or praise will be much greater than a few points or a different grade from a professor.

As I discuss in chapter 19, some courses tied to real-world experiences provide the knocks students need to gain experience, but the majority of them don't. Your child needs to supplement her course work by pursuing experiences that require activities outside of the classroom. Some of those activities may generate course credit, but in most cases they will not. This is the unfortunate reality of college today.

The "no pain, no gain" principle can't be overemphasized in the process of developing skills, building character, and exploring careers. The principle can be applied in some academic course work, but real-world experiences will be much more productive.

College provides an infinite variety of opportunities for failures that produce serious learning without the career-ending negative consequences that would occur in full-time employment. The range of experiences outside the classroom is infinite, and most colleges do a lot to help students get those experiences. In addition, businesses, government, and nonprofit organizations generate opportunities for experience. Increasingly, colleges are connecting to these organizations to help students get experiences and sometimes even college credit. I will discuss these options in chapter 19.

Taking Many Roads

Yogi Berra once said, "When you come to a fork in the road, take it." Career-savvy college students take both academic and nonacademic roads to develop skills, build character, and explore their career interests. Let me illustrate with a specific example.

Sarah, who had fun throughout her college career, primarily as a sorority girl, took many paths during her years at Syracuse. Her sisters voted her sorority president, which gave her access to top university officials and helped her develop leadership skills. She worked for a string of professors earning money to pay her sorority dues but in the process picked up valuable research and computer skills, not to mention outstanding references. She found time to tutor children at the local housing project and raise funds for charity on a sustained basis, which also appealed to prospective employ-ers. She managed to keep a 3.5 average, which showed her persistence and her intellect. Her efforts during her first three years of college led to a high-paying internship (over $6,000 and free room and transportation) between her junior and senior year. She was busy and frequently under stress, but it was worth it. She had a high-paying job offer with a consulting company in the early fall of her senior year.

She took many paths, but she never lost site of her mission—to leave college ready for a successful career. She made choices along the way that allowed her to move forward on her mission. Although your child may not be as high-octane as Sarah, she should allocate a substantial amount of her energy to gaining experience outside the classroom.

Yogi's advice, however, has its limits. It makes sense to be open to all opportunities, but at some point good time-management skills require that your child not take on more than she can do. As your child moves through college, more time should be spent on a smaller number of opportunities. Students should view all of their college experiences as many roads to travel, but by the time they are seniors, they should be reducing the number of forks in the road to two or three. They should try out a large number of paths as freshmen and choose a few to travel as seniors.

The activities outside of class can be critical in helping students to grad-uate from college, especially if the academic road is not for them. The joy and excitement of these activities can make the academic road bearable. Conversely, students who love the academic side of college can benefit from nonacademic experiences as a way to develop skills, build character, and explore careers in ways not provided by their course work. It can also help to reduce the chances that they will become perpetual students.

Chapters 16 through 20 describe the range of experiences outside of the formal classroom that your child can pursue. Some of these experiences, in the more progressive colleges, will generate academic credit. Most of the experiences, however, will not lead to academic credit, but they will be more than worth your child's time.

The chapters cover:

- Student activities, including student organizations, college-run ac-tivities, and especially community-service opportunities. They are the best places to start your world curriculum.

- Jobs during the academic year, which should be viewed as more than an opportunity to earn a little spending money. They can play a major role in career development.

- Summer opportunities for real learning, like jobs for which your child works from nine to five and hopefully even longer hours.

- Off-campus semesters, either overseas or in the United States, that incorporate field experience.

- Courses provided by outside vendors like the basic Dale Carnegie Training Institute Human Relations course or Microsoft training programs. They can add skill-building opportunities that colleges can't or won't provide.

Students can gain experience through volunteering, part-time work, and project-driven course work. Frequently, volunteers work up to paid positions or get faculty members to sponsor an internship. Volunteer activities are particularly useful to freshmen, who have fewer skills and experiences than juniors and seniors. The largest number and greatest variety of volunteer activities come from the student organizations on campus, which I will discuss in detail in chapter 16.

Many factors will determine whether an outside-the-classroom experience is a good fit for your child. She will have to weigh those factors and decide what opportunities to pursue based on her schedule, skill level, what she'll learn, and whether the experience will deliver what is promised.

Your child should explore at least one of these options early in her college career. Early involvement will allow her to pick and choose from several options and to build a "career" in that organization over time. If your child has what it takes, she will have an opportunity to develop her networking and leadership skills in the organizations. Employers like to see persistence and leadership.

An early start is also important because one experience builds on another. For example, a freshman who joins the organization that represents students on her dormitory floor can be on the committee that represents students throughout the entire dormitory the next semester and become a resident adviser the following year. If her work there is good, she might be selected for the college judicial board in her junior year. One door opens many doors. The sooner your child opens the first door, the more doors will open to her throughout her college experience.

Why Students Avoid Outside Experiences

Although the school of hard knocks may make a lot of sense to you, especially because you went through it, your child may resist. Nobody likes self-inflicted pain. Your child may try her best to avoid it, especially if you have been protecting her from bad experiences throughout her life. You'll need to help your child overcome some of her natural resistance.

Refusing to take a part-time job, accept a leadership role in a student organization, go off-campus for a semester, use the career center, or get a career-exploring and skill-building summer job may indicate any of the following conditions:

- Too resistant to change
- Too immature to seriously commit to a career mission
- Too committed to academic success and a high GPA
- Too busy to plan far enough ahead
- Too scared of the unknown and the risk of failure
- Too choosy in searching for the perfect placement

These are all typical behaviors and attitudes, not just among young adults but all of us. However, they are the kind of behaviors and attitudes that employers do not like in their employees.

If your child shows no interest in these activities, you should be concerned for two reasons. First, it may show a lack of engagement with college life, which should be taken as a signal your child may be thinking of dropping out or transferring to another school, or at least is seriously overwhelmed by the college experience. Second, these activities are critical in practicing many of the thirty-eight skills listed in chapter 1, building character, and exploring career interests. Unwillingness to participate in any of them will eliminate many of the most important opportunities to be career ready when your child graduates.

What Parents Can Do

You may have some difficulty in encouraging your child to focus so much energy on nonacademic opportunities. On one hand, you don't want to turn your child off to academic course work. On the other hand, your child could be so fixated on grades and completing the degree that she sees outside activities and employment as an unwelcome distraction.

This dilemma should not prevent you from encouraging your child to make commitments to volunteering and work throughout college. Keep a watchful eye and encourage balance. Suggest courses that will build on interests generated by activities outside of the classroom.

I have three specific strategies for encouraging a child to get a degree from the school of hard knocks while earning his college degree:

Strategy #1: Encourage your child to participate in volunteer and job activities on and off campus and to balance this with academics. Adhering to the Goldilocks Principle means you can't force your child to take advantage of these experiences. It also means you shouldn't discourage it. Parents all too frequently advise against these activities because they fear low grades.

If your child tells you he wants to do community service work, be supportive. Never say, "Your studies are more important," unless he's in danger of flunking out. You can counsel against overcommitment, but you can't prevent it. That's part of the learning process. Many students tell me that the busier they are, the better they do in their course work. In any case, a fear of low grades should not lead you to discourage a reasonable amount of outside activity. As discussed in chapter 12, a student with a 3.5 who has engaged in other activities will be more ready for a career than a student with a 3.8 who never ventured outside the academic zone except to play Frisbee.

But be on the lookout for what I call "volunteer junkies" and "student-activity junkies." These are students who need their "fix" of tutoring the cute little kids at the Boys & Girls Club every day of the week or of wheeling and dealing in student government until 4 A.M. Like all addictions, they are pursued in order to escape painful experiences like writing that term paper or going to class.

The best thing for you to do is promote the idea that experience is the best teacher, and that college is a place and time where there are plenty of opportunities to get that experience. Your child will figure out when enough is enough—an evaluation process that will serve her well in her career.

Strategy #2: Don't try to control your child's choices, but raise questions about skill development, character building, and career exploration. You may not like the idea of your daughter becoming president of her sorority. You would rather see her working at a soup kitchen or representing students on the college's board of trustees. But you should let your child select areas that she finds rewarding. Even if it's play, it can be a career-developing experience. Presidents of fraternities and sororities develop leadership skills, which employers highly value. In most cases, any type of student-group activity and outside work is better than none.

Strategy #3: See these outside activities as a test and convince your child that it's a test. Participating in activities outside of the classroom is an excellent test of both the skills and character that you hope your child develops in college. Observing how your child handles the challenge will tell you how well she will do in pursuing her career. Here are three things to look out for:

1. **Time-Management Skills.** Can your child spend fifteen hours a week working or participating in a fraternity and still maintain his grades?
2. **Work Ethic.** Does your child do her best in her volunteer position or job?
3. **Skills Development, Character Building, and Career Exploration.** Does your child see the value of experience in these areas?

Remember to advise your child of Aristotle's idea that excellence is a habit. If she is going to participate in activities outside the classroom, she should be the best she can be.

Useful Resources

Established in 1973, the National Program on Noncollegiate Sponsored Instruction (PONSI) is a part of the New York State Education Department in Albany, New York. According to the PONSI website, the organization "links learning experiences that take place outside of college classrooms to college degrees." It does this by evaluating learning experiences at noncollegiate organizations throughout the United States and overseas and making the results available to colleges. The colleges use this as a guide in awarding credit for noncollegiate course work. The member-organizations list contains some of the best-known names in corporate America as well as labor unions, government agencies, professional and voluntary organizations, cultural institutions, and healthcare organizations. For more information, visit http://www.national ponsi.org. Access to the College Credit Recommendations portion of the site is free.

Note

1.   Alan B. Krueger, "A Study Backs Up What George Foreman Already Said: The Job Corps Works," *The New York Times*, March 30, 2000, p. C2.

CHAPTER **16**

Student Activities

"You miss 100 percent of the shots you never take."

—Wayne Gretzky

The term *student activities* is collegespeak for the nonacademic programs supported by a college. Administrators put a lot of resources into student activities because they recognize their value even if faculty members don't. All administrators who care about their students know the 50-50 Principle well.

One student I know was her college's mascot, managed a national convention on campus, served as a teaching and research assistant, had several work-study jobs, helped organize homecoming events, and participated in several student activities. She established a consistent record from the time she was a freshman until she was a senior. It was no surprise that she had two excellent job offers in hand by December 15 of her senior year.

In addition to volunteer and job activities both on and off campus, the greatest strength of her resume were her student activities. She played a consistent and stellar role in many residential-life activities, and from that base moved into other areas, including jobs off campus and work with several academic offices. Being the college mascot was a goal she set for herself and was perhaps the highlight of her college experience, but to get there she had to start as a freshman, being "Ms. Student Activity."

Types of Student Activities

Colleges have hundreds of student activities. I have put them in the following five categories:

1. Athletics, which includes intercollegiate and club level, within or across campuses
2. Programs run by university staff to provide learning experiences
3. Fraternities and sororities, which could be social, service, or academic
4. Non-Greek student organizations, which include student government, groups representing various types of populations, groups with a political or service missions, religious groups, recreation organizations like the ski club, groups sponsored by the office of resident life, public safety groups, academic programs, and performing groups
5. Community groups run by university staff and by student groups

Here is a brief overview for each of these five types of activities.

Athletics

Intercollegiate athletics may be the single most important educational activity available to undergraduates who see college as a way to prepare for a rewarding career, regardless of the career field, and not necessarily in sports. Unfortunately, the public and some faculty, administrators, and students (including student-athletes) sometimes don't see it that way.

You should not make that mistake. A recent study published in the *Journal of Human Resources* reports that on average college athletes make more than nonathletes. One of the authors says that college athletes acquire "skills on the field that can be applied in their careers."[1]

Look at what the Syracuse University Athletic Department lists on its website: "The demands of being both a student and an athlete sometimes leave little time for getting job experience. What the athlete needs to realize is that participation in Division I athletics is very similar to holding a job. Athletes learn skills that can be transferred to any job situation." The website also notes the following attributes that employers are seeking:

Good time management
Teamwork
Goal-oriented behavior
Competitiveness
Confidence
Persistence/endurance
Loyalty
Discipline
Ability to take criticism

Ability to deal with setbacks
Leadership
Flexibility/adaptability

No one can argue with this list. It emphasizes work ethic and personal quali-ties that are in short supply in the workforce. Although the list is appealing to employers, some athletes, especially in the big-money sports like basket-ball, are pampered to the point of dishonesty. Whether they learn how to be honest or dishonest from this experience depends on the individual.

The list of skills and character could be expanded. Athletic programs around the country help student-athletes develop many more skills valued by employers beyond those listed above.

Employers place high value on the additional skills that athletes develop. They include the following seven skills:

1. Money Management. It's not easy to teach, even to adults, if mounting consumer debt and bankruptcies in the United States are any indication. Student-athletes have to watch their money even more carefully than most students because time demands placed on student-athletes often restrict their employment opportunities, and the National Collegiate Ath-letic Association (NCAA) is watching. Keeping track of travel receipts is a must.

2. Personal Communication. Conversing one-on-one is a critical but often overlooked skill. Teamwork is based on this skill, but it has value in many other contexts.

3. Public Speaking. Presenting to groups will be required of most pro-fessionals in any field. Student-athletes will frequently have the opportunity to do so.

4. Teaching and Mentoring. Teaching skills are required for any pro-fessional position. As juniors and seniors work with freshmen and sopho-mores, they can develop these skills. Mentoring, after all, is teaching.

5. Organization. Keeping and using records are part of athletes' activi-ties as they try to improve their own, as well as their teams', performance.

6. Applying Basic Math and Statistics. Using numbers and graphs to look at performance is commonplace and part of understanding any game.

7. Detail Awareness. Paying attention to detail is one of the most criti-cal but overlooked skills required in the business world. Athletes also have to pay attention to detail to comply with eligibility rules and to keep up with plays during games.

The skill areas listed are concrete. Athletes also practice high-level analytical skills such as gathering and applying information, evaluating actions and policies, and problem solving. Isn't that what good athletes do on the playing field and in preparation for games? Aren't these skills what undergraduate academic programs are supposed to develop and employers are looking for?

Even if your child doesn't make the team or lasts only one or two years, the experience can help. Some of my most successful students are dropouts from the crew team. They started freshman year, getting up at five in the morning to freeze their butts off—a perverse form of skill number one on my list (Kick yourself in the butt). This demonstrates the work ethic that employers want, but dropping out also shows they learned when enough was enough.

In addition to the skill and character development that comes from sports, students benefit from networking that allows for career exploration even if it doesn't directly produce a job. Having a common experience breaks down doors and gives athletes a decided advantage in the job market. It also opens the door for coaching, which allows the students who love the game to stay in it and make a living.

What if your child isn't up to the level of a division-I school? Encourage her to attend a division-II or division-III school. Or if that isn't possible, encourage her to play in club sports or even her dorm floor's volleyball team. If your nonathletic child is completely in love with the sport, he might want to explore becoming a team manager. I have taught several student-athletes in my teaching career and have found that their ability to handle the demands of managing logistics while completing degrees to be a great test of skill and character. The sidebar from one of the managers of the Syracuse University football team, Andrew Robinson, illustrates the point. He became a manager because he "wanted to continue to be part of a team." He goes on to say, "I played football in high school but wasn't a division-I recruit. I had been going to football practice every day after school for close to ten years. I didn't want to give that up." But as the sidebar indicates, he got a lot in return.

Athletes are pampered, especially in the big-money sports, and that leads to a sense of entitlement and laziness that no employer wants. You see it in professional sports all of the time. But a little bit of pampering is not a bad thing, because the good athletic programs try to help their students succeed in careers after sports. Plus the alumni, both the athletes and non-athletes, provide mentoring about careers and networks that can give students an extra advantage.

This is not to say that all athletes, especially at Division-I colleges and

Team Manager Is a Path to Career Success

As a student manager for the Syracuse University football team, my job in a nutshell is to make life for the coaches easier. Each manager is assigned to a specific assistant coach and we work with them setting up drills, and in some instances participating in the drills when the number of players is uneven. We are the people responsible for making sure practices run smoothly. On game days, managers are responsible for setting up and cleaning up the locker room before and after the game. Managers must prioritize well. Without this job I never would have learned how to become more organized. We spend sometimes forty hours a week at the football complex and must still find a way to get to all classes and finish all work. This will do nothing but help in the future. I have also learned the valuable skill of being able to complete tasks on time. Like the business world, some tasks designated to student managers have to be done by a specific time. If they aren't done, problems arise.

—Andrew Robinson, senior and manager of
the Syracuse University football team

universities, use the opportunities offered to them to develop the professional skills and character that employees want. My students who read drafts of this chapter asked me if I ever talked to athletes, because their experience suggests that athletes are not skilled and not motivated beyond their athletic programs. I know plenty of athletes who are skilled and do have good character. The point is that the athletic programs offer great additional opportunities to develop skills. Whether they use those opportunities is another matter. This is also true of all students in college.

Programs Run by University Staff

The list of learning activities provided by university staff is long but is usually hidden from public view. Staff members in various student-affairs programs frequently run workshops and training sessions related to the entire range of student activities. In some areas like residential life, the training for resident advisers is intense, but in other areas like orientation for student-group leaders, it is confined to a few workshops. Awards programs are used to increase learning for student participants. Some of these programs tend to be more useful than others. Those that have a lot of structure (like for tour guides introducing prospective students to the campus or working as peer advisers to help freshmen choose courses) require training and consistent performance that is usually evaluated. Those that are one-shot affairs like half-day "training programs" or lectures may raise some awareness but have little lasting impact without follow-up activities.

Some programs provide opportunities for students to attend regional, national, and even international conferences. For example, students who participate in residential-life programs regularly travel to conferences to discuss campus topics. These travels provide an introduction to the kind of professional-association travel and people in virtually every career field.

Don't underestimate the power of these formal and informal training programs for learning the skills and developing the character employers want. They can lead to career-exploration activities as students talk to one another and are treated to lectures from successful and accomplished speakers. Even in cases where the programs are disorganized and poorly run, which happens regularly, students can gain insight into conference management and still learn a lot from their peers.

Fraternities and Sororities

The "Greeks" are on about 20 percent of college campuses. There are 5,500 fraternity chapters located on 800 college campuses throughout the United States and Canada and 2,922 undergraduate sorority chapters on more than 600 college campuses.[2] On the Syracuse University campus about 20 percent of the students are in more than 44 fraternities and sororities on campus. You may be concerned about the image of the Greek system portrayed by the movie *Animal House* and the all-too-frequent reports of alcohol poisoning or some type of physical abuse. Drinking, drug use, and silliness are clearly part of the Greek scene, but as my students remind me, it's also part of non-Greek college life.

My advice is to keep an open mind if your child wants to join a fraternity or sorority. There are some negatives. The biggest downside other than the reckless behavior many Greek organizations promote is the time demands, particularly during the pledging period. I can always tell which students are pledging because suddenly their papers come in late and they fall asleep in class (if they show up at all). GPAs sometimes drop during pledging.

Colleges and the national organizations of fraternities and sororities work hard to make their organizations more about character building and networking than about unencumbered fun. There are many positives from a career perspective.

If your child is able to maintain his GPA, stay awake in class, turn papers in on time, and complete the pledging period as well as do the other "fun" things the organization provides, he has passed an important test of his time-management and character skills.

You may be surprised to find out that the GPAs of students in fraternities and sororities is on average not lower than the GPAs of students not participating in the Greek system. At Syracuse University, the GPA for members of fraternities and sororities is one tenth of a point higher than for nonmembers.[3] A similar pattern is found at Iowa State University, where Greek members have a 74 percent graduation rate, compared with a 63 percent graduation rate for non-Greeks.[4] At campuses across the nation, the graduation rates for Greeks are higher than for non-Greeks. Many of the organizations pressure their members to do well so they can win some kind of prize and make their national affiliates happy. But the higher GPAs may also be a result of a selection bias—students in the Greek system are more committed to finishing college and may have more financial resources than the general student population. Or, as one of my non-Greek students wrote, "Most of the frats and sororities keep assignments and tests on file to 'help' their members." This help could be instrumental in the higher GPAs, but not necessarily character building.

The upside is that fraternities and sororities are businesses. This means that the leaders of each chapter have the opportunity to develop their skills in management and finance. Employers recognize this and are ready to give students who were presidents or treasurers of Greek organizations added consideration. Getting your child's fellow members to choose him as their leader is a good indicator of skills like teamwork, leadership, and management.

Other Greek organizations are honor societies and community-service organizations. They use Greek letters, but they are completely different in purpose from the traditional fraternities and sororities. There are honors societies with Greek letters that are based on GPA and strength of program, like Phi Beta Kappa, and those attached to particular academic fields like Psi Chi (for psychology majors) and Alpha Kappa Psi (for business majors). There are also service fraternities like Alpha Phi Omega (which admits both genders). I mention them so you don't get frightened when your child comes home and says he wants to join one.

Non-Greek Student Organizations

At Syracuse University, there are more than 300 student organizations that range in size and visibility, from the student association to the chess club.

They present a continuing test of the skills and character employers want, because the organizations are only as strong as their members. Some of them do outstanding jobs.

Figure 16-1 is a selected list of organizations at Syracuse University. Any college or university has a similar list. From the list it is clear that students have a variety of choices. The range of groups includes almost every activity that you can think of, from politics to recreation to support groups.

Many student organizations are chaotic and disorganized masses that can be very discouraging to students. Students frequently don't take respon-

Figure 16-1. Selected student organizations at Syracuse University.

1. Profession Oriented
   a. Association of Black Journalists
   b. American Institute of Aeronautics and Astronautics
   c. American Institute of Architecture Students
   d. Fashion Association of Design Students
   e. SIFE (Students In Free Enterprise)
2. Recreational
   a. Dance Works
   b. Field Hockey Club
   c. First Year Players (Drama)
   d. Ultimate Frisbee Club
   e. Martial Arts Sports Club
3. Service
   a. Habitat for Humanity
   b. American Red Cross Club of SU
   c. Keep a Child Alive
   d. NYPIRG (New York Public Interest Research Group)
4. Major Related
   a. Psychology Club
   b. Women in Communications
   c. Society of Undergraduate Geology Students
   d. Health and Exercise Science & Physical Education Majors Club
   e. Music and Entertainment Industry Student Association
5. Political
   a. College Republicans; College Democrats
   b. Student Environmental Action Coalition (SEAC)
   c. Undergraduates for a Better Education
   d. Student Peace Action Network
   e. Green Party

sibility for their organizations. Students can also be ridiculous as they take on more than they can handle. Student governments can't get a quorum, student leaders call for a meeting and then forget to show up, the finances are a mess, and the bickering reaches almost congressional levels.

The chaos in the majority of student organizations can be viewed as an asset from the perspective of developing skills and character. Students who can attract hardworking members, raise funds, keep the books, and organize large-scale projects are students employers want to hire. Employers know the organizations are chaotic, so even modest achievements are taken as a sign that a student leader is a potentially good hire.

I get a lot of questions about honorary societies. I serve as a faculty adviser for one of them (the National Society of Collegiate Scholars). Parents call and ask if the onetime fee of seventy-five dollars is worth it. My response is that it is not a good value if they are buying the membership because they think it gives their child added prestige or looks good on the resume. If the purchase is designed to provide an opportunity for their children to network with students and develop leadership and other skills, it may make sense.

Community Groups

Community service overlaps the four previous categories. Athletics, programs run by college staffs, Greek and non-Greek student organizations, and even some public-service jobs provide ample opportunities for students to give back. Increasingly, faculty members, with the help of college staffs, are offering academic credit for community service. Figure 16-2 provides a list of community-service and volunteer activities at Syracuse University. All colleges promote these types of activities.

The most popular activities are fund-raising and tutoring children in schools and community centers. Think about all the skills students can develop in these two activities. People skills, communication skills, and problem-solving skills are tested daily.

Nonprofit organizations depend on volunteers and low-paid workers whose skills or commitment may be limited. These organizations have no choice but to use volunteers for important tasks in research and publicity because they lack the staff to do them. For example, a local community center might like to distribute a monthly newsletter but doesn't have the funds to hire a professional. If your child has some basic skills in Microsoft Publisher, for example, your child could volunteer to produce a newsletter. For someone with no experience, your child has an opportunity to be a newsletter designer, an editor, a writer, and a publisher. If he does a reason-

Figure 16-2. Volunteer and community-service activities at Syracuse University.

Category	Type of Service Opportunity	Organization
Adult Literacy	Tutoring	Literacy Volunteers of Greater Syracuse
Children	Tutoring/recreation	Boys & Girls Club
	Mentoring	Hawley Youth Organization
—Day Care	Caring for children	Atonement Lutheran Day Care
—After-School Programs	Tutoring/mentoring	Shea Middle School After-School Program
		Westcott After-School Program
—Tutoring	Tutoring	R.E.A.C.H Tutorial Program
		Lincoln Tutoring Program at the Reformed Church of Syracuse
—Mentoring	Mentoring	Big Brothers Big Sisters
Soup Kitchens & Food Pantries	Meal preparation and serving	Food Bank of CNY
		Meals on Wheels
Food Collection	Canned-food collection	Salvation Army
Women's Issues	Visiting patients, tutoring, cleaning	Rape Crisis Center
		Chadwick Residence
Nursing Homes	1:1 visits, special events, and activities	Eastwood Senior Center
		Iroquois Nursing Home
Arts	Greeting visitors, providing information, handing out programs, managing exhibitions	Cultural Resources Council
		Onondaga Historical Association
		Syracuse Stage
Housing	Helping to renovate and build houses	Habitat for Humanity Home Headquarters
AIDS	Public education, visiting with clients	AIDS Community Resources
		The Living Room
Environmental Cleanups	Trash pickup, park and trail maintenance	Beaver Lake Nature Center
		Centers for Nature Education, Inc.
Hospitals	Transporting patients within hospital, visiting, recreation activities	Crouse Hospital
		Community General Hospital
		VA Hospital

People with Disabilities	1:1 visiting, education, administrative	Exceptional Family Resources Aurora of CNY
Alternative Break Trips	Planning and attending service-based break trips	Habitat for Humanity
Clerical/Office	Administrative tasks	CNY Children's Miracle Network
Blood Donation	Donating blood	Red Cross

ably good job, he has a product to put on his resume or in his portfolio when he seeks a job.

Employers recognize these experiences are valuable in three different ways. First, volunteering off campus shows a willingness to take risks. Second, it demonstrates the skills associated with the work your child did. For example, tutoring nine-year-olds is a test of patience, communication, and focus—all of which employers value. Third, it shows that your child cares about something bigger than his own narrow self-interest and therefore has the character to be loyal to the company.

What Parents Can Do

Your role in the choices your child makes about student activities will diminish over time and may not be much, even at the beginning. Here are some strategies that provide some guidance in recognizing the limited role you are likely to play in your child's choices:

Strategy #1: Help your child understand that participation in some student activities is a crucial part of his preparation for a successful career. Exhibit a positive attitude and provide encouragement for participation in some student organizations. Many students tend to think that these organizations are extracurricular and not important for their education, when in fact they can be a determining factor in selecting a career and getting that first job.

Strategy #2: Encourage your child to participate in student activities sooner rather than later. Students who don't get involved in the first and second years are not likely to get involved in student activities later. The natural flow, in any case, is that students should move to more off-campus activities as they progress.

Strategy #3: If your child is participating, encourage him to treat it like a job. All of these student activities can end in disaster. A member of the crew team could sleep through his afternoon classes. A student-government representative could be verbally attacked not just in a meeting but also in the cafeteria. A student could discover he is not cut out for the bickering. The fraternity can be thrown off campus, and your son could be suspended. The university staff member running the activity could be incompetent. Living with this chaos and risk is a valuable preparation for what your child will face not just in his career but also throughout life.

Student activities present students with the opportunity to make choices. It's good for your child to be persistent. But it is also good for him to know when to collect his marbles and go home. This is part of everyone's career. You can provide counsel and support as he considers and reconsiders the decision to stay or go. Encourage him to reflect on that question periodically.

The ultimate test of the worthiness of participating in student activities is whether your child is serious about his responsibilities. Does he go to meetings? Does he take on leadership positions and act responsibly to complete them? Does he do the best he can do? Counsel him to take these activities seriously and to treat them as if he will be receiving a performance review on a job. Student activities are places where a significant portion of students behave badly by shirking their duties and acting like children. Those who show maturity and a professional approach will benefit immensely, and those that don't will be confronted with an opportunity to learn how to do better next time.

Useful Resources

How You Can Help: An Easy Guide to Doing Good Deeds in Your Everyday Life, by Bill Coplin (New York: Routledge, 2000). A no-guilt approach to doing good, this book provides a range of activities that you can undertake as a meaningful but limited part of your life. It also shows how to incorporate doing good in everyday life so that your child does not have to become Mother Theresa.

Notes

1. Daniel J. Henderson, Alexandre Olbrecht, and Solomon W. Polachek, "Do Former College Athletes Earn More at Work? A Nonparametric Assessment," *The Journal of Human Resources*, Summer 2006, vol. 41, no. 3, p. 558.

2. The North American Interfraternity Conference (http://www.nicindy.org/); National Panhellenic Council (http://www.npcwomen.org/).

3. Roy Baker, Director of Fraternity and Sorority Affairs at Syracuse University, in an e-mail to the author, October 10, 2006.

4. http://www.greek.iastate.edu/join/benefits/scholarship.html.

CHAPTER 17

Jobs During the Academic Year

"The harder I worked, the luckier I got."

—Dave Thomas

I wanted to use this quote from the founder of Wendy's to make the point that students shouldn't just look at their part-time jobs during the academic year as a way to make money. Much more is at stake for the career-savvy college student. Part-time jobs can help develop skills, build character, and explore careers as much or even more than 120 credits.

Why Part-Time Jobs Are Important for Career Development

When I ask high school students who work at fast-food restaurants if they only do it to make money, most of them say yes. I tell them, "Wrong answer!" A hamburger flipper who takes his job seriously and does his very best is well on his way to a successful career.

I had a student who worked for McDonald's in high school and continued to work there while she went to community college. She transferred to Syracuse University and today is a high-level government official in a state department of social services. I knew that she would have career success when I met her as a transfer student. She made an appointment with me to enroll for the major I advise. During the conversation, she told me that she became the location manager and was invited by the owner (who owns thirty-nine McDonald's restaurants) to work as his assistant. I offered her a job on the spot, and she became a mainstay of my office. She went to graduate school, had a successful career at a consulting company, and ended up with a high-level government position.

Aside from all the skills demonstrated by this student's achievement, her willingness to pay her dues appeals to employers in this day and age when too many college graduates think they are "very special."

Any job, no matter how mundane, will provide practice for the skills listed in chapter 1. If your child uses these jobs to practice excellence in all the required skills, the dividends will be enormous. If not, she will be missing critical opportunities. Commitment to excellence may sound like obvious advice, but as Asher Epstein notes in the sidebar, it is not so easy.

What could be more mundane than working at a refreshment stand in the Carrier Dome during sporting events? That's what one of my students did as a first-semester freshman. She demonstrated excellence and was given a managerial position the next semester. The following semester she got a raise and was put in charge of scheduling all 625 part-time student employees. With this experience, as a sophomore, she made more than other sophomore concession workers, and other supervisors sought her out. When she went to Albany for a semester as part of an internship program in the legislature, the experience and skills she developed in her previous part-time jobs allowed her to take on a lot of responsibility in an assemblyman's office. The office offered her a permanent job even though she had a semester left before graduation. They waited for her, and she became a legislative aid. When the assemblyman moved on to a higher political position, she moved along with him. From this base, she had many career options, both in politics and business.

Part-time jobs not only contribute to skills and character; they also pro-

Asher Epstein on Excellence

It is better to be good at something than okay at five different things. Narrowing down what you are going to focus on allows just that. You are able to focus on the keys to developing career opportunities. You told me this, and I didn't forget it as I was working over the summer. "Wherever you work," you said to me, *"practice excellence."* And there were definitely moments when I was tired or felt like giving up, but I stuck it out and practiced excellence.

vide a chance for career exploration. Your child may not want to go into the fast-food business, but if she is good enough to become an assistant manager, she may find that she enjoys the responsibility of managing others. Management is not usually something college students see as a path to career success, but it's a skill area in very short supply. Crunching numbers as a research assistant for a professor may help your child realize she wants to work as a consultant for a management organization. In other words, the types of skills independent of the field are important to explore. Skills are transferable across career fields. Part-time jobs will provide an opportunity for your child to test her interests and talents.

In addition, your child may actually enjoy the field. Resident advisers will find out if they want to go into psychological counseling. Working for campus technical support may open up careers in the computing industry. Students may not want to become computer engineers or programmers, but they will see that computer companies need all kinds of salespeople.

The value of these part-time jobs on campus is that your child can try several different ones without the disruption that would occur if she took a permanent job after college and decided it wasn't for her. The part-time positions will help her get summer internships or jobs by having prior relevant experience and at the same time will help her choose a summer position more intelligently.

I have talked about the upside of part-time jobs, but the downside can be significant. The biggest problem facing students who are excellent workers is that the employers will pressure them to work more hours. Offered more money doing something they are good at and may even like, students could sacrifice not just their academic performance but their chance to take on other opportunities. In many cases, the employer will try to convince a student to take a full-time position with the company, and the student might take the offer to stay in his comfort zone.

I had a student who had been working part-time for a medium-size, independently owned grocery store since high school. The owners wouldn't let go of him because, among other things, he hired, trained, and closed up for them. The student's loyalty and guilt kept him there. I had some paid projects for him that could have expanded his considerable skill base, but he didn't have the time and missed out on the opportunity.

Although he could excel in almost any career, he could also end up at the grocery store for life, which he said he did not want to do. Fortunately, he joined the Peace Corps, and I doubt the grocery store owners will fly him in from Kenya during the Christmas rush.

This example raises a point about character. This student exhibited the rare and valuable quality of loyalty to his long-time boss, but he showed a weakness in not being able to say no. The boss was getting a store manager worth $20 an hour for $7.50 an hour, but the student didn't protect his own reasonable self-interest. Loyalty has its limits, and perhaps he will learn that about character as he reflects on the experience.

If after graduation your child moves from a part-time to a full-time position with an employer, it may or may not work out. Guilt and the comfort of staying where she is already top dog could cloud her judgment. You have limited influence ultimately on this choice. The best way to help broaden your child's perspective is to encourage her to see that part-time jobs are places for skill development, character building, and career exploration. I like it when a student tells me that she didn't return to a part-time job because she had no more to learn from it.

On-Campus Jobs

Campus jobs are plentiful for two reasons. First, the need for seasonal workers makes it necessary to hire part-timers, and students are part-timers. Second, federal work-study programs usually cover 50 percent of the cost for students who are work-study eligible. Although there's an ample supply of students, there's an equally ample supply of jobs.

I recommend jobs on campus for the first two years of college. Staying on campus for a job saves time and travel costs. During the junior and senior year, an off-campus job is frequently a better option. College employers have a tendency to coddle their students. They are usually desperate to keep those who show up on time and are halfway competent. Staff members frequently become attached to their student employees, treating them more like their children than employees. This is not a good thing. It allows students to think that all employers will treat them like forgiving parents.

The types of on-campus jobs are varied. Here is a list just to give you and your child an idea about the range of opportunities:

Types of On-Campus Federal Work-Study Jobs

Administrative Intern
Certified Personal Trainer
Child Care Aide
Clerical
Driver
Drivers for Shuttle-U-Home
Dome Concessions
Food Court/Snack Bar Employ
Catering Server

General Employee, Residence
Dining
Warehouse Café Employee
Graphic Designer
Interactive Media Lab
Consult
Laboratory Attendant
Library Student Assistant
Main Desk Assistant

Office Assistance/Audiovisual	Teaching Aid
Support	Video Production Assistant
Student Building Manager	Web/Electronics Media Assistant
Student Consultant	

SOURCE: Syracuse University Department of Student Employment Services.

On the question of which job your child should choose, the answer depends on many things including her schedule, job availability, and salary. Your child should take a position that will help her develop skills and possibly even explore careers. At this point in her development, the skills are more important. For example, a telemarketing job for the alumni fund would be more useful for a student intending to become a stockbroker than doing data entry for a professor studying the stock market.

From my experience, the top campus jobs are:

■ Resident adviser programs, which offer students room and board and sometimes additional compensation to be in charge of a floor of students. The money is good but the experience is better. Just getting the position is evidence to employers that the student has great skills. Because of the significant amount of money involved, competition for these positions is usually stiff. Most programs have a rigorous selection process and an even more rigorous training process. Surviving and excelling in the position is a remarkable feat because it requires dealing with a micromanaging bureaucracy and thirty students, usually freshmen. Most resident advisers find the bureaucracy more aggravating than the students.

■ Alumni telephone fund-raising, which means cold calling, is one of the most plentiful jobs on campus. If your child is good at the position, she has an advantage in getting sales positions. This job not only shows good communication skills but also the capacity to take rejection. Sales jobs are very lucrative with the right company.

■ Student services, which usually require dealing with other students and working with staff members who are usually overcommitted and don't provide much supervision. The best position is in a career-services office because the employee gets first shot at all internship and job opportunities that come into the office. The student also gets trained in career counseling.

■ Research and teaching assistance, which can be paid, volunteer, or for credit and gets a high level of respect from faculty members. These positions demonstrate that a faculty member has confidence in the student's intellectual ability and sense of responsibility. These positions are particularly valuable for students thinking about careers as college professors or high school teachers. They help on graduate school applications and allow students to find out if they are talented enough to go into these fields. They also build research skills, which are increasingly valuable in today's work world.

■ Low-activity positions, which are jobs where the student sits at a desk and checks people in and out, usually as a part of campus security. Residence halls have students in these positions overnight. Libraries also have similar positions. Although they're not as focused on skill development, these jobs have the advantage of permitting academic work while earning money for the time-strapped student.

Off-Campus Jobs

Most students take off-campus jobs only for money and scheduling reasons. Sometimes they have worked for companies back home and have access to other branches near campus. As is the case for on-campus jobs, students should not just consider convenience and money. Here is a list of typical off-campus jobs:

Types of On-Campus Non-Federal Work-Study Jobs

Accounting Associate	Customer Sales/Service
Administrative Assistant	Delivery Driver
After-School Program Counselor	Drivers
Appointment Setter	Expeditor
Assistant Gymnastics Instructor	Guest-Services Agents
Assistant Manager/Closing Manager	Gymnastics Instructor
Birthday Party Supervisor	Hostess/Host
Brand Ambassador	Kitchen Helper
Cashier/Receptionist	Landscaping/Mowing
Cashier/Showroom/Gameroom/	Legal Secretary
Kitchen Help	Lifeguard
Child Care Aide	Line Cooks and Dishwashers
Childcare Substitute	Marketing
Cleaner	Mixologists/Bartenders (but check
Clerical	the age requirement)
Computer Support	Nanny
Cook	Part-Time Receptionist
Counter Person/Pizza Maker	Part-Time Sales Consultant
CSD Relayer	Package Handler

Pharmacy Technician
Pita Maker
Preschool Teacher
Production Assistant
Receptionist
Restaurant Positions
Sales Associate
Sales Support/Bussers

Sales—Telemarketing
Sandwich Artists
Security Officer
Servers
Teacher/Tutor
Teaching Assistant
Waitstaff & Dishwashers
Web Developer

SOURCE: Syracuse University Department of Student Employment Services.

Students should look to their part-time jobs off campus as opportunities to develop skills, build character, and explore careers. Their connections to the college may help them find such positions. Local businesses, nonprofits, and government organizations frequently contact university staff for recommendations on part-time employees. Students who develop good reputations in class and in student activities are likely to be selected.

In addition, students who are heavily involved in community service or in course activities that take place in the community frequently find that this experience leads to a job. One of my students did a study for the city on the maintenance records of the Department of Public Works vehicles as part of a course. He was offered a part-time job as a result of that study. Although money is always tight in nonprofit and government agencies, employers who find someone with skills and character miraculously discover the money.

Public and private employment agencies can also help students find jobs. Searching with these agencies for a part-time job will not only lead to a job; it will also give the student practice in job searching for when she is a senior. Temp agencies, which supply workers on a nonpermanent basis, are always looking for skilled people.

Most jobs are not directly related to a student's desired career field. Students may be in a lucky position of getting a research job at a research consulting, nonprofit, or government organization that is directly related to a specific desired field. However, all students can develop their skills and character in even the most mundane jobs. Door-to-door sales or cold calling looks great on a resume because it shows a commitment to hard and boring work. Waiting on tables and bartending may be the best of all jobs because they can pay extremely well and provide contacts with future employers. The downside to bartending especially is that it can be so much fun that students will devote too much time to it, and the late-night hours are bad for health and doing homework.

Finding off-campus jobs is sometimes difficult because of class schedules. Working at businesses around the college is more convenient but also may not pay as well. Students should look to the traditional sources like newspapers, bulletin boards, and friends. They may also want to contact local staffing firms. They pay more, sometimes provide training, and provide access to companies that could eventually offer full-time jobs.

What Parents Can Do

Once again, let the Goldilocks Principle be your guide. You can't micromanage your child's work life. I suggest three strategies that you may be able to apply in varying degrees:

Strategy #1: Don't discourage working. Many parents are afraid that a job will detract from studying, just as heavy participation in student activities may. This is a reasonable concern but be open-minded. The guideline is moderation. No paid part-time work may be advisable if your child is heavily involved in student activities or volunteering in a structured situation like working with a professor on a book or a research project. But a position that requires responsibility and reporting to a supervisor during your child's college experience is essential for her career mission.

Strategy #2: Advise against too much work. How much is too much depends on answers to four questions:

1. **How heavy is your child's academic course load?** The consensus is students should not work more than twenty hours a week. Figure nine hours of class work and homework for each class taken. That's forty-five hours a week for a fifteen-credit semester. Let's take as a given a sixty-hour workweek as a challenging but doable workload. That would leave fifteen hours to work.

2. **What are the hours and days?** Working on the weekend might allow for more hours as long as your child gets her studying done during the week. Working all night may not be a good idea because it could result in students sleeping through classes. However, some people have internal clocks that allow for sleep disruption. The one thing your child should watch out for is work hours resulting in stress about getting to class on time or even missing class. This is clearly a no-no.

3. **What kind of work is it?** Students working in the library or on security in the dorm can usually study while they are working, which means working ten hours a week may be too little, especially if there is no socializ-

ing and it "forces" your child to sit still and study. Other jobs might not permit studying. If the job is stressful or tiring, each hour might count as two. Sometimes work can be fun, like tutoring in a school or working at a community center, so it might count partly as "playtime." But one of my students who was tutoring in an inner-city school, said, "[It was] the most depressing, stressful, and exhausting work I've ever done."

4. Does your child's job help his skill development and career exploration? If so, the extra time required may be worth it as long as some balance is maintained.

These questions will help you decide if you should counsel your child to reduce her work hours. If she is driven by financial concerns, you may want to increase your subsidies to her education as long as your child agrees to reduce her hours of work.

Strategy #3: Counsel excellence. With respect to skill development, your child needs to embrace excellence as a habit. Treating any job as an audition for a future career will lead to broader skill development. Doing an outstanding job means learning new things and honing existing skills. Excellence on the job will also lead to a good job reference.

Useful Resources

The best sources of information for jobs during the academic years are the student employment and career-services offices of the college or university your child attends. Want ads in the student and local newspaper and word of mouth are also good sources.

Your child may also want to access some websites. The site http://www.snaga job.com provides job leads as well as some advice for the college student looking for part-time work. Another source of part-time jobs that most students don't think about is provided by what are called "staffing companies," "employment agencies," or "temp agencies." Most areas have companies that do this. Students who have skills in customer service, computer software like Excel and Access, or data inputting can get relatively high-paying part-time positions. Students can locate these companies in their area by going to the phone book or by searching on Google.

CHAPTER **18**

Summer Is a Time for Real-World Learning

"There is no education like adversity."

—Benjamin Disraeli

There's something to be said for the idea that summertime should be a period of rest and relaxation. But the almost four months between the end of the spring semester and the beginning of the fall semester should not be one long vacation for the career-savvy college student. Think about it. Adults typically take two- to three-week vacations; most college students have twelve-week summer vacations plus another four weeks between August and May. A college education should help transform your child into an adult. I can't see how a four-month vacation does that.

At the other end of the spectrum, many college students spend those four months earning money to help defray the high cost of a college education. Although this may be a necessity, your child also needs some of that time off from college to develop skills and explore careers. As I will suggest in this chapter, some compromise is necessary.

Summer should be viewed as a time to prepare for a successful career. Whether it's a job, a paid internship, or an unpaid internship, students can learn more of what they need to know in a concentrated ten-week period in the summer than during the academic year when peer-group play is a constant distraction and irregular sleeping hours are the rule. Innovative programs offered by universities may also make sense if they have an internship component.

Why Summer Jobs and Internships Are Important

The summer internship or job experience, six to ten weeks of day-to-day work experience, is more important for developing professional skills and exploring careers than a semester or even a year of college. The sidebar contains a testimony to the value of internships from a graduate of my program who has been a successful CEO of several health-care companies over the past twenty-five years.

Every year, alumni return a questionnaire providing advice to my current students. By far the most frequent recommendation is to get several internships.

Colleges are making great strides in helping students get internships and other kinds of field experiences in the summer because their leaders know the importance of such experiences. More to the point, companies report that more than 59 percent of those they hired had internship experience.[1] A significant percentage had internships with the companies that hired them.

Internships are not the only way to get experience. A job in the summer might provide more of an education. Working as a camp counselor at a summer camp makes a lot of sense for students who want to go into educa-

The Value of Internships

At some point your office connected me with a researcher doing a project with troubled youths in Syracuse. I was offered a paid part-time research position. That position became a full-time summer job so that I didn't have to return to the family farm and mend fences or work as a house painter alongside my father. I continued to work on this project until graduation. The ability to do this changed my life in many ways. First, I learned skills needed for the working world that I would never have learned in class. Second, it embedded on my brain the idea of "doing good things" and "giving back." Third, it allowed me to go straight from Syracuse University to the Wharton School of Business at the University of Pennsylvania. I was, I believe, one of less than ten people out of a class of over 600 who came directly from undergrad to the MBA program at Penn.

—Bob Watson, President and CEO, Concuity, Inc.

tion, for example. No matter what field, telephone or door-to-door sales jobs develop critical communication, time-management, and work-ethic skills. Paid internships range from a token $500 to cover transportation to serious money ($6,000 or more for an eight-week stint). The money is not as important as the experience.

Don't get confused over internships versus summer jobs. Organizations might call their summer jobs internships to avoid fringe benefits or a flap from the unions. Some programs may even require that the student purchase academic credit. These organizations are usually in high-profile areas like media, sports, and politics. It would be nice for you as a parent if your child didn't have such refined tastes so you didn't have to pay the extra tuition. Better he gets that experience during the summer than dream of such a job when he is a senior. Dreams uninformed by experience could send your child looking for a job he can't get and back into your house before you know it. If he gets the job, he may realize that he doesn't really want that career after all.

Summer jobs may be just as educational as paid or unpaid internships. Many organizations—business and government—have employees who like to take summer vacations. Interns may actually end up doing their jobs. For example, during her junior and senior years, one of my students was working at a small research bureau. After being at the organization for about four weeks, her supervisor went on vacation right when a survey of municipal services was mailed out to 10,000 people in the city. Because this student had gained the supervisor's trust, she was put in charge of managing this survey while the supervisor was on vacation. This student had to receive the surveys, code the results, create the database for the survey results, and manage questions from the public.

Your child can have a better experience in a summer job than in an unpaid internship because the organization is likely to pay more attention to the jobholder. The pay is usually for work that has to be done because it is vital to the company's cash flow.

A student who worked for me as an editor during her freshman year was hired as an intern for a state political party. She got one of five positions (for which there were over eighty applicants) because of her experience as an editor. She said, "I quickly developed a reputation as a good writer among the party staff and was given the opportunity to write mass e-mails, website updates, and letters on behalf of the party chair. After six weeks, my boss made me the party liaison to one of the state's congressional campaigns. I got to know the candidate very well and within two weeks was asked to join her full-time staff as a paid deputy campaign manager." This student took the fall semester off to work for the campaign and as a nineteen-year-old was a key staff member in the campaign.

As a parent, you should see summer internships or jobs as important to your child's preparation for a successful career. Each summer can build on the previous summer. The course work, student activities, and part-time jobs during the academic year can provide the essential skills that will get your child a great summer experience. He can bring this experience back to campus the next year to prepare for an even better experience the next summer. Your encouragement and financial help can make the critical difference.

A key benefit to getting a useful summer job or internship is the process of pursuing the position. It's a replica of what your child will do his senior year when he pursues a job. To get the summer position, he will have to plan early, do a thorough search, get the help of the career-services office, produce a resume, participate in interviews, and decide among options. The process alone, even if your child winds up not getting a position, is a critical step in his career development.

The most important reason that a summer internship is necessary, even if the student already works a part-time job during the academic year, has to do with the routine of getting up early in the morning and getting through the entire day. College life is a day at the beach compared with a full-time job. Working full-time does not mean running back to the dorm and taking a nap from one o'clock to three o'clock.

Roadblocks to a Career-Developing Summer

Several things stand in the way of your child getting a successful summer work experience through either an internship or a job.

Immaturity

The first roadblock is the possibility that your child may not want to take a summer internship for a variety of reasons that have to do with play. Lifeguard positions are frequently the culprit here, as are caddying jobs on the golf course. I don't recommend returning year after year to the same summer position unless there are substantial additional job responsibilities. Unfortunately, you can't micromanage this one very well. If your child wants to play, he wants to play.

Pickiness

The second roadblock is that your child can't get a position he would like. Students tend to have unrealistic expectations. They don't want to be gophers. They also want to work where everyone wants to work, like in TV or in sports. They tend to emphasize the career-exploration aspect over the skill-development aspect. Both are important, but door-to-door sales in the summer may be a better path to a job in entertainment than getting coffee for the assistant of the assistant of some second-rate entertainer. Most successful people, especially in the entertainment field, did door-to-door sales even if it was for Girl Scout cookies or Little League raffles. They know how much grit it takes. Tim Russert, who is a top TV interviewer, worked on a garbage truck in the summer. Lucky for him, this fact caught the eye of the late Senator Daniel Patrick Moynihan, who gave his career a big boost.

Flawed Recruitment Processes

Another roadblock is that the recruitment process for internships is subject to nepotism and cronyism. The Web apparently gives everyone equal access to thousands of positions through search engines, but it's no match for the personal connections available to those whose parents are themselves connected. Your child needs to use existing formal systems for contact as well as networks to which he has access. The role of informal networks may be more important in an internship search than a job search, but it exists in both. The faster your child understands that life is not fair and that he should use informal networks, the better. The internship search, like the internship experience, is an important introduction to what it will be like once he graduates.

Your child needs to put as much planning and thought into getting a summer position as he did in planning his senior prom. Self-reflection and systematic information gathering are essential to getting such positions, especially as the competition grows. Ten years ago, less than 10 percent of my students used to come to me early for advice on the summer. Now, 50 percent of my students contact me in the fall. Students are increasingly aware that they need good summer positions.

A little help on your part is recommended. Provide some networking leads from friends and business associates. Some parents forbid their children to use friends and family, which is noble and teaches character. But I think it is okay to suggest that they use personal and family contacts. The one caveat is that you don't make the contacts yourself or get your child the position. Suggesting a lead is reasonable; treating your child like he is incapable of taking the initiative will not build the character employers want him to have. Nor will arranging a job or internship that your child does not even want and then forcing him to take it.

A Lack of Skills and Character

The key to landing a valuable summer experience is for students to demonstrate they have valuable skills and character. Most important, they need to demonstrate a strong work ethic. Students also need to understand that they have to pay their dues as interns. I knew an intern once who quit when a paralegal asked him to make a copy of a contract. Presumably, he thought he should be writing the contracts, not copying them.

Contrast that with another student of mine who took a job with a public-interest lobbying group in D.C. He told me that all the interns were sitting around complaining about having nothing to do. He volunteered to do all the copying that he could during the first two weeks. The next week he was put in charge of a major campaign for the organization, and the complainers were working for him. Students who tell me that they were given nothing to do by their supervisors are telling me that they failed to gain the supervisor's confidence. There can be bad supervisors, but I find that bad interns greatly outnumber bad supervisors.

Whether getting a job or an internship, students should see themselves as apprentices. They are making a bargain with the organization to serve as such. That bargain requires them to pay for their education with their services, even if it means mopping the floor.

Students have real bargaining power to learn more if they have something to offer their bosses. In addition to being hard workers who have good attitudes and good people skills, students should exhibit other skills that are in short supply. They include Web design, ability to use Microsoft Office software, and writing skills.

These skills get the attention of supervisors and can lead to an experience way above expectations. A student working for an established public relations firm told me recently, "The people here just think I am a genius because I can make things 'pretty and organized' as they say. Today was the icing on the cake—when the principal of the firm came to me and asked if I was able to do something in Excel, then put it into a Word document and hyperlink that document. I completed the task while he was standing there. I honestly think he would have hired me on the spot."

Like everything else in life, developing skills and character is a process that builds upon itself. You have to have some to develop more. Students need to earn the opportunity to gain valuable summer positions, and that requires them to have some of the skills they expect to develop further on the job. That's why it's so important that students gain experiences during the academic year that will allow them to develop and demonstrate the skills that employers and intern supervisors want.

The students who will go the longest distance in pursing their career missions are those who get summer internships or jobs between their freshman and sophomore years. The sooner your child gets into the real world, the better. It will create a track record so that each summer your child will get a better internship or job than the summer before. It's a lot easier to climb a ladder one rung at a time.

Money

If I have convinced you that a summer job or internship is an essential activity for your child's college education, now comes the hard part: money! If you are like most parents, you will want your child to earn money in the summer to help defray costs. This is a reasonable expectation, but if it means turning down a great unpaid internship, it may not make much sense.

If your child makes $2,000 less over the summer because he is pursuing a valuable skill-development and career-exploration experience and you're both spending $100,000 over a four-year period, the $2,000 is only 2 percent of what you're already spending. You should consider covering the additional expense. It could lead to a first job and a successful career that makes your entire college investment pay off.

Here's some more bad news about money. To get the best internships and jobs between their junior and senior years, students should have internships for the two previous summers. So, it might not be subsidizing for one summer but for three.

To further add to the monetary misery, some organizations offering internships will require that your child be registered for academic credit during the summer. This can substantially add to the cost. If your child must register, buy only one credit and see if you can get it from a community college to reduce costs. The only exception to buying as few credits as possible would be paying tuition for summer internships that would enable your child to graduate earlier. A couple of additional credits from summer work will usually not lead to earlier graduation.

But all of the news isn't bad. Money can grow on summer-internship trees. Paid internships might pay $500 to cover transportation or they might pay $6,000 or more. The ones that pay serious money, offered by corporations like Microsoft or GE, are highly competitive, as are high-level government internships such as those with the FBI and CIA. Investing in your child's summer experience between her freshman and sophomore years may lead to one of these "to-die-for" internships the next summer.

Summer School Is Not Usually a Good Choice

Students frequently choose to go to summer school for the following reasons:

- Get pesky requirements out of the way, such as general science requirements.
- Graduate early.
- Take special programs.

Any of these three reasons could make sense but only under special circumstances. In general, it makes more sense for your child's career mission to use the summer to get a job or internship experience.

Students who attend summer school should try to still have a job or an internship. Many colleges offer one-month or even one-week courses or two summer sessions in which the first one is over by the end of June. These are preferred to eight or ten weeks of summer classes.

Many students would rather avoid the large freshman classes that meet general graduation requirements. They frequently go to community colleges where they can pay a reduced price for their tuition. I'm not a strong advocate of this option because it's mainly a way to reduce pain. A six-week summer-school-required class is shorter and perhaps easier than a fifteen-week course during the academic year. Summer-school classes are more grueling but also more compact and ultimately easier. Students may also choose them to keep low grades out of their GPAs. These are not strategies to increase skill, but if they allow for more flexibility during the academic year, they may make sense.

In some cases, students can graduate a semester early by picking up six to twelve credits during the summer. From a financial and career-development point of view, this may make sense. It deprives the student of a summer to explore careers through an internship or a job, so the trade-off needs to be weighed carefully.

Colleges and universities see summer programs as profit centers and for years have been creating interesting programs. Many of these programs can be good choices for career-development purposes. Given the 50-50 Principle, the more these special programs involve travel, internships, fieldwork, or hands-on research experience, the better the choice. A two-week course at an archaeological dig in the Caribbean could be a great skill-development and character-building experience even if the student is not interested in archaeology. It could be useful at cocktail parties or when a job interviewer happens to have had a similar experience.

The availability of such special course work can be appealing, but I would not place it above a solid internship or job experience for career-development purposes unless it includes a required internship of at least three weeks. As in most cases, students need to weigh the trade-offs.

Some universities, especially in D.C., have courses that provide an internship as part of the program. The quality of the internship varies and in some cases, after the student enrolls, the universities just hand the student a list. Most students I have talked to about these programs in D.C. have very positive responses, except about the high cost. I'm not sure that these students couldn't have landed the internships without paying the fees, but it's a viable option. If your child decides to take one of these programs, advise him to seriously investigate the internship component.

The big downside to these special programs is that they are expensive. Some grant money is available to offset the price, but a student could pay from $2,000 to $5,000 for one of these special programs. The cost may be the deciding factor, because ambitious students can build a great summer learning experience without paying a university to organize it. If you and your child are on a tight budget, I recommend not using these programs. There are plenty of options through networking and the Web.

What Parents Can Do

Given summer's critical importance for your child's career preparation, you should be a cheerleader and, if necessary, provide financial support. I suggest three strategies to help your child get a valuable summer job or an internship:

Strategy #1: Encourage your child to start early, which means plan early. Begin talking to your child about his summer plans nine months in advance. A student who approaches me as a freshman to get my help on directing him to an internship or a work experience is a student who will have a successful career path after college, if my experience is any guide. A summer work experience between freshman and sophomore year will give your child a leg up the next year. It's hard for rising sophomores to get great jobs or internships, but any position will be a great asset.

The sooner your child starts thinking about and researching options, the better. Most students wait until March or April, but most deadlines are March 1 or before. Some of the highest-paying and most-useful positions have fall deadlines. Encourage your child to start the search for next summer's internship by mid-October at the latest. Getting a summer internship or job is like getting a permanent job after college.

Because summers are so critical to your child's career development, encourage careful planning and systematic thought for whatever he plans to do. He should consider cost, the job or internship's appeal, skills he will learn, and careers he might explore when making his choice. Putting summer internships and jobs into the initial plan you develop before entering college (as outlined in chapter 6) is a good idea no matter how tentative. Each summer should lead to increasingly better opportunities.

Strategy #2: Emphasize skills over career exploration initially. Students want a perfect fit between what they think their career interests are and their internships. This attitude could lead to no summer position. Moreover, student career interests shift, so finding the perfect fit may make no sense particularly between the first and second years of college. The primary focus should be on skills between freshman and sophomore years. If your child has a clear and long-term career interest in mind, then a more career-specific internship the second and third year makes more sense. But even then, I would suggest choosing skill development over career exploration. A student who develops good computer skills on the job between his sophomore and junior year, even for the Association of the Most Obscure and Distasteful Thing You Can Think Of, might get him that coveted internship with a movie producer the next year.

Strategy #3: Offer some subsidy. It may have not been in your original budget to take another $2,500 hit for your child's education. Many children are afraid or too guilty to ask. Instead, they drive a forklift for a third summer when in fact their parents would have been happy to provide an additional subsidy. I had a student who drove a forklift for fifteen dollars an hour for three summers. A very bright student, he spent five years after college trying to figure out what career he wished to pursue. This didn't seem to be a good decision to me or to him five years later. Perhaps if his parents had offered some subsidies to him for the summer before his senior year, he would have been on a more direct career track when he graduated. There may have been severe financial pressures operating in this case, but if not, his parents should have provided additional financial support or encouraged him to take additional debt if he had a solid summer-internship possibility.

Useful Resources

Internships for Dummies, by Craig P. Donovan and Jim Garnett (New York: John Wiley & Sons, 2001). This book is the most comprehensive general source of advice for any type of internship. It tells you how to search for and land internships and, most important, how to have a good learning experience.

Idealist.org lets you search thousands of public-service internships, fellowships, summer jobs, and volunteer opportunities by country, state, area of focus, and time period. The site also includes a "Career Center" with lots of resources and helpful hints for those interested in the nonprofit world.

National Student Internships and Jobs (http://www.internjobs.com) is a database of internships available globally and nationwide. Browse or search by keyword or locations. Employers can also post their internships and entry-level jobs openings online.

The Riley Guide (http://www.rileyguide.com) website has lots of information to help guide your job and internship search. Resumes, cover letters, networking, and interviewing are all covered. Best of all, you can search thousands of internships, apprenticeships, volunteer opportunities, part-time and temporary jobs, and occupations by discipline and industry.

Rising Star Internships (http://www.rsinternships.com) is a website for posting and searching for internships. Students can post their resumes and search for internship openings by field, from accounting to zoology. Employers post internship and job openings and search for interns who match their qualifications.

Internship Programs (http://www.internshipprograms.com/) is a free site that requires registration but gives you access to thousands of opportunities in cities across the country. You can also post your resume on this site and allow prospective employers to recruit you. This site is certainly not comprehensive but will give you ideas and leads.

Note

1.   National Association of Colleges and Employers, "2004 Job Outlook Survey."

CHAPTER **19**

Get off Campus for at Least One Semester

"You will see something new. Two things. And I call them Thing One and Thing Two."

—From *The Cat in the Hat*, by Dr. Seuss

I am a strong advocate of off-campus semester programs. Many of my best students take their entire junior year off campus—one semester overseas and one in Washington or elsewhere. Although the cost will be higher than staying on campus, and some off-campus programs are more about play than career preparation, taking at least one semester off campus is a smart move.

Skill development from these off-campus programs will be enhanced even more if the programs involve traveling seminars and internships integrated into the course work. If the off-campus programs are just traditional college courses in another location, the added benefit will be minimal. Generally, this is not the case. Colleges have more flexibility in these off-campus courses because administrators have more freedom in shaping the courses and hiring the faculty.

Another advantage to these off-campus semester programs is that they are uniformly recognized by graduate schools and employers as valuable preparation for their programs. Admissions officers know that students who like to deal with new situations and are able to take risks to improve themselves usually pursue off-campus programs. Employers value foreign experiences because many participate in the global economy, and, frankly, they tend not to trust the course work at the undergraduate level from any institution.

All employers like to hire people who can accept the risk of new challenges. Employers also highly value internship experiences, which are associated with many off-campus programs both in and outside the United States. A semester spent working for a legislator in a state capitol will not only help a law school application; it will also appeal to lobbying firms.

Overseas Experiences vs. Experiences in the United States and Canada

When advising your child on where she might have her off-campus experience, one question is whether overseas is better than domestic.

Going out of the United States and Canada is better than staying in the country because students will be stretched and tested more. As the United States becomes more diverse and the world becomes more integrated, an intense cross-cultural experience is critical to developing the skills and character employers want. For that reason alone, every college student should have such an experience.

However, there are several reasons why an overseas semester might not be your child's choice. First, there's the money question. Just getting across the Atlantic or Pacific requires a significant travel expense. Second, for students with a specific interest like politics or medicine, an internship-based semester working as a White House intern or for the National Institutes of Health would benefit more than a trip across the pond.

More than 190,000 U.S. students participated in study-abroad programs in 2003 and 2004, the last years for which data are available.[1] That is triple the number of students who went abroad fifteen years earlier. Although the majority of students go to Europe (63 percent), the trend is more toward programs in Latin America and Asia. The most popular options are one-semester programs, although some experts advocate a full year abroad.

Almost any student who has had an overseas experience will rave about it. A former student, Sharon Awadalla, who now works at NBC Universal, wrote me two years after she graduated about her experience in Hong Kong:

> I grew up in Iowa, where our high school had one minority student out of 800. For eighteen years I lived in a homogeneous bubble where Caucasian, middle-class Christians were the overwhelming majority. Diversity was a concept, not a reality. New York was enough of a culture shock! But I took a risk, hopped on a plane, and came back a different person—more edu-

cated and open-minded. Hong Kong was a learning experience education-ally, culturally, and professionally. I gained international experience that employers value in today's economy. I interned for the Fortune Global Forum where every year, *Fortune* magazine hosts this forum for over 250 of the world's top CEOs with prominent guest speakers. During my intern-ship the forum was held in Hong Kong, where I met and worked with such well-known leaders as Gerald Levin (CEO of AOL Time Warner), Bob Selt-zer (CEO of Ogilvy), Bill Clinton, Thaksin Shinawatra (prime minister of Thailand), Jiang Zemin (president of the People's Republic of China), and Jack Welch (CEO of GE). The forum was surrounded by political contro-versy and it became my responsibility to inform the Hong Kong and New York contacts of the international events around the world. Just last week I sat prepping a senior financial analyst for GE, who was traveling to Shang-hai for a possible sales-expansion opportunity, about the people, culture, and what to expect in Asia's economy today. You don't get that kind of exposure sitting around your sorority house.

An off-campus experience within the United States and Canada will present fewer day-to-day challenges if only because differences in language will not permeate everything. However, students are still faced with new geography and the daily chores that were much easier at college. A domestic off-campus experience can provide more career-exploration and skill-building experience than overseas programs.

An off-campus semester within the United States and Canada requires that your child be more selective about the nature of the program, the qual-ity of the course requirements, and the value of the internship or work environment she finds herself in. In general, the stronger the local control by the university over the courses and hands-on experience, the better.

Most domestic off-campus programs require an internship experience of at least two days a week and as many as five full days a week. Plus, they have assignments and classes. Together, this experience will make your child work much harder than she works on campus. The biggest challenge for many students with whom I have talked is that they have to learn to deal with "a real professional job."

Course Work and Credit

In any off-campus semester, your child should earn the academic credit she needs to graduate on time. Although many colleges accept most credits from many programs, students should check this out very carefully. You don't want your child spending an extra semester at school because the college refused to accept nine of the fifteen credits taken off campus. Require your child to get a written commitment either in a policy statement by the college or in a memo confirming what she says the college has decided. Never accept the spoken word in a matter related to degree progress.

The best way to be sure a student will get the credit is to enroll in a program run by her own college. If the school does not offer such programs, it probably has formal relationships with other colleges and organizations that do. If so, the next best choice would be to enroll in one of those programs.

Going outside of the student's college programs will create more administrative hassles and probably more costs. Students have to make sure the home college and program will accept the credit and may have to take a leave of absence from the home school and enroll in the college providing the experience.

Students usually take twelve to eighteen credits during the off-campus experience. Most programs are designed to generate fifteen credits. If your child is ahead in the pursuit of her degree, drop to twelve credits because more free time will allow her to explore the new environment or just to have fun.

Some Negatives to Consider

The biggest single downside to off-campus programs is that no matter what they tell you, it will cost more. The tuition may be the same but that doesn't include travel, additional moving expenses, and ending up in places where daily expenses are higher. Students have trouble getting jobs in other cities or countries. On some occasions, off-campus programs that require a substantial internship could carry a stipend, or the intern-hosting organization could provide a salary. Sometimes grants are available, but don't count on it.

The next biggest risk that students face in taking a semester off campus is breaking the continuity of their academic programs. If your child takes a course in the fall, leaves in the spring, and gets back in the fall, she may not be able to take a subsequent course until the next spring. Students will also break the continuity of the extracurricular and academic commitments that they've developed during their first two years in college. This can be a major drawback, especially if going off campus means losing a good job or the progress made developing some program or initiative in a student organization.

The only surefire way to mitigate this drawback is to adequately plan ahead. The planning document described in chapter 6 becomes an important tool to avoid the dislocations that can occur from one or two semesters away. If a student knows in her freshman year that she is going to be study-ing off campus during the spring of her junior year, she can plan around that semester.

The chaos caused by going away one semester can waste time and energy that would be better put to skill development or career exploration. It could increase stress and cut down options for summer jobs and upcoming oppor-tunities. A student who wants a summer internship in New York City but is in Austria for the spring semester will face additional obstacles in landing a satisfying summer position. The same goes for scholarship applications. E-mail is wonderful, but that doesn't always work. Some job and internship sites like to conduct personal interviews.

The break can be even more serious for students who aren't sure what they want to do once they graduate. In my experience, most students put thoughts about the future on hold while they are away, especially overseas. The intensity of the experience seems to prevent long-range planning. Stu-dents away during the fall semester of their senior year will miss most of the campus visits by the large corporations and get back in the spring in a funk. Graduate school applications and (and their accompanying standardized tests) are usually due no later than February 1, which gives little time for preparation.

Finally, consider the student's safety and health, which could depend on the location of the off-campus program as well as specific living arrange-ments. They also depend on how careful the student is about keeping safe. The risks may be slightly but not significantly higher than remaining on campus. Other than staying away from countries where there is a civil war or the potential for one and taking the health precautions recommended for tourists, most overseas locations are at least as safe from criminal acts, traffic accidents, and disease as the home college.

What Parents Can Do

Several strategies can help you help your child explore the possibility of taking a semester or two off:

Strategy #1: Encourage your child to go off campus at least one semester and plan early. Many of my students have parents who encourage off-campus semesters. They see the value in broadening horizons and taking risks. Some parents however are not enthusiastic and may even oppose such experiences. They may be concerned about the costs, the risks to health and safety, and the disruption to their children's academic programs. These are legitimate concerns but on the whole not serious enough to prevent students from taking a semester or two away from campus. The benefits are much greater, especially if your child carefully plans ahead of time.

Students sometimes don't anticipate the consequences of taking a semester or two off with respect to both housing and degree completion. Students sign yearlong leases and then by September decide they want to go off campus the second semester. This can cost money but will definitely cost time and aggravation in finding a new lessee.

Degree progress is the most important long-term consideration. About one out of every five students I advise thinks about an off-campus semester in the second semester of his sophomore year or the first semester of his junior year and then realizes he can't graduate on time if he goes. Course sequencing and availability always play a role. The best strategy is for your child to get requirements—major and liberal arts or general education core—out of the way as quickly as possible to allow for flexibility. This is another reason that choosing a major early is a good idea.

Strategy #2: If your child appears to have little interest in leaving campus, take that as a warning sign about career development. Sometimes students don't want to go off campus because they are so heavily involved in extracurricular activities like sports or a music group that they feel irresponsible if they leave. Sometimes it is because they just can't get it together enough to plan a semester away or they "don't see the point." These excuses may indicate some long-term limitations in looking for a job. It constitutes a tendency not to want to take risks or confront new situations. These are severe limitations in an increasingly changing and diverse world. Carefully probe why your child will not even consider the possibility. You may not like the answer, but you will be prepared when the same behavior occurs during the senior year, when your child is searching for a job.

Strategy #3: Watch out for party time. Parents should be concerned if their children seem to be most interested in sightseeing or how many of their friends are going too. Many students are not serious about the learning potential of these experiences and are looking for a good time. I always question students who have already been to London three or four times and then want to take a semester abroad in London. There is not much you can do about the choice except to encourage your child to list the benefits to skills development, character building, and career exploration.

Useful Resources

The Council on International Educational Exchange (CIEE) has a valuable and friendly website (http://www.ciee.org/) that provides comprehensive coverage of study-abroad options. CIEE offers some good services, but the study-abroad programs it lists are strictly its own. It administers work-abroad and travel-abroad programs such as international volunteer opportunities and teaching English in Asia.

The Washington Internship Program's website (http://washingtoninternship .com) provides information on opportunities for a variety of semester-long internships and course programs (not just government) in Washington, D.C. For programs outside of Washington, use the sites listed in chapter 18.

Studyabroad.com is a user-friendly site that provides comprehensive coverage and claims to be the number-one online search site for this topic. This site takes browsers directly to sponsors' Web pages, unlike others.

The study-abroad search section of the Peterson's site (www.petersons.com/ stdyabrd/) is one of the Web's best comprehensive online resources, and it is especially user-friendly.

The Institute for the International Education of Students (IES) (www.iesa broad.org) has strong relationships with universities in more than a dozen countries and will help you transfer credit to your home college.

The Institute for International Education (IIE) (www.iie.org) has some substantial financial aid and scholarship programs for undergrads and graduate students studying abroad, particularly in Asia and other non-Western areas.

For general information about funding opportunities, visit www.finaid.org. This site provides information on available sources of financial support for overseas programs.

Note

1. Institute of International Education, "Opendoors 2005 Fast Facts." Available at http:// opendoors.iienetwork.org/file_depot/0-10000000/0-10000/3390/folder/48524/Open + Doors + 2005_FastFacts_FINAL.pdf.

CHAPTER 20

Look Elsewhere for Skill-Driven Courses

"I took the [road] less traveled by, and that has made all the difference."

—Robert Frost

Have you ever wished you didn't have to purchase an entire package for cable TV so you didn't have to pay for all the channels you'll never watch? Unbundling would be great for college also. A college that allowed students to pick courses and programs that built specific skills would be ideal from a career perspective. But there are other purposes to a college education, and besides, higher education as we know it would disappear. The cash cow of undergraduate tuition would dry up if students were free to choose not only courses but the number of credits they had to take to be ready for careers.

With cable, you have to buy a package that includes channels you would never watch, and then you have to buy the extra channels that you want to watch. The same is true for getting your child the courses he needs to get ahead in this highly competitive global economy. Many courses that would help college students pursue their career missions are not available in the package of most bachelor's degree programs. Your child will have to look elsewhere. The good news is that these short courses and credentials are available and will only cost a small fraction of the money you are spending on the entire package of a college-degree program.

Very few parents of college-age students are aware of the tremendous resources available for helping their children develop the skills employers want. In many cases, they have already benefited from such courses but haven't connected the dots between their midcareer educational experiences and what would be good for their children. Businesses, government, and nonprofit agencies send their employees to seminars all the time for training not just in technical skills like Microsoft Access but in many of the "soft skills" like teamwork and human relations. These courses are expensive in some cases, but when compared with the high costs and low career-preparation value of many college-level academic courses, they are a great buy. In addition to the training seminars provided by commercial vendors, many for-profit colleges and continuing-education programs at traditional colleges offer short and targeted training opportunities.

I am not suggesting that your child should not go to a traditional two-year or four-year college and should just take his own customized bundle of these specialized courses instead. It would be a road less traveled and a path to success for some students. However, because many employers use degrees as a preliminary screening device, specialized courses should supplement degrees from traditional programs. Students who are eighteen to twenty-two years old may benefit from the traditional bundle of courses if only to allow them to grow up. However, if students could build their own bundles of courses and not worry about degrees, they would be better off. If your child is having trouble sustaining enthusiasm for a traditional four-year program, he may want to take some of these courses as he takes on a full-time job.

The educational programs discussed in this chapter are a blend of the 50-50 Principle. They are formal classes, some of which carry college credit, and they're on the academic side. But they have adult learners and are integrated into business- and government-training programs and are therefore close to the college of hard knocks. When soundly designed and delivered, they represent the best of both worlds.

Where to Find Add-On Courses

A variety of institutions offer add-on courses: college and university continuing-education programs, for-profit institutions, commercial training companies, professional associations, and high school adult-education programs. I will briefly touch on these in this section to help you and your child think about the infinite number of programs.

I have already mentioned how summer-school courses and off-campus semester programs tend to be more valuable for career development than traditional academic programs. They are better because administrators have more flexibility in serving the needs of students and, more important, because the competition for summer-school and off-campus dollars is so fierce that the programs are more likely to survive if they provide value to students. Whereas the majority of traditional academic courses have a captured audience coerced by degree and major requirements, the nontraditional courses have to meet the needs of the student more directly.

The first place to look for valuable, skill-based courses is in the night school, now usually called *continuing-education program*, of the college your child attends or one nearby. On some occasions, your child may be able to take these courses as part of her traditional program, but usually there are roadblocks to this. If there weren't, the traditional students would overrun these classes and the programs wouldn't generate cash. Many of these programs are also not deemed worthy of academic credit for reasons that have to do more with fear and snobbery. Faculty members at traditional institutions frequently call these courses "vocational" to drive home the point that a four-year degree is about culture and the educated person.

Many high schools offer skill-based adult-education programs at night. These courses are a great value because they are usually inexpensive and they may be taught as well as, if not better than, courses offered by colleges.

For-profit institutions such as University of Phoenix also provide some useful courses on a part-time basis. A growing number of specialized vendors offer programs that may not carry academic credit anywhere but could be valuable for developing skills. These specialized vendors are successful because they have developed programs to meet a specific need. One of the needs is generated by corporations that find that their new employees, with their newly minted college degrees, lack essential skills. They call in a private company to provide those skills.

Because these vendors are market driven, the courses can be better taught and more valuable from a career perspective than those offered by colleges. Courses offered through outside vendors or part-time colleges are evaluated more thoroughly, and (especially with respect to private vendors) instructors are more heavily managed than typical college faculty members. Corporations will pay the Dale Carnegie Training Institute $1,400 to send an employee to the introductory course in human relations. At a private college, you will pay over $2,500 for three credits of Psych 101. If the goal is to develop human relations skills, as mentioned in chapter 12, there's no contest which is the better value!

Dale Carnegie tried to get hired by colleges in New York City but had to offer his programs at venues like the YMCA, even though, as he reports, "In a public address to approximately six hundred people at the Yale Club in New York on the evening of Thursday, February 23, 1933," a conservative and eminently successful Harvard graduate "declared he had learned more in the fourteen weeks through this system of training about the fine art of influencing people than he had learned about the same subject during his four years of college."[1]

In addition to being more customer driven, these courses are usually better designed and delivered than most college courses. Instructors with poor ratings from students are more frequently replaced than traditional college instructors if only because tenure means that instructor will have to teach something. Evaluations are more comprehensive and quickly analyzed, leading to continuous improvement. Instructors usually practice in the fields they teach, which means students take them more seriously. And as Bruce Hamm, an administrator at a continuing-education program, writes in the sidebar, adult learners add substantial educational value.

Like everything else, particularly in the service industry of part-time education, the quality and relevance of these nontraditional courses varies tremendously. Check the credentials of the entities offering the training. Programs don't necessarily have to be accredited to be worthwhile, and you should note endorsements by professional associations and/or offerings by reputable companies. The best thing to do is to ask former students and the employers who hire them about the quality of the programs.

These sources of education play an increasing role in the education of college graduates. They still serve very few traditional students in college. Parents who help their children take these nontraditional courses, even if they cost more and don't carry credit, can give them the extra education they need to succeed in today's highly competitive workplace.

Adult Learners Create a Richer Educational Environment

Traditional-age students may make contacts and find internships from studying with businesspeople. They also learn that people who have real lives can add richness and a whole new diversity to the learning process, that people who are paying for their own education take their studies much more seriously, that people who know why they are in school ask probing questions informed by their own backgrounds, and that people who bring experience and maturity to the classroom will not *tolerate* inadequate instruction that is not relevant.

—Bruce Hamm, director of the Legal Studies Program and University College, Syracuse University

Some Examples

It's not possible to cover the entire range of options, but I've provided some sources for identifying outside vendors at the end of this chapter. Here are two good examples of the variety of programs available:

1. **Dale Carnegie Human Relations Training.** More than ninety-two years old, Dale Carnegie Training operates in sixty-five countries and has more than seven million graduates. Each of its programs is carefully developed, continuously evaluated and updated, and hugely successful. The Carnegie introductory course, which involves twelve sessions of three hours each, in addition to outside assignments, introduces Dale Carnegie's theories of human relations and encourages participants to practice those principles each week. Students must give two brief speeches each week. I completed the course in 2004 and saw a remarkable transformation in the twenty-five people who attended. Individuals who mumbled during the first speech won speaking awards by the end. It changed my approach to dealing with students and colleagues, and I have incorporated some of the approaches into my classes. The cost of this course is $1,400, which is less than a three-credit course at a private university. Some colleges will give academic credit for the course. Regardless, this might be a very good investment, particularly if your child is shy or has trouble in public speaking. An added benefit is that those who attend these seminars are usually from the business community, and your child may get a job or an internship out of it.

2. **Wall Street Prep, Inc.** Founded by a group of investment bankers formerly from Goldman Sachs, this company provides programs at prestigious institutions like Middlebury College, Harvard, Northwestern, Oberlin, and Vanderbilt. A two-day course they call Investment Banking Boot Camp costs less than one credit even at most public institutions. The company operates a weekend-blitz seminar for those who want to go into finance. The educational value is most likely viewed by students and employers as equal to or greater than a typical three-credit finance course. Students are not required to go through existing institutions and can also take the course online. Liberal arts majors who want to prepare for careers in investments and finance often take the courses.

There are an infinite number of possible educational opportunities from private vendors that can be crucial in obtaining jobs and pursuing satisfying careers. Professional certification in various computer applications, such as those provided by Microsoft, Sun, Cisco Systems, and Oracle, are already available to part-time students in many universities. Other programs, such as the HIPAA Academy, which provides training in HIPAA and its Administrative and Simplification Act, might also be included. The American Council on Education (ACE) and the National Program on Noncollegiate Sponsored Instruction (National PONSI) list and evaluate formal education courses offered by businesses, industries, professional associations, labor unions, and other noncollegiate organizations. See the sidebar for a list of some of the corporations providing education provided by PONSI. Many of these programs generate college credit at most schools—an added but not crucial bonus.

Test-Preparation Centers

I have considerable ambivalence about recommending Kaplan and other courses to help your child do better on tests like the LSAT, GMAT, GRE, and MCAT. On one hand, they are costly in time and money, and they send the wrong signal to students that their futures depend on getting into the more selective programs. I doubt how much they increase scores in comparison to the many manuals and computer programs out there. On the other hand, they symbolize a commitment to going to graduate school and in some cases they may appreciably raise scores.

One reality about test-preparation programs is that graduate schools place a lot of weight in their admission decisions on test scores. Law and medical schools even publish the average scores as a way to tell potential applicants whether to bother. But the scores become less important to graduate school admission the longer the applicant is out of undergraduate school.

If your child is going to seriously consider graduate school, he should take the tests while he is in college or right after graduating. He will be in the study and test-taking mode at the time. Graduate programs will usually accept test results for several years.

This suggestion raises a point that I discuss in more detail in chapter 21. Except for students who are thinking about a career requiring a graduate degree, they should not automatically think they need graduate degrees. In addition, every student, no matter what graduate program she goes into, will be much better off working or taking a community-service position for a couple of years right out of college.

Taking the test could encourage your child to go into graduate school too quickly. Taking a commercial study course could make him feel that he has invested so much that he might as well as go to graduate school. If he does well on the test, he might think he's meant for graduate school. If he does poorly, he may actually be better off.

Partial List of Corporations Providing Education Programs

Academy for Film and Television
Academy for Healthcare Management
American Express
Apex Technical School
APICS—The Association for Operations Management
Arnot-Ogden Medical Center School of Radiologic Technology
Association for Hebraic Studies Institute
Bridgeport Hospital School of Nursing
Builders for The Family and Youth, Inc.
Career Tech Services/Instant Train
Center for the Study of Expertise in Teaching and Learning
Children's Trust Fund of Missouri
Citibank School of Banking
Consolidated Edison Company of New York, Inc.
Constellation Nuclear
Dale Carnegie & Associates, Inc.
First Energy Corporation
The Global Institute for Finance and Banking
The Institute for Supply Management
International Claim Association
Joint Apprentice Committee of the Electrical Industry-Local Union 3
Lighthouse International
Link-Systems International, Inc.
LOMA
Manhattan Institute of Management
Memorial Sloan-Kettering Cancer Center
Nassau County Emergency Medical Services Academy
New York Institute of Credit
New York State Department of Correctional Services
New York State Department of State
New York State Division of State Police
New York State United Teachers
North Shore University Hospital
Public Safety Education Institute
World Trade Institute
Xerox Corporation

If you want to err on the side of caution, support your child's decision to take a test-preparation course. It will be another opportunity for him to exercise work ethic, attention to detail, reading and writing skills, and excellence. It should not do serious damage to his intellect. If he doesn't do well after all his hard work, it could incorrectly lead him to the conclusion that he doesn't have the ability to succeed in that field. As noted throughout this book, career success is dependent on a wide array of skills but is not dependent on scoring in the 90th percentile on some standardized test.

What Parents Can Do

Parents can't force their children to take advantage of courses outside of their main college program, but they can pursue several strategies:

Strategy #1: Increase your awareness of these options and introduce your child to them. You can alert your child to these opportunities. He's not likely to notice them without your help given the overwhelming presence of traditional college in his thinking about his own education. If your child asks for support to take one of these programs, don't dismiss the idea on the grounds that you are already investing enough or the value can't be as great as the college your child is attending.

Strategy #2: Advise your child to carefully investigate the quality and relevance of the course. Your child has to be very careful in selecting these programs. The quality of the programs varies widely and the degree of relevance to your child's career goals may be less than the advertising suggests. But the same can be said for college programs. Look at what's promised, consult with graduates of the programs, and check with employers. It would be less useful to ask college faculty members about these programs. They may have little knowledge of them and be predisposed to oppose them for competitive reasons. The career-services office at your child's college may be helpful. As noted above, some of these programs can be poorly executed, so thoroughly study the organization's credentials. Comments by recent students are a must.

Strategy #3: Consider enrolling your child in the basic Dale Carnegie Human Relations Course. I am not paid by Dale Carnegie, so this is a suggestion based on my own experience. Not everyone is satisfied but most are, and I have witnessed firsthand its impact. Too bad the course is not part of our high school or lower-division college curriculum!

Useful Resources

The National Program on Noncollegiate Sponsored Instruction (http://www .nationalponsi.org) offers ways to find experiences that can carry college credit. Click on the College Credit Recommendations (CCR Online) link for a full list of and links to the various programs.

Dale Carnegie, *How to Win Friends & Influence People* (New York: Simon and Schuster, 1981).

Note

1.   Dale Carnegie, *How to Win Friends & Influence People* (New York: Simon and Schuster, 1981), p. x.

PART SIX

Post-College Paths

Your child will face many new choices as graduation approaches and passes. Developing skills, building character, and exploring careers still need to be the mission.

CHAPTER 21

Graduate School Should Not Be a Default Option

"It's déjà vu all over again."

—Yogi Berra

If four years of college does not prepare a student to get a job that leads to a viable career, why would more college do the trick?

I will demonstrate in this chapter that graduate school is an expensive proposition that may have limited benefit for many new college graduates. If a college degree and four quarters is worth a dollar, how could a master's degree or a Ph.D. be worth any more? It's the skills, character, and career focus that determines whether your child pursues a desirable career path. That comes first and then maybe—and I mean maybe—graduate school is needed.

There are plenty of other paths to a very successful, lucrative, and rewarding career. If your child gets a job in the GE Financial Management Program, for example, he'll receive training equivalent to a master of business administration (MBA) while earning a good salary and moving up the ladder at GE. If he shows he's a great asset to the company, GE will send him to the graduate program of his choice and possibly one that can be completed on weekends. And then he'll be ready to be the chief financial officer of one of GE's thousands of businesses or land somewhere high up in the corporation. This is what's happening now to one of my students, ten years after starting at GE.

To put it another way, if your child has the right stuff, graduate school isn't needed right away. If he doesn't have the skills and character, graduate school might get him a couple of jobs, but he's going nowhere. Like too many undergraduates who think the degree will make them a success rather than their skills and character, too many students seeking graduate degrees think they can write their own tickets with a master's degree. If the master's degree is all they have to rely on, they are in for bitter disappointment, as are their employers.

The success of the Policy Studies undergraduate program I run at Syracuse University demonstrates that skills, not mere degrees, are the keys to success. Over the years, many of my strong students with only bachelor's degrees have triumphed over graduate students for prize jobs. Students of undergraduate programs that emphasize skills and experience, especially co-op programs, have the same positive experience.

Graduate programs are proliferating. There used to be law and medicine and Ph.D. programs in the arts and sciences. Over the past seventy-five years, professional master's programs have developed in business, social work, psychology, education, public administration, or public policy. Today the variety of master's degrees seems to be increasing daily as college and university administrators envision additional tuition dollars. The number of people receiving a master's degree is 38 percent of the number receiving bachelor's degrees. More than half of those are in education, where a graduate degree is required for employment, and business, where a graduate degree is not required for employment.[1]

My message in this chapter is that unless your child plans to enter a profession like education, medicine, or law, where a graduate degree is required as a union card, he should not treat graduate school as his preferred option. He should get a job for a few years or a fully paid internship and then he should look at graduate school. If he does that, odds are he'll never go to graduate school because he'll already have a successful career. If he does go to graduate school after he has been employed, his employer might pay for it. Moreover, he can go at night or on weekends and keep the money flowing in. If he seems to be getting nowhere in his career after two or three years, he may have a better idea of what kind of graduate degree he wants to get.

A Quick Overview of Graduate Programs

I can't give you a comprehensive review of the tens of thousands of graduate degree programs offered in this country, but I can give you basic information so you have a better picture of the landscape.

There are four types of graduate degrees: professional degrees, general master's degrees that are not considered direct paths to a profession, certificate programs, and Ph.D.'s.

Professional degrees are frequently some type of master's degree or specialized degree like law or medicine. In some fields like law, medicine, education, and social work, a professional degree is required. In others, such as business and government service, they are not required.

Universities have been offering a variety of master's degrees, which are not to be confused with professional master's degrees—those lead to very specific types of jobs. These nonprofessional master's degrees, primarily in the liberal arts field, are for individuals who do not want to earn Ph.D.'s but who want to study the field for its own sake. Students who earn them are frequently no farther along in their career paths after their completion.

Colleges are increasingly offering certificate programs, sometimes only to college graduates and sometimes to anyone who wants to pay the freight. I described some computer-software certificate programs in chapter 20. However, certificates exist in almost any field. Students may need to look at continuing-education programs for these courses rather than programs offering formal master's programs. They are a good choice if your child finds a career fit, because they are usually shorter and more focused and therefore less expensive than a master's program.

For example, your child may think she wants to be a lawyer but might get a certificate as a paralegal first, then get a job that can eventually pay close to $100,000 a year, and then go to law school. The advantage would be that she could have a career in law without the cost and horror of law school. If she decides to go to law school, she will be better prepared than any of the other students who had not gone that route.

Ph.D. programs make no money for universities except when they generate grant support, and then it's not really clear if there is a net profit. Ph.D. programs are highly subsidized in most universities by undergraduate and master's programs. Any student a department considers worthy will receive a subsidy, which can be as much as $160,000 over a four-year period. The subsidies exist because Ph.D. programs have two big negatives. First, for fields outside of the hard sciences—the professional schools and economics—Ph.D.'s have trouble getting jobs in their chosen fields. Second, although officially a four-year program, it takes on average seven years to complete and is sheer torture for many students. The subsidies usually run out after four years.

The fact that Ph.D. programs attract so many students is a testament to the relentless effort of so many faculty members who want to find and nurture professional scholars. The Ph.D. is a very specialized degree that leads directly to a small number of jobs in almost any field. Although people in fields like consulting and mental-health counseling can benefit because their clients are attracted by higher degrees, the quality of the services is more a result of experience and talent than formal training.

Students need to look carefully at graduate-school options. They should be wary of the promises made in the brochures and consider the fit between the curriculum and their career needs.

What Graduate Programs Can Do

Graduate school can do four things for your child:

1. **It can essentially provide a union card for some fields.** By union card, I mean you don't have a career if you don't have the degree. Relatively few fields have this requirement although more will in the future. Professions push for higher standards—sometimes for good reasons and sometimes because it will limit the supply of new people in the field.

2. **It can provide a network for landing a first job and building a long-term career.** The programs' staff, students, and alumni can help you launch and grow your career.

3. **It can provide crucial knowledge about the field.** This means being socialized into the terminology, history, and culture of the field.

4. **It can provide skills needed to be successful in the field.** Many of the skills are the thirty-eight skills listed in chapter 1, but some are technical tools specific to the field. Graduate programs do a much better job than undergraduate programs in training students because the good ones provide extensive field experience.

Higher-ranked schools may have larger and better-connected alumni networks, but most graduate programs pay attention to placement of their graduates. Prestigious schools might not do such a good job in the last two areas because their faculty members are so research-oriented that they don't have the inclination to provide students what they need or they are very busy doing outside consulting. Graduate programs without extensive fieldwork or clinical experience should be crossed off your child's lists. Fortunately, most do put resources into fieldwork activities.

Some studies on MBA programs show that the prestige of the school is not strongly correlated with the financial success of its alumni. This should not be surprising because hopefully by now you have accepted that skills and character are more important than a degree.

Statistics show that people with graduate degrees make twice as much money over their careers as people with bachelor's degrees. Professional degrees tend to pay more than Ph.D. degrees. From a monetary point of view, pursuing an advanced degree seems to be a good decision. The confounding variable is that students who pursue graduate degrees are usually more focused and committed to career success. Just like students who apply to and are rejected from prestigious colleges are likely to do well, students who apply to graduate schools are also likely to be more successful. The unknown is whether the graduate program made a significant difference.

Although most students complete their graduate programs if they go full-time, whether they get the jobs they intended to get is not as certain. Their chances of finding worthwhile careers increase greatly if they take some time off between undergraduate and graduate school.

Taking a Hard Look

Graduate school is becoming increasingly popular; maybe too popular according to an editorial in the *Chronicle of Higher Education* titled "The Dirty Little Secret of Credential Inflation."[2] The author writes, "Many people believe that our high-tech era requires massive educational expansion." He also states, "In principle, credential inflation could go on endlessly, until janitors need Ph.D.'s, and baby sitters are required to hold advanced degrees in child care." This comment is extreme but makes the point.

The most popular graduate degree by far is the MBA. An article written by two Stanford Business School researchers, Jeffrey Pfeffer and Christina Fong, maintains that with the exception of graduates from some of the elite schools, an MBA is not correlated with higher salaries over the long run.[3]

For most other fields, a master's or even a Ph.D. is not required. Students who get these degrees are sometimes told they are overeducated for the jobs they want. The best advice is for the student to explore the graduate school option by systematically asking the following five questions:

1. Does the degree have the necessary approval of accrediting bodies?
2. Is the degree really a union card, or can I enter the field without it and complete it later?
3. Are the alumni and students in the program part of a network that could help current students secure jobs, and how good is the placement of its graduates?
4. Does the program provide the technical knowledge I need to get the job I want? (This knowledge includes the history and culture of the professions as well as technical language the profession uses.)

5. Will the program help me develop the general professional skills and technical skills essential to the field?

If a student cannot answer yes to these questions, entering the program makes no sense. If students don't know enough to answer these questions, they need to get more experience and information about the field and the program.

Other Alternatives

Getting a job right out of college is the obvious alternative to going to graduate school. A college graduate can pursue jobs for two very different purposes. The first purpose is to see the job as a start of her career. A permanent position in business or government right out of college can lead to a long career in that organization or, most likely, in several different organizations. The second purpose is to develop more skills and character, to learn more about herself, and to learn more about the particular field she has entered. The job may last for only a year or two, and she should be clear about this when she interviews for the job. Leaving a job that was supposed to be permanent after a year or two does not send a good signal to future employers.

Either way, getting a job is going to the Graduate School of Hard Knocks and getting paid. The obvious advantage is that your child will be paid, and he will not be paying. That is at least a $50,000-a-year monetary differential and quite possibly more. If your child has worked with the career-services office and seriously looked for a job, he'll find getting a job an attractive alternative to going to graduate school. Chapter 22 discusses how you can help your child get that first job.

Not only is getting a job better financially; it is better educationally. Working for a real boss in a company or agency has to be a better learning experience than satisfying professors with papers and tests. Experience is always a better teacher if your child is committed to applying his talents. Graduate programs usually provide fieldwork and therefore the necessary experience. However, short periods of fieldwork, in-class simulations, and case studies are not the same as the experience to be gained from a job.

Going after a job in business, especially with established corporations, is the most common alternative new college graduates choose. Although the job market is competitive, persistence pays off. This alternative not only makes sense because your child gets paid, but also because it provides a solid learning experience.

Some of the largest corporations offer paid two-year positions that do much better jobs than most graduate schools, and they pay reasonable salaries while they're doing it. One of the oldest, best-known, and largest programs is the Financial Management Program at General Electric, which I referred to at the beginning of this chapter. This two-year program combines four or five rotational assignments across different GE businesses with formal classroom studies that focus on specific skills needed for jobs like financial analysis.

Most Fortune 500 companies have training programs for new hires. In part, these programs are designed to socialize new employees into the culture of the corporation and the procedures that need to be followed. Many programs, however, go far beyond that by providing formal training that ranges from three months to two years. Applicants should always ask about training programs, which may be the most important factor in choosing a job.

Students who can't find a job directly with an employer can always find a job through a temporary agency. Employers hire temporary agencies to screen and select temporary employees, but "temporary" can mean two years or more—and many of these positions lead to full-time jobs. For example, Aerotek, Inc. is a staffing company that provides employees to many of the nation's top companies in a wide range of industries. These companies depend on Aerotek's experience and specialized resources to track down the best candidates. At any time, over 50,000 contract employees are working through Aerotek all over the country. An Aerotek client may hire an employee on a temporary basis to check for a good fit and to ensure he or she has the required skills. Once that's established, the client can take the employee on permanently. Some of the jobs are technical and require extensive job experience. Others are not. Temporary agencies like Aerotek are great places to find jobs that can provide better experience than going directly to graduate school.

Students can also apply to one of the many programs offered by nonprofit organizations and supported by AmeriCorps. AmeriCorps supports a wide range of nonprofit organizations, like the Boys & Girls Club, that hire people on a one- or two-year basis. Such a position means a salary, some money to pay off student loans, and an invaluable experience serving others.

Joining the military is also a reasonable option. People with military backgrounds are in high demand in the business world, in government jobs—especially law enforcement—and in the nonprofit sector.

Arguments Students Make for Going Directly to Graduate School After College

Here are five arguments that your child might make on why he should go to graduate school right after college:

1. **"I need more general professional skills."** I don't like to hear this one because it means the student didn't develop general skills in college or at least he thinks he didn't. Unfortunately, this is frequently the case, and therefore graduate school may make sense as a remedial treatment. Graduate school can accomplish what a college education did not. Most graduate programs have more skill-based courses and fieldwork experiences than undergraduate programs. If you were unable to get your child to buy into the program offered throughout this book or you are picking up this book late in your child's college career, you may want to support some graduate school. I would still recommend a year or two in the work world first.

2. **"I need to have a network in the field I want to pursue."** There are three reasons why this is a legitimate argument. First, faculty members in graduate programs are usually accomplished in their professions or have had at least some experience. Moreover, some of the students in the program will have already been in the field, and your child can learn a great deal from them. Second, any good graduate program will have a lot of resources devoted to getting its students jobs or at least internships leading to full-time positions. Third, your child's grad-school friends will be in his field. Consequently, your child will have a built-in network that will help him find and keep jobs.

3. **"I look too young and need a few years to be taken seriously."** This might be called "the growing-up factor." Many people in the work world are not ready to take anyone under twenty-five seriously for obvious reasons. For students who feel they look young or are not ready to deal with professionals over thirty, taking a couple of years to grow up may not be a bad idea. Lack of self-confidence and unwillingness to take on adult responsibilities is going to create problems for that student for a considerable period of time, and the year or two of graduate school may not do the trick. Don't forget the possibility that your child's desire to go to graduate school to "grow up" may mean he doesn't want to go into the real world.

4. **"I am very confused about what I want to do with my life and graduate school will help me."** This frequently expressed opinion shows a serious misunderstanding of the nature of a good graduate program. Students will be asked to start jobs or summer internship searches within two months of arriving at the program. For students who graduate in May and start job searches in October, what could happen in that short time to get them ready for jobs or even job searches? Going into a first full-time job, even if it's temporary, will allow for greater career exploration and skill building when they go to graduate school at a later date.

5. "I was too busy to do a job search, so I want to go to graduate school." Your child may not be honest enough to give you such an explanation for going to graduate school. It is frequently the case, however. I have had many students admit this to me. Applying to graduate school is easier than searching for a job. It's easier than sending out hundreds of resumes and getting involved in the interview process. True, college seniors have to take another standardized test, but once that's done a graduate school application is not much work. Moreover, it's not hard to get into the majority of graduate programs, so parents can't count on their children being rejected everywhere they apply. Just as there are some colleges that will take even the most unprepared student with or without a high school diploma, there are graduate programs that will take any warm body, and I am not talking about diploma mills.

I had a student who had close to a 2.0 GPA and was so irresponsible and so limited intellectually that she just barely made it through her undergraduate program. She decided to apply to graduate school, against my recommendation, and she was admitted to a graduate program that was highly ranked. The really sad part for this student was that she made a good impression and could have had a well-paying marketing job if she had really wanted to work hard and search for a job.

The message about graduate school is mixed. Except for professions requiring the credential, it should not be viewed as an automatic decision. Even in those cases, two or three years of work will bring clarity of purpose to the decision to go to graduate school. The primary value, however, of most graduate school programs is to help students explore careers and enter career networks. That means your child will have to select and get into a program that actually does that. Your child will need to do serious research.

What Parents Can Do

In the majority of cases, no student should go to graduate school right after college and many should not go at all. Students should think long and hard about the graduate-school option. Here are some things you can do as a parent with respect to graduate school.

Strategy #1: Do not pressure your child to go to graduate school right out of college. Parents pressure their children to go to graduate school out of fear that their children will never get advanced degrees and will end up in dead-end careers. Although it's less likely that students will go to graduate school after they start working, it doesn't mean that they will be worse off financially. Many of my most successful and wealthy students did not go to graduate school right out of college, and less than half of those went at a later date. If you have followed the Goldilocks Principle in dealing with your child while in college, you will know not to apply pressure. Don't let fears of your child never being able to support himself lead you to push graduate school right after he completes his undergraduate degree. If your child doesn't have skills, character, and career focus, graduate school will not give him a viable career path and, if he goes, you or he will end up with $50,000 more in expenses or debt.

First, let's deal with the fields that require a graduate degree like medicine, law, social work, counseling, and education. If your child wants to go into one of those fields, obviously she has to go to graduate school. She would probably benefit from a year or two hiatus from school before she enters the program. She needs to be sure that it's what she wants to do for at least five years after graduate school. I say five years because you never know.

This general advice holds except for the field of law. About half the students I talk to today who plan to go to law school say they don't want to be practicing lawyers. Instead, they see the law degree as giving them added juice over those with just an undergraduate degree, or they rightly see a field like being a legislative aid to a congressperson as almost requiring a law degree. Several of my students who got their law degrees worked for law firms for two years and then became teachers.

Viewing a law degree as a way to "think like a lawyer" and build up more education is like eating a second and third helping at dinner. Beyond the satisfaction, what's the point? To look at law school as a broad education for people who are not going to be lawyers doesn't make a lot of sense. Of course, the fact that many people with law degrees can't pass the bar examination doesn't make a lot of sense either. Don't forget we are talking about another $100,000 or more in expenses.

A colleague of mine wrote the following:

> What is perhaps more frightening is that law school is very much the same as undergraduate liberal arts programs. Reputed to be a "professional school," you encounter the same attitudes among the tenured faculty that you speak of at the undergraduate level. It is only when you encounter the "adjunct" professors (or professors who have been in the field) that you begin to get a sense of what practicing law is all about. Not all students will find themselves clerking for judges, which appears to be the educational purpose of most law school programs.
>
> Law school graduates wind up taking a bar review course at the end of law school to "prepare" for the bar exam. Coupled with the suspect bar

pass rates at many institutions, you have to ask, "What is law school for anyway?" In law school you never get a course on running a business, or how much to charge per hour, or where to find the courthouse for that matter. You can go the entire three years without accumulating any "practical" skills. Perhaps even more frightening is that on most bar exams they test on at least twenty different areas of law, while "required" courses in law school only number six or seven. If you're not careful, you could miss two-thirds of the courses you need for the bar exam.

Strategy #2: Recommend that your child go to graduate school only after he works or does some other sustained activity for at least two years. If you and your child are lucky, he will be employed by a company that will pay for his graduate school. He'll go at night or on the weekends to get the piece of paper, and everyone will be ecstatic. This could even work for law school. If he goes full-time, he will get into a better graduate program and benefit much more from the experience. Working for a couple of years is definitely recommended for the MBA and the master's of public administration or public policy. In any case, the better the graduate program the fewer students it will admit right out of undergraduate programs anyway. They want to see two to five years of on-the-job experience.

Strategy #3: If your child decides to go to graduate school, don't pay for it. This may sound a little harsh and perhaps you could help out, but not with more than 30 percent of the tab. In many cases, graduate school will help your child make more money, so why should you take the hit? This stance, even if you decide to give a little at a later date, will force your child to really think hard about the decision. If your child thought college was a day on the beach, he might think the same for graduate school. This may or may not be the case depending on where he goes and how slick he is at getting work done with little effort.

Strategy #4: Suggest your child research a variety of options thoroughly. With graduate programs, "buyer beware" is even more important than undergraduate programs. The placement rate for graduates is absolutely critical. Your child should get hard employment data supported by interviews of randomly selected recent graduates before he takes the plunge.

Useful Resources

AmeriCorps is a network of national service programs that engage more than 50,000 Americans each year in intensive service to meet critical needs in education, public safety, health, and the environment. For more information, visit www.americorps.org.

Idealist.org lets you search thousands of public-service internships, fellowships, summer jobs, or volunteer opportunities by country, state, area of focus, and time period.

The military section of the Lucas Group website is one of many websites that help place former members of the military. The range of jobs that ex-military people get and the salaries are listed on the site. Visit http://www.lucasgroup .com/military/.

Congress formally authorized the creation of the Peace Corps in 1961, and its mission is to "promote world peace and friendship." There are 7,000 Peace Corps volunteers currently serving in seventy countries around the world. All assignments are for two years plus three months of training in your country of service.

Teach for America (www.teachforamerica.org) is a national corps of outstanding college graduates of all academic majors and backgrounds who commit to teach for two years in urban and rural public schools.

Notes

1. *The Chronicle of Higher Education,* Almanac Issue 2006–2007, p. 22.

2. Randall Collins, "The Dirty Little Secret of Credential Inflation," *The Chronicle of Higher Education,* September 27, 2002.

3. Jeffrey Pfeffer and Christina T. Fong, "The End of Business Schools? Less Success Than Meets the Eye," *Academy of Management Learning and Education,* September, 2002.

CHAPTER **22**

Securing That First Job

"Act and you shall achieve."

—Anonymous

Once upon a time, on a cozy campus in southwest Ohio, there was a young lad who met with a recruiter from a regional bank. About fifteen minutes into this interview, the recruiter looked at the aspiring professional and calmly stated, "You don't have the background or the skills that we require to be a banker. Plus, it doesn't sound like you really want to be a banker. Let's not waste any more time. This interview is over."

This scenario happened to me as a college senior for a reason: I was unclear about a career direction.

Ever since that cold slap in the face in 1983, it's been my mission to learn effective employment strategies. Along my career journey, I have read countless guidebooks, attended how-to seminars, picked the brains of hiring managers, and acquired streetwise tips. Further, I've been a practitioner of various techniques while mentoring young adults to secure entry-level positions. Interestingly, what began as a part-time passion evolved into my full-time occupation as a career counselor.

By Tim Conway

Tim Conway operates Ignite Young Adults to bolster the college and career choices of individuals nationwide (ages 16 to 30). He assists in the selection of an academic major, college, internship, first job, graduate school, and career change. Tim can be contacted at 847-749-1394 or timconway@igniteyoungadults.com.

This chapter provides a wide-angled view of the labor market, shares perspectives of what it's like to pursue "a real job" for the first time, spells out the six stages of a productive job search, and recommends parental dos and don'ts. This advice will enable you to coach a twentysomething to land a rewarding job.

Job-Market Reality Check

Because your child will pursue employment in a rapidly changing world, you need to be familiar with seismic shifts in the labor markets:

- Economic volatility that translates into minimal employment security

- Expanded technology and globalization

- Less full-time hiring by Fortune 500 corporations and more freelance contractors as needed

- Demographic fluctuations such as the upcoming retirement of 78 million current workers[1]

For entry-level candidates, the impacts are significant due to new roles, scaled-back training programs, and uncertain upward mobility.

Amid a chaotic labor market, there are other variables to keep in mind. About 15 million jobs per year turn over, which means there are always openings (because professionals change employers, companies reorganize, and people retire). So don't fall for student remarks that "there are no jobs." With the increased use of the Internet, employers have larger pools of applicants. Ironically, this makes the classic human resources adage that "people hire people"—those they get to know and like—even more important. Employers heavily rely on internships and cooperative-education programs because employers gain a broader impression of candidates over an extended period.

Employers actively seek those who are able to collaborate on teams. Candidates should provide evidence of prior experience as team members or leader. Plus, speaking an in-demand second language—such as Spanish or Arabic—separates your child from the masses in certain industries (e.g., health care, retail, hospitality, government). The sidebar provides some facts affecting hiring.

- -

Job Market for New Graduates

- Small and midsize businesses—under 250 employees—are actually where 80 percent of job growth occurs, but few undergraduates look there (most just concentrate on megaorganizations).
- Seventy percent of job placements come from word-of-mouth referrals (this statistic is slightly lower for collegians because some get jobs through on-campus interviews).
- Only 10 percent of jobs are found via online job boards.[2] But twenty-somethings are naïve about the poor results of these sites. Many are seduced by the ease of posting a resume; some assume job boards will magically deliver employment offers with minimal effort.
- Hiring managers are typically high achievers, in their forties, male or female, with master's degrees; they are time starved, risk takers, and savvy self-promoters who want to hire go-getters with business-building ideas.[3]
- Each organization has its own hiring time frame (corporations are bureaucratic and take longer to process applications and extend offers than small businesses).

- -

Process for Job-Search Success

First-time job hunters need to be wary of the following:

■ **Warning #1: Negative emotions can surface.** An individual will feel overwhelmed, discouraged, stressed-out, and angry while pursuing employment. These emotions bubble up because a job hunt is an activity that he or she lacks expertise in and can be intimidating. These emotions increase with each rejection.

■ **Warning #2: Getting motivated is tough.** First-time job seekers resist beginning a job search, making cold calls, and going to networking events. Think of this hesitation as being similar to attempting a new dance. At first, people think they can just "wing it." Then they struggle to get interviews and realize that it's better to learn the steps. After a few false starts, inertia may set in. Afraid of underperforming, failing, or being embarrassed, they become immobilized. A job search: It ranks up there with giving a speech or going for a root canal.

■   **Warning #3: Planning is always on the short side.** The start-to-finish time frame for a comprehensive employment search is six to eight months minimum (although your college student will probably debate this timing). Students must allocate extra time during their junior and senior years because a job search requires months of diligence. Procrastinators should take lighter course loads and use time-management tools—such as to-do lists with deadlines—to attain desired outcomes.

As with other activities in this book, pursuing employment fosters valuable skills (e.g., writing, project management) along with character (e.g., work ethic, persistence). Your child must grasp that a job search is a *process*, not a quick fix to begin forty-five days before departing campus. There are several ways to earn a job offer; some approaches are better than others and tactics vary by industry.

Once acquired, a person must redeploy these core search methods throughout his career (because Americans change jobs seven to ten times). In fact, the initial time invested to learn the process pays long-term dividends.

The six elements of an effective job search are:

1. Self-awareness
2. Research
3. Personal packaging
4. Outreach
5. Interviews
6. Closing the deal

Students who have spent their college years developing skills, building character, and exploring careers as suggested throughout this book will find these steps a lot easier to complete.

1. Self-Awareness

For peak performance during a job search, first-time job seekers must become comfortable talking about their skills and character. They shouldn't react with a deer-in-the-headlights gaze when asked to name their top strengths. In fairness, some people are modest and don't want to "brag." But all first-time job applicants should ponder these kinds of questions:[4]

■   Who do you want to be (e.g., computer guru, health-care expert, renowned author)?

- What comes easily to you (and what do you do better than your peers)?

- What subjects are you curious about and want to keep learning about?

- What job title(s) intrigue you (e.g., financial analyst, psychologist)?

- What industries do you favor (e.g., software, advertising, transportation)?

- What prior experiences can benefit employers?

- When do you perform your best (e.g., group project, under intense deadline)?

- Where do you want to work/live? Are you willing to relocate?

- Why are you qualified for a specific role (talents, education, skills, and traits)?

To expand their self-knowledge, students should visit the career-services office. They should have been working with the career-services office throughout their college years if they followed the advice in this book. The career-services office is worth investigating because it can provide job leads and alumni connections that could help secure a first job. On the other hand, a student should not expect it to generate a full-time job offer.

The quality of the career-services office varies from campus to campus. State universities have larger budgets for objective assessments. Smaller colleges have leaner staffs that may not have time to work one-on-one with students. Size and quality of staff as well as the evolution of the career-services program can make a big difference. Seniors should use these resources, but they must own the process.

2. Research Jobs, Organizations, Industries, and Hiring Managers

This is a key stage in nailing down employment. An individual must thoroughly research job titles, organizations, and industries. A reasonable objective is to compile information on twenty-five to thirty target organizations in a chosen geographic area.

To begin, a young adult should visit a library, the career-services office, and career-related websites to scan widely for opportunities. Here are criteria to follow to gather meaningful details:

- **Macroeconomic Trends.** What variables are affecting labor markets (such as aging U.S. population, opening of Asian markets)? What industries/

organizations are booming (e.g., nanotechnology, computer services, Homeland Security)? Which product/service categories are expanding due to consumer buying habits? What are the high-growth fields?

■ **Geography.** Which companies are in a thirty- to fifty-mile radius from home (a one-hour commute)? What regions or cities are worth considering?

■ **Organizational Culture.** Which organizations match my personality and work style? What is senior management's leadership style? What are work expectations for employees (e.g., travel, weekend hours)? What are the benefits (e.g., flextime, telecommuting, training)?

■ **Contact Names.** Who are employment decision makers within an organization (hint: someone with profit/loss responsibility)? What are the hiring executives' titles, addresses, phone numbers, and e-mail addresses? When is the best time to reach them and arrange face-to-face meetings (e.g., before 8 A.M., lunchtime, after 5:30 P.M.)? What are the preferred communication methods (in person, phone, e-mail, or letter)?

Once candidates have adequately researched potential employers, they can craft messages that will resonate.

3. Personal Packaging

There has been plenty of buzz in magazines and books about the concept of personal branding. The theory is that professionals are responsible for their career moves and long-term reputations. Applying that logic to first-time job hunters, a student should take calculated risks to stand out. The perfect time to establish a differentiated image is when a young person is being compared with hundreds of others.

The goals of the personal-packaging stage are to grab the attention of harried executives and receive more callbacks from organizations (which lead to additional interviews).

A conventional resume—chockful of action verbs and assorted puffery—doesn't cut it anymore. Granted, the one-page resume has been a staple for college students to convey credentials since the typewriter was invented. But computers now scan resumes to automatically filter candidates (especially those who don't align with a job description). On occasion, a resume is still useful (e.g., if an employer demands one). However, this antiquated document should no longer be the sole device to introduce a candidate to prospective hiring staff.[5]

Hiring executives want to make fact-based decisions to reduce recruitment expenses and improve retention rates (on average, rookie employees depart in just two years). By getting to know prospective employees, hiring managers can make wiser selections. If a young adult reveals personal details—motivations, top skills, character traits, biggest obstacles overcome, or career aspirations—she can boost the number of callbacks. So convince your twentysomething to "tell her story."

An undergraduate can discuss and write about academic, employment, and volunteerism experiences; what makes her tick; and how she will contribute to XYZ, Inc. This approach is the employment equivalent of a college-application essay. By openly sharing key parts of her life, a candidate demonstrates the number-one skill that hiring managers look for: stellar communication.

In job-search communication—whether on the phone, in person, via letter, or via e-mail—young people must understand that messages cannot center only on them. Instead, an applicant must explain how her talents will enhance future operations. This is done by highlighting her past accomplishments, which hiring managers believe are indicators of on-the-job performance. Examples might be "cut sorority operating expenses by 16 percent," "supervised twelve retail cashiers during holiday season," "improved manufacturing efficiency 8 percent during co-op project," or "directed fifteen volunteers to raise $7,500 for campus walk-a-thon." For more ideas, see the list of thirty-eight skills in chapter 1.

Results-oriented communications that showcase achievements will probably be a mind-set shift for a twentysomething. However, to be hired, it's imperative that a young person use *quantifiable* messages that portray him as "an impact player ready to make a difference at XYZ, Inc." Custom messages should be prepared for each organization.

Here are some innovative door openers to try:

- A show-and-tell portfolio of school/work/community service samples.

- Case studies using this format: situation, actions, results (one paragraph per section on topics such as customer service and teamwork).

- A biography or personal statement explaining ambitions (begin with an inspirational lyric, movie quote, or anecdote).

- A pitch letter with bold lead paragraphs (e.g., a quote from company founder, CEO, or mission statement); it should address the company's needs based on news coverage, executive speeches, or Wall Street reports.

- A results-oriented resume with key words from the job description to highlight education, skills, character traits, and a track record of success. Examples include "3.25 GPA," "received $5,000 academic scholarship," "funded 75 percent of educational expenses," "sales award winner," "Toastmasters International member," "lived in France for five years," "nationally ranked in martial arts."

- A congratulatory note to an executive (start by tracking local employment announcements in business journals—staff changes may point to hiring; then call to arrange an informational interview).

- An offer to work for *free* (up to thirty days with an agreed-upon review date).[6]

- Emerging self-marketing tools such as a video resume (a two-minute tape of a candidate on camera); an audio resume (a brief recording embedded as a link in an e-mail message or sent as a cassette or CD); or a visual resume (a summary of academic, work, and volunteer history in an appealing two-sided, color-printed page or as an electronic screen layout).

Compelling door openers can increase the number of callbacks, position a candidate as a proactive employee, and boost the odds of being hired.

4. Outreach to Hiring Managers, Senior Executives, and VIPs

Because 70 percent of job placements come from personal referrals, a twentysomething must stay on the radar screen of influential people. The objectives of this critical stage are for your student to be top of mind when VIPs hear of openings and to receive warm referrals to hiring managers.

A proven technique is to schedule thirty-minute informational interviews seeking advice (but not a job). To set up these sessions, your undergraduate should rehearse a concise phone pitch and voice-mail message (one-minute maximum). These informal meet and greets can be used to practice a smile, firm handshake, and eye contact; reply to a mix of questions; and fine-tune interviewing skills. A young adult should still prepare because casual conversations can transition into employment interviews if the chemistry and timing are right. Before leaving an informational interview, a student should always request the names of two or three other contacts.

A few comments about those who comprise about half of the population: introverts.[7] The art of self-promotion may be awkward for a timid individual. However, the job search is not the time to be shy. Humble individuals should recruit job-search buddies for role-playing interviews and to attend networking events together.

You can assist by telling enthusiastic people—neighbors, coworkers, family lawyer/doctor, health-club colleagues—about your preferred job titles, industries, and organizations. Be specific about target organizations so your contacts are more likely to supply referrals.

Here are some additional techniques young adults can try:

- Attend speeches by company representatives, speed-networking events, and trade shows to mingle with executives and distribute business cards.

- Access professional-association databases to reach industry executives (via phone or e-mail).

- Tap databases of university, fraternity, or sorority alumni ("Professor so-and-so told me to call you for insights on the exciting field of . . ." or "We met at last year's reunion . . .").

- Participate on industry sites or listserves; casually mention your career objectives and request mentors.

To cement networking relationships, an employment candidate should periodically check in with companies he's interested in for a "job-search update." This subtle tactic conveys persistence without being a pest.

5. Interviews

A student will be nervous about employment interviews (a normal reaction). Keep in mind that she is pursuing a *first* job—essentially a career starter to nurture skills and explore the world of work. Contrary to what many twentysomethings believe, an initial position is not a lifelong commitment. This misperception is affirmed by U.S. Labor Bureau data that show professionals change jobs three or four times by age 30 (which reflects a popular saying that "thirty is the new twenty" for career commitments). So expect a young person to experiment with roles and employers.

To obtain a high-quality position, an individual must overprepare for interviews:

- Before the interview, review the company's marketing documents, and if the company is public, review its financial statements.

- Visit a library to skim business directories, journals, trade magazines, annual reports, competitors' websites, lists of fastest-growing public/private firms; compose three or four interview questions from this information.

■   Do online searches on the interviewers to find background details for use as ice-breakers (e.g., education, employment history, professional accolades, and leisure activities).

■   Go over anticipated questions; rehearse use of show-and-tell portfolio and case studies.

Upon entering a hiring manager's office, an individual can quickly check a room for details to use during conversations (e.g., diplomas, photos). At the beginning of an interview, a young person should inquire about current business needs to clarify what is expected from a new employee. By verifying immediate priorities, a candidate can direct his replies to the employer's explicit needs (which will be music to the ears of executives).

An interview is a chance to spotlight skills and admirable traits. If an undergraduate seeks a specific role—such as accountant, engineer, or teacher—she should mention a license or certification. An individual with a background in liberal arts, humanities, or social sciences can stress transferable experiences and "soft skills" (e.g., a can-do attitude, empathy, relationship-building skills).[8] For example, a student government member can use his supervisory and organizational skills as a hospitality-management trainee at a hotel, convention center, resort, or restaurant chain.

Throughout an interview, a candidate should be sociable and optimistic, review her skills and character, express keen interest in the position, state her desire to make a tangible contribution, and ask informed questions to facilitate two-way communications. The use of a show-and-tell portfolio enables an individual to address questions with evidence of past accomplishments (an advantage because peers won't think to use one). At the conclusion, the applicant should inquire about "next steps" (e.g., additional interviews, timing for a decision).

6. Closing the Deal

Soon your twentysomething may have a job offer or, better yet, multiple offers. To finalize the process, an individual should:

■   Send handwritten thank-you notes to each interviewer reiterating that she wants the job along with highlights of her skills and character.

- Call back within five days to reinforce her interest and determine if any more information is needed to make a decision (e.g., transcripts, references).

- Hesitate to state a dollar figure for a starting salary; instead probe about a salary range (because there is a compensation "band" of several thousand dollars for most positions).

- Request that an employment offer be made in writing (if the hiring manager refuses, rethink the cultural fit of the organization).

- Accept an offer by sending a brief letter restating salary, bonus, start date, and vacation period.

- Take time to celebrate her first job with family and friends because this is truly a significant moment!

- If rejected, stay in touch with executives in case another person turns an offer down or if openings occur in the future.

What Parents Can Do

This perspective and advice will be daunting to students seeking their first full-time jobs. Your child will need ongoing support during the ups and downs of a job hunt. By following the advice throughout this book, your child will be able to articulate how her academic program and activities outside of the classroom built her skills and character. Here are some strategies to use at your discretion.

Strategy #1: Resist the urge to do the heavy lifting for a young adult. A job hunt is a classic "rite of passage" on the pothole-filled road to adulthood that your offspring should accomplish (mostly) alone. You can lend a hand and provide pats on the back to assist with the rough spots.

At least encourage your child to look in the mirror and pledge to complete the six steps of a job search. This ensures that he will take control of his employment, be energized to do the necessary groundwork, and follow a disciplined plan. Here is the bottom line: Your twentysomething must accept responsibility for the outcomes. Heck, it's her future at stake. If she doesn't own it, who does?

An exercise to do together is to write job-search goals, such as make fifteen phone calls per week; send ten pitch letters by December 1; and go on six interviews per month. A college junior or senior may see this task as a burden he doesn't have time for, but insist on it because goals matter when he "hits the wall." Goals allow a young adult to monitor progress, maintain hope, and feel proud of extra efforts. Remember, a job search is

Dos and Don'ts for Parents When Job-Search Coaching

Dos

- Periodically mention your child's strengths: what she has always liked to do or shown a passion for, when she seems to be in a groove, adjectives that describe personality traits.
- Share your positive and negative job-search experiences; if you've had hiring responsibility, explain how you selected candidates.
- Accept that the job-search game has new rules (e.g., resumes are not as effective; networking is king; it's okay to self-market).
- Recommend recruiting job-search buddies to practice being enthusiastic during interviews, because executives want to hire optimists.
- Encourage "immersion" into the job search (the sooner the better) through self-help books, websites, career-services seminars, part-time jobs, internships, networking luncheons, and mentors.
- Reinforce that a job candidate should "work smart" by concentrating on productive tactics such as networking with friendly university alumni.
- Invest some dollars in a personal-packaging campaign for your job seeker: business cards, thank-you notes, leather folio, fancy pen, electronic portfolio, interview suit, shoe-shine kit, regular haircuts, manicures, travel budget, or conference fees.
- Consider retaining a career counselor (to administer and interpret assessments that identify strengths), a copywriter (to draft resume alternatives), and a graphic designer (for page layouts of show-and-tell portfolios or websites).
- Suggest job-search performance goals (e.g., number of phone calls, letters, and interviews); offer to track progress via project-management software; hold regular phone calls for status reports.
- Act as a "career leader" by offering upbeat comments such as, "I know it's awkward to put yourself out there," "You can do it," "Take it one step at a time," and "Before long you'll look back and chuckle." Remind a collegian that "No" is a normal part of the process and that only *one* job offer is needed to begin a fulfilling career! Make sure to reward little victories.
- Give the gift of self-help for a birthday or holiday: a bookstore gift card for career guidebooks, subscriptions to industry publications and magazines (e.g., *Fortune*, *Fast Company*, *BusinessWeek*, *Inc.*, and *The Wall Street Journal*), memberships in professional organizations, and work-

shop fees (Toastmasters International, Dale Carnegie training, American Management Association).
- Watch for signs of delaying the job search (spending too much time on websites), complacency (resistance to making cold calls; overreliance on electronic job boards/classified ads), and situational depression (being oversensitive to rejection, giving up).

Don'ts
- Don't pressure your child into an occupation that you think is right for her. Remember, this process is about her long-term happiness, not yours. If you must propose occupations, make sure to give reasons or justifications.
- Don't overreact when a student is negative about the labor market or job-search process. Young adults have unrealistic expectations for their first jobs, are the least loyal to employers, and feel the most distressed.
- Don't force yourself into your child's job-offer decision (by giving a laundry list of pros and cons). This is his big moment; unless asked for input, stay out. Hopefully by now, you've done your part. Trust your offspring to make a sound choice.
- Don't fret if a young adult's job choice doesn't precisely match her academic background. Most people majored in something different from the fields they ended up in. As a backup plan, taking a temporary position that's in the same industry as a dream job is a sensible move.

arduous—especially for a first-timer. When a twentysomething achieves little victories along the way, she should be rewarded (e.g., a heartfelt "attagirl," special meal).

As part of your guidance, encourage your child to use all of the career services the college provides.

Strategy #2: Coach a young adult using these dos and don'ts. A twentysomething should simply admit that she doesn't know much about conducting an employment search. Why? A young adult has never been trained to job hunt. Have a laugh together about this sad-but-true fact. A lighthearted approach allows an individual to shed the typical attitude of "I know how to get a job" or "I can do it by myself." Instead, you want agreement that looking for employment is "tough sledding" and that it's okay to ask for help. Someday your offspring may realize that job hunting is a skill that can carry her a long way.

When discussing an employment search, recognize that your opinions count because your offspring still seeks assurances. For instance, state that it's okay to join a midsize or small business (where a high-energy individual can be promoted earlier). Look over the dos and don'ts in the sidebar. Some tips may help you figure out what to do to ensure an individual completes a successful job search.

Strategy #3: Persuade your child to think like an employer. Because companies look for reasons to hire or reject applicants, it's crucial for a twentysomething to put herself in the shoes of an employer. She should ask herself challenging questions such as: What skills do you bring our company? What needs can you fill? What problems can you solve? Will your personality mesh in our culture? What's in it for my organization to hire you?

Here are other matters your child should take care of:

- Change e-mail and voice-mail messages to convey a professional image. Cheesy e-mail addresses such as ladiesman1@yahoo.com or partygoddess247@gmail.com can damage an individual's reputation with employers.

- Dress to impress on a first interview with a dark two-piece business suit, a light-colored shirt or blouse, a tie or scarf, shined shoes, dark socks, and a conservative hairstyle. Men should not wear earrings or cologne. Women should avoid miniskirts; cleavage; and excessive makeup, jewelry, or perfume.

- Be aware of proactive recruitment initiatives for minorities in certain industries (e.g., female civil engineers, African American pharmacists); negotiate a signing bonus or added benefits.

- Individuals with an entrepreneurial streak can look into start-up ventures (e.g., Silicon Valley, high-tech incubators near Boston, New York, Austin, Seattle, or many universities). These organizations often delegate more responsibility in shorter time frames. Know that small-business owners can be micromanagers, very demanding, frenetic thinkers, and mavericks. Many prefer to hire multitaskers who will "get their hands dirty" and work long hours.

- For extra income, be a part-time sole proprietor to apply underused talents (e.g., computer installation, private tutoring, real estate investing); multiple income streams can grow savings and maintain a desired lifestyle.

Useful Resources

Tim Conway's college and career planning services for college-bound teenagers, undergraduates, and university alumni are available at www.igniteyoungadults .com.

The Riley Guide (www.rileyguide.com) is an in-depth, all-things-careers site. Check the A-to-Z index for relevant topics.

America's Career InfoNet (www.acinet.org/acinet/library.htm?category=1.2) is part of Career OneStop, a suite of national websites sponsored by the U.S. Department of Labor. The site has information about different occupations and industries, as well as the wages and skills associated with them.

Hoover's (www.hooversonline.com) provides company and industry profiles worth reviewing before job interviews.

The Job Hunter's Crystal Ball: Read the Minds of Employers and Influence Their Decisions, by Stanley Wynett (Cincinnati: Adams Media, 2006). This book explains the reasons for hiring from the employer's side of the desk. It gives suggestions to "humanize" a resume and cover letter along with tips on interviewing etiquette.

Interview Answers in a Flash: 200 Flash Card–Style Questions and Answers to Prepare You for That All-Important Job Interview, by Pat Criscito and Dee Funkhouser (New York: Barron's, 2006). A novel way to prepare for the toughest interviews.

Bring Your "A" Game: The 10 Career Secrets of the High Achiever, by Rob McGovern (Chicago: Sourcebooks, 2005). In this book, the author explains that exceptional job candidates know what they want to do, can articulate an exact job title to target organizations, match their career desires with entities that actually have work, shamelessly promote their capabilities, and visualize the "top box" of a career pyramid (e.g., surgeon, chief financial officer).

Business networking sites: Young adults can create Web profiles to increase referrals to corporate professionals, small business owners, employment agencies, and peers on sites such as www.linkedin.com, www.hooversconnect.com, www.jigsaw.com, www.ryze.com, www.spoke.com, www.zoominfo.com, www .ziggs.com, www.doostang.com, and www.fdnetwork.org.

Notes

1. American Association of Retired Persons, available at www.aarp.org.

2. Richard N. Bolles, *What Color Is Your Parachute?* (Berkeley, CA: Ten Speed Press, 2006).

3. John W. Hobart, *Hire Education: What Every College Grad Should Know About Landing That First Job* (Pittsburgh: Lighthouse Point Press, 1998), p. 4.

4. Gregg M. Levoy, *Callings: Finding and Following an Authentic Life* (New York: Harmony, 1997), and Dr. Melvin D. Levine, *Ready or Not, Here Life Comes* (New York: Simon & Schuster, 2005).

5. Jeffrey J. Fox, *Don't Send a Resume: And Other Contrarian Rules to Help Land a Great Job* (New York: Hyperion, 2001).

6. Brandon Toropov, *303 Off-the-Wall Ways to Get a Job* (Franklin Lakes, NJ: Career Press, 1996), and Bob Weinstein, *I'll Work for Free: A Short-Term Strategy with a Long-Term Payoff* (New York: Holt, 1994).

7. Paul D. Tieger and Barbara Barron-Tieger, *Do What You Are*, 3rd ed. (Boston: Little Brown, 2001), p. 17.

8. Daniel Goleman, *Emotional Intelligence: Why It Can Matter More Than IQ*, 10th ed. (New York: Bantam, 2006).

CHAPTER 23

Succeeding in the Workplace

"Toto, I've a feeling we're not in Kansas anymore."

—Dorothy, from *The Wizard of Oz*

Nearly 50 percent of newly hired employees will fail within eighteen months on the job, according to a study by Leadership IQ, an executive education and research company.[1] Technical skills are not the primary reason for the failure; poor interpersonal skills dominate the list. As noted in chapter 1 and the 2007 National Association of Colleges and Employers (NACE) Job Outlook report, the skills employers most often identify as lacking in recent college graduates are communications, interpersonal skills, teamwork, and work ethic. Let's hope your child is one of the success stories! To be successful, your child must recognize that the workplace is a very different world from the academic world. This new world requires a skill set and level of maturity not previously demanded of your child.

Lack of Maturity

A good friend of mine, "Damon," is a fairly recent Ivy League graduate. He got good grades and participated in a variety of activities. He is not only bright, but friendly, fun loving, insightful, curious, and honest. He confided

By Andrea T. Dolph

Andrea Dolph is coauthor of Hit the Job Running: Your Guide to Developing Essential Job Skills and Handling Workplace Issues.

this to me about a year out of college: "My friends and I are all walking around afraid to be grown-ups. We're afraid of making commitments, we're afraid of taking responsibility, and we're afraid of losing our freedom. We're afraid of making mistakes and we're afraid of being found out. You can't imagine how much stress we're all carrying around." Damon's confession is supported by comments I hear every year when I ask corporate entry-level trainees what their biggest shock is coming into the workforce. With regard to maturity, typical recent-graduate comments are:

- I just realized I may never get another summer break until I retire. I don't think I can survive without one.

- It's hard not being able to sleep whenever I want.

- I still like to go out drinking every night. It's hard dragging myself in on time in the morning.

- I'm afraid I'm going to make a mistake and commit to a career I don't like. I don't want to get stuck doing something I hate for the rest of my life.

Surprisingly, too many recent grads act on these feelings—sleeping in late or arriving at work hung over. Many refuse (overtly or covertly) to find steady jobs in order to avoid the commitment. Not a good start to a career or adult life.

I also ask employers what their biggest problems are with the recent graduates. They say:

- Many new graduates don't seem to realize the office isn't a fraternity house or college dorm. Too many of them yell over their cubicles and spend too much time talking about last night's game, hot cars, or weekend plans.

- The way many new graduates dress is appalling. They don't understand the image they portray when they wear jeans and T-shirts. They don't understand this attire communicates an attitude of immaturity. And more important, it limits their potential—I can't put them in front of important customers or people at higher levels of our own organization.

- Too many young women seem to view the office as a place to find a boyfriend or a husband. Their provocative dress makes it impossible for some of us to concentrate. If a woman wants to be recognized for good ideas and an ability to achieve them, she shouldn't wear tight, low-cut tops and overly short skirts!

Have you ever seen signs in your office's coffee area reading "Your mother doesn't work here, please clean up after yourself"? Most supervisors have enough to do that they can't—and don't want to—be surrogate parents, therapists, or best friends with their new hires. They need their new hires to be efficient and effective professional contributors.

Wrong Expectations

We call this business acumen. Many recent graduates never give a thought to why their company is in business or the mission of their nonprofit or government organizations. Many interpret business decisions as being "antiemployee" rather than considering the underlying financial or strategic rationale for the decision.

I think of Rachel, a young woman who, after about six months on the job, went into her boss's office demanding a raise because her current salary wasn't allowing her to "live the lifestyle I want to live." Furthermore, Rachel had friends in other industries who were making more money. She expected to be paid the same. Almost every job has a basic pay range, influenced by such factors as geography, success of the particular organization, and economic conditions for that particular industry. For example, entry-level teachers can expect to make money within a certain range, depending on what part of the country they live in and the demand for any special skills they may have acquired. An electrical engineer in the defense world can expect a different salary range. Basically, organizations have figured out what they can pay and still be competitive. Rachel didn't recognize this, and she came across as immature and selfish with her demands.

I also think of Eric and Bryan, two really talented engineers who worked for me in the software-development field. They complained bitterly that I wasn't letting them get all the training they wanted or go to all the trade shows that interested them. Instead, I kept assigning them to projects for real customers with real due dates. (Imagine that!) One day I finally accused them of having the motto "This would be a great job if only the customers would go away." They unabashedly agreed. So then I asked, "And where would the money come from to pay you for all that training and travel you want?" Their answer: "Not my problem. If the corporation wants to keep me, they need to figure this out." Wow!

Basically these guys felt entitled, not recognizing that all organizations—be they for profit, nonprofit, or government—are bound by one formula: Profit = Revenue − Expenses. For nonprofits, revenues come from funding, and the expenses cannot exceed the revenues. The purpose of the business, agency, or organization is to deliver products and/or services in a way that doesn't cause them to lose money.

* * *

The workplace is different from academia in so many ways. In the introduction to the book *Hit the Job Running*, we use figure 23-1 to illustrate just a few.

Underlying figure 23-1 are three key concepts: cultural differences between college and the workplace, differences in the nature of the personal mission, and the presence of workplace skills.

Office Culture

The culture of the workplace is vastly different from college life—and even significantly different from business to business. Fail to understand the new culture and how you fit in, and . . . you fail. I will never forget Jack, a very nice employee I had many years ago—a sharp, motivated, recent graduate from a respectable university. Shortly after joining my group, our part of the company moved its office space from one building to another across town. When I asked my team members if they wanted me to make seating assignments or if they wanted to figure it out themselves, they opted for the latter. I gave them the new floor plan with our assigned cubicles identified,

Figure 23-1. Differences between college and work.

College	Workplace
• Appearance & etiquette have little bearing on academic performance.	• Appearance & etiquette have significant impact on perceptions of professionalism.
• Fresh start every semester.	• First impressions are often final.
• Definitive assignments (e.g., well-defined due dates and outcomes).	• Open-ended assignments with partial details.
• Relationships have little bearing on grades.	• Effectiveness of relationships can influence appraisals and promotions.
• You select your friends.	• No choice of coworkers; you must get along with all.
• Assessment and promotion based on grades.	• Assessment and promotion based on multiple subjective factors.

Source: Reproduced with permission from *Hit the Job Running*, by Andrea Dolph and Ray Sarnacki (Wayne, PA: Rise & Shine Press, 2005).

and off they went. In the culture of our organization, location and amount of assigned office (or cubicle) space was a sign of seniority. Typically cubicles were set up in rows perpendicular to large outside windows. The closer to the window you were, the more senior. The view was better and you were farther away from general office traffic.

Jack failed to observe that important perk of seniority. I later found out that when my team members negotiated among themselves for cubicle assignments, Jack was adamant about getting one next to the window. I learned that he was so stubborn that finally the team gave in—but not without a price. From then on, Jack was never treated like a team member. He wasn't invited to join the others at lunch or join in important office chitchat. Consequently, Jack didn't pick up key information about projects and other office happenings, which is often shared informally, rather than formally. He was treated as an outsider and didn't feel accepted—he wasn't. The team never forgave his error in assessing culture. Eventually he left—his work wasn't rewarding and he wasn't able to accomplish tasks a person with his skills should have done easily.

Many college graduates think their university experiences gave them exposure to a diverse set of students, professors, and ideas. Probably not—at least, not compared with what they will find in the workplace. Chances are your student didn't have to work very closely with a single mother struggling to keep her head above water or a curmudgeon with thirty-five years of experience who truly has gathered infinite wisdom but is now focusing on his retirement in just a few months. Your student didn't have to work side by side with such diversity, didn't need to be able to communicate effectively with people and their own biases, interpretations, and inclinations.

Personal Mission

As a student, the mission is to learn information and demonstrate through tests and papers how much information was understood and retained. In the workplace, the mission is to "make things happen" and "achieve assigned outcomes" by bringing to bear all appropriate knowledge, experiences, skills, and resourcefulness you possess. It's not how smart you are; it's what you make happen. To illustrate, consider two former employees of mine.

Gene was an absolutely *brilliant* theoretical scientist. He continually researched and synthesized the latest developments in his field. He was published internationally. Gene was also arrogant and couldn't get along with anyone. He couldn't figure out how to apply his very advanced concepts to real-world projects and made disastrous blunders sounding off to my superiors about what he didn't like about the company. In other words, he had *no* business acumen. I was always in damage-control mode with him—and eventually I couldn't justify keeping his research position, because it wasn't producing tangible benefits for the company. I also couldn't justify the amount of unproductive time I spent getting him out of trouble, repairing destroyed relationships with coworkers, and ultimately hiring people to replace the coworkers who couldn't work with him. Eventually we strongly encouraged Gene to find a new position.

Raphael had a 2.65 GPA from a decent state university. His technical skills were fair, but he got along outstandingly with the clients, really understood their needs, was able to communicate with them, and lead teams of more proficient engineers to deliver products on time and within specification. Raphael was barely three years out of school when he started receiving key leadership roles and even received stock options in recognition of his outstanding achievements.

The difference: Knowledge versus outcomes. The latter wins out every time.

Lack of Workplace Skills

The differences I've already highlighted between college and the workplace already suggest a set of skills your child may or may not have developed. They include:

- The ability to size up a new culture and adapt accordingly.
- Business acumen, which includes an understanding of the organization's mission, strategies for achieving the mission, and subsequent priorities. The ability to apply this knowledge, correctly interpret why business decisions are made, and align personal contributions at work is crucial.
- Effective teamwork and communications skills that truly demonstrate respect and appreciation of diversity.

Many universities and even high schools will argue that they develop these skills, but they don't. Year after year the NACE job outlook report identifies variations of these skills, which the surveyed employers report as lacking in their recent college graduates.

But that's not all. Most new employees have the academic (or technical) knowledge to do their jobs, but they don't have the workplace skills needed to actually do the work efficiently and effectively. In our book, we call these performance skills. Basically, they include:

■ **The ability to ask the right questions.** Employees should clearly understand what is expected of them, thus avoiding wasted time and energy doing the wrong things. We've talked to young "high-potential" employees who admit to sitting in their cubicles for days, staring at the walls, not knowing what in the world they've been asked to do, and not having the confidence to ask for clarification.

■ **An ability to plan and execute work.** Some high schools, even middle schools, now require students to use planners, but recording when assignments are due only scratches the surface of real planning. Good employees know how to decompose and schedule tasks, manage resources, identify and mitigate risks, and track progress. The complexity of challenging work demands proficiency in these skills.

■ **Job mastery.** This means doing more than exactly what you've been told to do. There are different levels of job mastery—the level reached usually differentiates the level of an employee's success.

■ **The ability to accept and benefit from feedback.** Interestingly, employers complain that their recent grads' inability to deal with feedback is a top problem with young workers.

What Parents Can Do

Before choosing strategies, I always think it's important to identify my goal. In this case, I believe the goal of a parent, particularly the parent of a child now in the workplace, is to raise a happy and self-sufficient adult. The keyword here is *self-sufficient.* If you don't agree with my goal, consider this scenario: When I graduated from college, I had a friend, Pete, who was a smart, good-looking, and engaging guy. He graduated from a prestigious state university with an engineering degree. Pete's father was a wealthy and successful entrepreneur and property owner who let Pete become his partner in innovating unique engineering solutions for the federal government. Dad also let Pete live in his lake house, took Pete and his new wife on vacations, and paid for the windsurfers, sailboats, and other entertainment. Pete was allowed to work whatever hours he wanted (less than forty a week!) and take off when he needed a vacation. I was so envious of his life! It was all about having fun, being tanned . . . oh, and sometimes work. After a couple of years of this, Pete's dad died unexpectedly at the same time as the bottom fell out of the real estate market in their area. Suddenly Pete didn't have the financial backing, but worse, he still acted like a kid and couldn't mentally adapt to being a self-sufficient adult. I lost touch with Pete years ago, but last I knew, he and his wife were living in a beat-up trailer. Pete couldn't keep a job, so his wife had to go back to work, leaving a small child in day care, which they couldn't afford. Their stress was extreme. Their situation showed no sign of improving. In the last Christmas card I ever received from them, Pete's wife told me things were really difficult for them. I often wonder what happened.

If you've followed the advice Bill has given throughout this book, you've probably been pretty successful in raising a happy, self-sufficient young adult. I hope you believe that after graduation there's little you can do as a parent to help your child succeed. That doesn't mean you should abandon your recent graduate. Nevertheless, this is the time—before your child makes serious commitments to things like a mortgage—to let your child figure out her own style, which might even include several failures along the way.

Strategy #1: Resist the urge to get personally involved. I don't have any friends who admit to doing this, but I've heard from many career-placement centers that parents go with their children on job interviews, call employers to negotiate salaries, and even yell at supervisors for poor appraisals. If you're thinking about jumping in to help your floundering child, resist the urge! In two regards, you're not doing your child any favors. First, I've asked employers if they would hire a young person whose parent came to the interview. The answer is always no. By actively becoming involved, you communicate to the employer that your child is not capable of being a responsible, self-reliant employee. Employers can't afford to hire new employees who require a lot of hand-holding. Second, you've just robbed your child of an opportunity to develop new professional skills: interviewing, negotiating, resolving conflict, etc. At some point, your child needs these skills. Now is a good time to start!

Strategy #2: Don't tolerate whining without action. A rule in your house should be "No complaining unless you're willing to do something about it." I think one of the most important personal attributes a parent can foster in a teenager or young adult is ownership of his or her life. Everyone faces disappointments, setbacks, if not disasters, sometime in life. It's how we constructively deal with those adversities that determines success. "Victims" don't make good employees.

Let's say your child loses out on a plum assignment to another new employee in the office and whines bitterly to you about it. The first question to ask would be, "What do you think the manager saw in that other employee that you need to develop?" Emotional responses such as, "The other employee is a brownnoser" suggest your child isn't taking ownership for his own performance. I remember complaining when I was younger that it wasn't fair that someone who put in a lot more overtime than I did got promoted faster, even though the feedback on my own performance was very positive. It took a while, but I finally took ownership of that fact that although working weekends was important to getting ahead in our office, I wasn't willing to do that—and I'd just have to accept (without complaining) the consequence of seeing others get promoted faster. It's often best to wait a bit for the emotion to die down, but eventually you can try to coach your child to identify the real reason for the setback—and then see if she is willing to take action. In many situations, it's okay not to take action—but don't whine about the consequence.

Strategy #3: See things as they are, not as you wish them to be. As CEO of GE, Jack Welch was adamant that all employees needed to see things as they are, not as they wished them to be. This is an important element of maturity and ownership. I have a friend who periodically complains about how unfair it is that she isn't paid more as a public school teacher and how it has limited how she and her husband have been able to live their lives. Sure, we all wish we were paid more, but the reality is that schoolteachers make a certain salary, and if my friend needed more money she should have pursued a different career. The same can be said for the importance of showing up on time for work, for why new employees don't usually get critical assignments, or any of the many other things your recent graduate might be complaining about. If you can encourage your child to identify the reality of her situation, it should make it more acceptable.

Strategy #4: Encourage your child to establish his own personal financial plan. Up until this point, most parents will have provided most of the financial planning for their child. Now that your child is out of school, it's time to let him figure it out for himself. He may have different goals and a different way of achieving them from the way you and your spouse have done things. What's important is having a plan and being able to follow it. Handing over that responsibility is likely to motivate responsible fiscal-decision making— sooner or later. In *Hit the Ground Running*, all of chapter 14 covers managing personal finances. Your child's financial plan should include short-term management—setting up and managing a budget—as well as a long-term plan that includes lifetime goals and strategies for achieving them. If you and your child communicate well, you may be able to help define a financial plan that's right for him. There are many other ways to gain this knowledge:

Get advice from professionals, read, join an investment club, or take a class. A word of caution: At this point, the vast majority of young adults do not need expensive advisers. Start with the free or inexpensive options first.

Strategy #5: Focus on process, not solutions. Again, despite the fact the goal is to encourage self-sufficiency, I'm not advocating totally abandoning your child! Just as the people in my life whom I respect and know care about my well-being, I still seek my parents' input from time to time on various challenges in my life. If your employed child has problems with a difficult boss or a tough career decision, try to limit your coaching to the process of making a decision rather than suggesting a solution. Maintaining a process orientation not only teaches your child how to make future decisions (don't give her a fish; teach her to fish), but it also keeps the ownership of the decision in her court.

Let's say your child asks if she should switch jobs. Coach her through identifying evaluation criteria (e.g., better pay, more chance for advancement, job location), possible alternatives (e.g., stay in the job as is for a while longer, stay in the current job but seek additional responsibility, or look for a similar job with a different company), and potential consequences or outcomes of each choice (e.g., develop greater mastery of the position, get better pay, or move farther from home). When the decision is hers, your child will be more likely to see it through successfully rather than blame you if things don't work out.

Useful Resources

Andrea T. Dolph and Ray Sarnacki, *Hit the Job Running: Your Guide to Developing Essential Skills and Handling Workplace Issues* (Wayne, PA: Rise & Shine Press, 2005). In our book, written specifically for college interns and recent graduates, Ray and I describe essential workplace skills and specific steps for developing them. During layoff situations we experienced, these are the skills people who were let go lacked—regardless of their industry or level in their respective companies.

Ram Charan, *What the CEO Wants You to Know: How Your Company Really Works* (New York: Crown Publishing Group, 2001). This easy read effectively explains key concepts of business acumen. Even a first-year employee can benefit from Charan's insights.

Stephen R. Covey, *7 Habits of Highly Effective People* (New York: The Free Press, 2004). Everyone should read this classic. Stephen Covey's seven principles of life management will help readers develop a positive mental approach to achieving goals at work or in their personal lives.

Ron Hein and Lauren Vicker, *The Fast Forward MBA in Business Communications* (New York: John Wiley & Sons, 1999). New employees will use this for years as a guide for improving both their written and verbal communications skills. The book is part of the *Fast Forward MBA* series, which is an excellent set of practical reference guides on a variety of topics.

Eric Verzuh, *The Fast Forward MBA in Project Management* (New York: John Wiley & Sons, 2005). This book may be a little more detailed than needed for many people new to the workplace, but this easy-to-use guide describes both key concepts and real-world applications of good project-management skills.

Note

1.   Mark Murphy, "Leadership IQ Study: Why New Hires Fail," *Public Management*, March 2006, vol. 88, no. 2, pp. 33–34.

Index